THE GAIA ATLAS OF
FUTURE WORLDS

14.96

THE GAIA ATLAS OF
FUTURE
WORLDS

*Challenge and Opportunity
in an Age of Change*

Norman Myers
Foreword by Kenneth E. Boulding

ANCHOR BOOKS
Doubleday
New York London Toronto Sydney Auckland

A GAIA ORIGINAL

Written by
Norman Myers

Project editor
Jonathan Hilton

Designer
Andrew Barker

Editorial
Philip Parker
Joanna Godfrey Wood

Direction
Patrick Nugent
Joss Pearson

To generations to come, from whom we have already stolen a good part of their future, in the hope they will forgive us; and to all those students and other young people embarking on their future, who show by their commitment to the futurist cause that it could be tough for any problem that gets in their way.

Norman Myers

"We are global citizens with tribal souls."
Piep Hein, Danish poet

AN ANCHOR BOOK
PUBLISHED BY DOUBLEDAY
A division of Bantam Doubleday Dell Publishing Group, Inc.
666 Fifth Avenue, New York, New York 10103

ANCHOR BOOKS, DOUBLEDAY, and the portrayal of an anchor are trademarks of Doubleday, a division of Bantam Doubleday Dell Publishing Group, Inc.

Library of Congress Cataloging-in-Publication Data

Myers, Norman
   The Gaia atlas of future worlds: challenge and opportunity in an age of change
/Norman Myers. — 1st ed. in the U.S.
"A Gaia original."
ISBN 0-385-26606-5
1. Environmental policy.   2. Economic forecasting.   3. Human ecology.   4. World politics – 1985-1995.   5. Technological innovations – Economic aspects.   6. Gaia hypothesis.   I. Title.
HC79.E5M95   1991
306'.01' 12 – dc20   90-39354
                    CIP

Printed and bound in Spain by Mateu Cromo, Artes Graficas, S.A. Madrid

FIRST ANCHOR BOOKS EDITION: February 1991
RRC

Previous page: a detail from the Mandelbrot set.

National Book Service

Foreword

by Kenneth E. Boulding

There is little doubt that when in the course of the evolutionary process *Homo sapiens* arrived on Planet Earth, this event created a potential for a major environmental crisis, which is now being realized. This is not the first environmental crisis in the evolutionary history of the earth. Every transition from one geological age to the next seems to be marked by a major crisis, with a wide extinction of existing species and the opening up of niches for new species. Certainly if the crisis, whatever it was, that exterminated the dinosaurs had not happened, either we would not be here today or we would look very different. Nevertheless, the present environmental crisis may be of unusual magnitude. And as it is the first environmental crisis that any of the participants have been aware of, this one is different.

The idea that the earth has operated for a very long time as a total system with an astonishing capacity for keeping within certain physical limits which has permitted the evolution of life is what underlies the "gaia" concept of Dr James Lovelock. This does not mean that the earth is an organism or a goddess, except insofar as these are metaphors with which to express our love for this extraordinary planet. The earth is more like an ecosystem than it is an organism. An organism has somebody or something in charge of it, whether this is DNA, which is an unconscious organizer, or whether it is our own conscious mind which organizes our own lives and organizations. Pre-human ecosystems, however, even when they have nobody in charge, do observe corrective responses to disturbance (this might be called "quasi equilibria"). Forests regenerate after fires; if we take fish out of a pond, the population will recover roughly to its previous level if we leave the pond alone.

We have to recognize, however, that with the coming of the human race evolution on this planet went into a new gear, just as it did with the coming of DNA and life. As far as we know, humans are the only species that not only have know-how (which all fertilized eggs have, at least), but know-what, that is, images of the world and of the universe in their minds. This has enabled the human race to produce an enormous variety and quantity of artifacts far beyond the capacity of the beaver or the termite, and all human artifacts enter into the total ecological system of the world. The distinction between the "natural", that is, nonhuman, and the "artificial" is not really very important. An automobile, I have often said, is a species just like a horse. It just has a more complicated sex life and it has detachable brains which guide it. The genes of a horse are contained in the stallion and the mare; the genes of the automobiles are in human minds, plans, perhaps computers, and so on, that organize the process of production in the womb or the factory. Humans have been in the business of producing

Kenneth E. Boulding is Distinguished Professor of Economics, Emeritus, and a Research Associate/Project Director of the Institute of Behavioral Science at the University of Colorado at Boulder. He has written over thirty books, including works on social systems of our global community, with some special emphasis on holistic and spiritual values at stake in our changing world. *Three Faces of Power*, published in 1989, speaks of the need for a "hugging" community on Earth.

biological artifacts by human selection and domesticated animals for a long time. We now seem to be on the edge of producing wholly new genetic species, which is exciting though perhaps very dangerous.

One of the reasons for the human environmental crisis is that humans are the first species which has occupied virtually every ecosystem on the planet. We have been to the top of Mount Everest and to the deepest depths of the oceans, even to the Moon. Because of this, the biological world has become much more of a total system than it ever has been before. We have introduced very large numbers of species, plants, animals, and bacteria, into ecosystems which have never had them before. It is not surprising that we have produced a great deal of extinction. The pig never reached Mauritius until humans introduced it, and the pig then exterminated the dodo. Whether we like it or not, we are creating the environment all over the planet of ecosystems in which many previous species are becoming extinct because of the pressures from human beings and human artifacts. On the local scale, this has been happening for three billion years, with mutation creating new species which have displaced older ones, mostly, however, at the local level. There does seem to have been one previous catastrophe on a planetary scale, when the first forms of life consumed the carbon dioxide which then dominated the atmosphere and turned much of it into oxygen, which largely killed them off, but not before mutation produced other species with perhaps greater potential which could use the oxygen. Pollution is a very old story. The critical question is whether mutation can develop species which can utilize the pollutants.

It is important to recognize that the earth has always been an open system in regard to energy, with throughput from the sun, so that on earth the Second Law of Thermodynamics does not strictly apply to the energy level. The entropy principle applies somewhat more at the materials level, where the earth is largely a closed system. However, with continental drift and all that, vulcanism continually rearranged the materials of the earth, although, here again, the human race has introduced a new dimension into this process through the mining of metals and other materials and through the burning of fossil fuels. We could almost say that all the catastrophes which the human race has been imposing on the earth have happened before. Mother Earth has been pretty crotchety at times, and the idea that there is something called "nature" outside the human race which is benign is hardly borne out by the history. What the human race has done is to speed up things. The human catastrophe is certainly faster than any catastrophe that the earth has known before in terms of ice ages, global warming, changes in the atmosphere, and so on. And this may be the greatest threat, simply because nonhuman organisms and ecosystems are slow to adjust and genetic mutation is extremely slow by human standards, though we may be on the edge of speeding it up.

There is a story going around that Woody Allen made a commencement speech in which he warned the students that there were two choices before them, one road leading to extinction and the other to catastrophe, adding that it was very important to choose the right road. This is perhaps the first time in three billion years in this part of the universe that there has been a road going towards extinction and the end of the evolutionary process on this planet. It is very important that we do not follow it. There is no question that the human race is a dominant species on this planet at the moment. No other species has the future of the planet in its hands. There are those who are disturbed by the great biblical verse (Genesis 1:28), where humans are urged to "be fruitful and multiply, replenish the earth and subdue it, and have dominion over the fish of the sea and over the fowl of the air, and over every living thing that moveth on the earth."

Nevertheless, we cannot deny that we are a unique dominant species. All previous dominant species, like the ponderosa pine, by altering the environment in which they grow, change the ecosystem that surrounds them. It seems probable that they don't know what they are doing, whereas we do know what we are doing, and this is unique in the history of the earth. We take delight in the existence of species that we do not interact with or utilize. Environmentalism, which looks like the coming major ideology of the next century, involves our having an image of the earth as a total system and loving it. This means loving not only the ecosystem which exists at the moment, but the whole evolutionary process which created it and will go on creating other systems. We may even produce our evolutionary successor. Then we could become extinct in peace. This, however, is a long way off.

The immediate problem which this volume addresses so eloquently, is how to make a better world in the future by those human evaluations which evolve as the human race itself evolves towards maturity. There is a certain magic about the number 21 in our society, and perhaps the 21st century will be an age of maturity by comparison with the adolescent centuries of wild growth and disorder that have preceded it. If this is to happen, we must have very widespread images of the future that will lead us towards it. This delightful volume is a step in that direction. Its aim is to instruct us in the present in ways that will lead into a better future. The author and the many people who have put it together are to be much congratulated. The more people read it, the better chance we have of passing through the almost inevitable crisis that lies ahead of us, into a more mature and better world.

Kenneth E. Boulding

Contents

Introduction

What is the future?

We all have an interest in the future. That is where we plan to spend the rest of our lives. Yet we all give too little thought to it. We even suspect the future is unknowable even while we have a gut feeling that our future world will be a world of change, change of many sorts, often surprising change, change to affect all our lives.

That much is obvious. What is not so obvious is the speed and scale of change in our future world. The onrush of change is so great that many people find it hard to grasp what is going on around them. They recognize many of the signs of change, and they sense many of its impacts, yet they cannot come to grips with its full scope. They realize they are living through an era of intense change already, and they would like to know more about what the future holds for them. Yet they cannot tune in to the essence of change overall. Rather than allowing their lives to be dominated by it, they would prefer to mobilize it in their own interest – to "ride the wave" – since it is a process with vast potential to enrich their lives. Yet the process is too diffuse, too pervasive, for them to grasp the true nature of change, still less to exploit it for their own purposes.

All too often, then, the process of change ends up as a prospect that, far from exhilarating as it should be, becomes threatening – increasingly so as the pace of change accelerates into the future. To cite the analyst Alvin Toffler, we sometimes suffer from "future shock". So we need a systematized sense of how our lives are being moulded by change in dozens of ways – and how we can shape the future to suit our needs.

After all, we can choose much of our future world. It is this element of choice – golden choice – that should inspire us to embrace change rather than resist it. We can choose from among the multitude of changes that sweep around us already – if we choose to choose. Far from being daunted by the prospect of ever-more change, we should see ourselves as the most privileged generation of all time. By comparison with past societies, we can enjoy a variety of experiences that amounts to packing several lifetimes into one. And the present scene is just for starters. The more we understand change, and grasp its potential to work for us, the more we shall welcome it, no matter how tumultuous the process.

So let us confront our future worlds with optimistic spirit. How readily can we resist the gloom-and-doom prognoses that presage a time of trouble ahead of us. Brighter future, here we come!

A wave of change

How can we anticipate anything worthwhile about the future? Some people say that all assertions about the future will be wrong – including that one. Given that we tend to think of the future as a blank, we take refuge in the past, supposing that the future will be a continuation of what we have known. But that is like travelling forward with our eyes firmly fixed on where we have been. It is plainly off target to say the future will be a simple extension of the past: it will be anything but. Indeed it will be a period of wave upon wave of change. As is evident in this book, we already live in a world that is undergoing a tumult of change. In many respects 1990 has been as different from 1980 as that year was from 1900.

Our need for structure

As people watch the process of change with its growing complexity, they look for structure in the process. In a world where complexity grows by quantum leaps and where the information din is so high that we must shriek to be heard above it, we are all hungry for structure. With a simple framework we can begin to make sense of our future world – and we can change that framework as the world itself changes. We yearn to perceive pattern in change, so that we can feel more at home with it.

All bets are off
"If God had intended that man should fly, He would have given him wings. The airship business is a 'fake', and will always remain so."
Rear Admiral George W Melville, US Navy, 1901

Gaian future

We live in a Gaian world of two sorts. Both will constitute a major part of our future, all the more as they converge. First is the Gaia hypothesis propounded by Professor James Lovelock. This scientific analysis postulates that the planet's physical environments and their living creatures have engaged in co-evolution, each affecting the other. So tightly coupled have the two processes become that the upshot is a single entity, a planetary ecosystem that is alive and operating as a kind of superorganism. Moreover, the living passengers on Spaceship Earth modify their environments to an extent that perpetuates and optimizes conditions for life. Lovelock names the system Gaia, after the mythical Greek goddess for Earth.

The implications are profound. Life itself is a mechanism that actively feeds back on to its environments in ways that are far more significant than we have supposed. It engenders homeostasis, or the capacity to maintain a stable state; and life is like a warm-blooded animal with body-temperature control. This means that if we deplete life's panoply on Earth by, for instance, eliminating tropical forests or extinguishing large numbers of species, we could well disrupt Gaia's workings to a degree that will entrain gross impoverishment for life's processes, including all we are as humans. Plainly the path of prudence is to intervene in Gaia's workings with as little disruptive impact as possible, especially while we are so ignorant of its processes. Yet we are ravaging Gaia ever-more widely and deeply. We are rushing into unknown territory as if with impunity, yet at potentially extreme peril to ourselves and all other forms of life, even to the Gaian organism itself.

Not all scientists agree with the Gaia hypothesis. No matter, responds Lovelock. While waiting to be investigated further, it serves a valuable function as a metaphor for our planetary ecosystem, an entity where co-evolution is an accepted fact, where highly integrated functioning is a key feature, and where we cannot study one feature in isolation from others. We see it all and whole, or we are not seeing what we look at. This runs counter to much conventional science with its reductionist approach: dissect an entity into its "manageable" parts in order to understand better the bits and pieces separately. The illuminating genius of the hypothesis is that it reminds us of a central factor of organizations – that the significance of a part derives from its contribution to a higher level of the system. It is not only that everything is connected, meaning that we can never do only one thing. It is that we can understand the true nature of what we do only by checking its relationships, generally within its higher-level context.

Interdependence in a Gaian world

We are all interdependent through the proliferating economic ties that bind us into one global economy. Equally we are interdependent environmentally: we share a common climate, winds recognize no frontiers, we all have a stake in tropical forests, and so forth across the environmental spectrum. Even more important, our economic and environmental interdependencies are themselves interdependent: fossil-fuel burning disrupts climate through the greenhouse effect, and our trade policies affect tropical forests through consumerist demand for specialist hardwoods. Still more interdependencies arise through personal values, lifestyles, and cultures with their technological and political linkages. Result: a super-interdependency that permeates all aspects of all our lives, and intimately ties in with Gaia.

Gaian democracy

The 30 million species on Earth, with all their diverse communities, make up a system where each can make its voice heard – but only to the extent that one does not shout down the others. This contrasts with humankind's attitude to its fellow species, a highly undemocratic response.

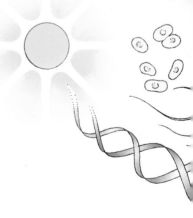

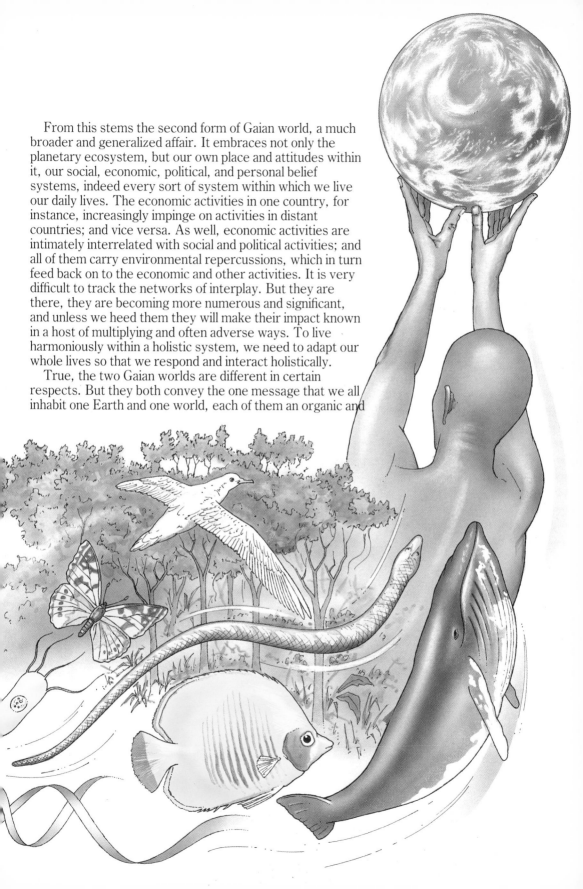

From this stems the second form of Gaian world, a much
broader and generalized affair. It embraces not only the
planetary ecosystem, but our own place and attitudes within
it, our social, economic, political, and personal belief
systems, indeed every sort of system within which we live
our daily lives. The economic activities in one country, for
instance, increasingly impinge on activities in distant
countries; and vice versa. As well, economic activities are
intimately interrelated with social and political activities; and
all of them carry environmental repercussions, which in turn
feed back on to the economic and other activities. It is very
difficult to track the networks of interplay. But they are
there, they are becoming more numerous and significant,
and unless we heed them they will make their impact known
in a host of multiplying and often adverse ways. To live
harmoniously within a holistic system, we need to adapt our
whole lives so that we respond and interact holistically.

True, the two Gaian worlds are different in certain
respects. But they both convey the one message that we all
inhabit one Earth and one world, each of them an organic and

self-organizing entity. Unless we tune into this Gaian message, we shall start to hear some highly discordant responses.

Hence the concept that Gaia is not only a planetary science, it is a transforming image, a global awareness, even a spiritual consciousness. Hence, too, it is much more than a concept: it is a way of life to be expressed through all our daily doings, a movement to make the world a better place in which to live – and not just for us but for all life, primarily for the ultimate life that is Gaia.

This means we can all have our interpretations of Gaia. Indeed this is as it should be. Variety is more than the spice of life, it is the crux. Our own views and experiences, our own lifestyles and relationships, reflect our individual under- standing of Gaia. It is up to all of us to come up with our personal response to the prime challenge of our future worlds: what is it to be a Gaian citizen?

Human change and political vision

In our Gaian world we shall all find we confront choices of abundant types. Many of these personal choices will best be expressed through the human world of politics, economic systems, and social structures. How will we actually achieve change? Will it arise through groundswells of opinion leading to sudden breakthroughs? Or will it rather emerge through an enlargement of vision as well as through step-by-step planning, for instance by envisaging our longer-term future and then engaging in a deliberate process of "getting there from here"?

Some may protest that people cannot change – even though we are changing all the time anyway, and will experience an onrush of change in the future. We already enjoy a wide variety of arrangements for work and leisure: home computers may soon be as significant as commuters. So too there are new definitions of family, indeed a vast array of lifestyles generally. We not only live in a global village, we inhabit a global household: within the lifetimes of many of us we shall move from a stage where it took months to send a letter halfway around the world, to a time when we can send a whole library anywhere on an instantaneous beam of light.

Yet it is difficult for us to *see* change in the world around us, and hence to adapt through the world within us. What is needed, for each and every one of us, is to stretch our imaginations until we perceive the radically altered world that is already here, and the altogether different world that

The Mandela phenomenon
The April 1990 concert for Nelson Mandela at Wembley Stadium in London was seen by 1 billion tele- vision viewers around the world. At a stroke, the event took the steam out of the "go slow on apartheid" brigade. As in the case of Bob Geldof's Live Aid concert, pop cul- ture in conjunction with global tele- vision can now mobilize political support from a large sector of humankind. We are entering an era of politics by the populace.

Reception of a new idea
First it is dismissed as wrong. Then it is said to be against religion. Finally it becomes something that everybody has known all along. Luckily the pace is quickening in the technological sphere at least. From its conceptual origins, television needed about 65 years before it became widely available, the video- tape recorder only 6 years.

Old-time politics
Talk about the new Germany lining up with what remains of the Soviet Union, or of China and Brazil be- coming "almost superpowers", is rooted in by-gone thinking. The new challenges range from population growth, environmental rundown, energy shortages, and climate change to mass migration, terror- ism, and international crime. These all demand a degree of collabora- tion that is light years ahead of the old power politics.

Two faces of the '90s
Vaclav Havel (above) delivers a
speech on democratic reforms in
Czechoslovakia to the Parliamentary Assembly of the Council of
Europe, Strasbourg.
   Nelson Mandela (left) salutes the
people of Soweto on his release
from prison.

lies ahead. This is all the more important in that many new trends are emerging from the bottom up – and there will be scope to generate many more initiatives by those who are able to think globally while acting locally.

Equally rapid is political change – or rather the speeding-up pressure for political change. And not only at national level, but at local and international levels too. The nation-state has become too big for the small problems, and too small for the big problems. If only through force of circumstances, we need to shift our vision from a world of many states, to the state of our one world. No one nation, however advanced economically, technologically, or even militarily, can hope to meet the challenges of global change on its own – just as no nation can protect itself from the action, or inaction, of others. Ironically, political leaders (so-called) are among the slowest to respond – and when they do read the political tea leaves, they often resist change as long as they can.

Even more than their citizens, however, political leaders must engage in "visionary leaps", accepting that the old order is superannuated beyond recognition. For instance, they need to recognize that markets are now more vulnerable than territory, information more powerful than weaponry. Even more importantly, there is not only an effective end to large-scale war, there is a fast-declining difference between war and peace. Fortunately the premium on governmental collaboration of unprecedented scale is facilitated by a burgeoning growth of awareness on the part of the governed, fostering a new sense of shared purpose West and East, North and South.

But we should not underrate the visionary challenge for individual and leader alike. We are poorly adapted to recognize change, we are more comfortable with continuity. Unfortunately sameness lulls the senses, reducing our alertness to change. For an individual or leader who is accustomed to viewing the future year by year, and the past in terms of a single lifetime, even cumulative change is hard to pick out. Consider the growth in human numbers: whereas it took 10,000 lifetimes for the world's population to reach 2 billion, a single lifetime today is enough for it to soar from 2 billion to 10 billion, and just the next decade will see the arrival of an extra 1 billion. There is a similar pattern in the planet's present loss of forests, topsoil, groundwater stocks, wilderness areas, wildlife species, stratospheric ozone, and climate stability. Yet these profound changes are matched by all too little change in our personal responses or in our political leadership. We all need to engage in a "growth spurt" if we are to attain the giant stature that alone will match the giant rates of change around us. Nothing less will restore our sense of "ecolibrium".

Collective endeavour

Just the present world's challenges demand collaboration way beyond the recent experience of citizens and politicians alike. But we can take heart from collective endeavours of the past, when entire societies were mobilized to build the Pyramids, the Great Wall of China, and the Gothic cathedrals of Europe. Only a few decades ago the Marshall Plan inspired Americans to devote 4% of their GNP to rebuilding post-war Europe – by contrast with today, when the US spares a mere 0.2% of its three-times-larger GNP to supporting the developing world. We do not lack the means, we are hopelessly short on vision.

Change of many sorts

There are different types of change. Some are plainly constructive, as when a new crop variety appears. Some are outright destructive, as is the case with earthquakes. Some are grossly disruptive, as when a stock market crashes. Other are gloriously disruptive, as when the dinosaurs were swept away and thus allowed the mammals to enter their heyday. Some forms of change are deliberate, others are a matter of chance. Some can be predicted and shaped, others simply emerge. Some are easy to see, others resist recognition even when they are all but upon us.

We are programmed to gradual change. The cycle of the seasons, growth and decline, life and death and new life again – all these are familiar. The same applies to new ideas and enterprises that come upon us slowly; and the same with new trends and patterns. They are all grounded in our everyday experience, hence they are acceptable to our established perception of change. Moreover they all contribute to change with dynamic continuity: ever changing while still stable overall. This condition of homeostasis is, we believe, the norm. The more things change, the more they remain the same while ever again changing.

Sometimes, however, homeostasis is overtaken by sudden change of a scale drastic enough to "flip" the system into a new equilibrium, whereupon it persists with homeostasis of a different sort. This has occurred in the geologic past through climate shifts (albeit at a speed a mere fraction as fast as today's shift). Sometimes too a "lurch change" leads to a system's collapse, as when a civilization comes to an end through environmental overloading after the fashion of Babylon or the Mayas. Again, system transformation can occur when a number of small changes accumulate to reach a critical mass of change, resulting in overwhelming change, and either breakdown or breakthrough.

The times of greatest change in human history appear to have arisen when things have reached a state of extreme flux. This is the "crisis and opportunity" situation proclaimed by the Chinese as a time when the old order breaks, everything is up for grabs, fresh outlooks flourish, and new ideas spring up on every side – culminating in crisis-scale change that engenders a new and better order. Something of this sort may have occurred during episodes of great flowerings of the human spirit, for example in ancient Athens, Elizabethan England, Renaissance Italy, and pioneer America.

Today we are at a time of crisis supreme. This offers stimulus to perceive crisis as challenge, and then convert it into bountiful opportunity. But to achieve this we shall need to engage in creative change of unparalleled type and scope.

The inspirational leap

Creative change is more than the fabrication of change. It represents an inspirational leap into a realm of hope and uncertainty. The Ancient Greeks could not get beyond post-and-lintel architecture because they could not visualize the arch; nor could ancient American civilizations achieve the breakthrough represented by the wheel. It takes both flair and courage to shatter the mould of conventional thinking. What creative changes are we denying ourselves today because we cannot achieve the inspirational leap?

Population off balance

For 600 million years of major life forms, species' populations have remained in general balance with their environments. Primarily through limits of food supply, births have been matched by deaths, or by slow adaptations to make more efficient while still sustainable use of environments. But from the 1950s onward – or the last 0.000007% of the 600 million years – humankind has supposed it could escape the inexorable confines of population growth. It is not that parents have been breeding too prolifically, it is that their children have no longer been dying in vast numbers. For too many of us, however, it has meant a switch from a life that is nasty, brutish, and short, to a life that is little better than nasty, brutish, and prolonged: the change in the survival prospect has not been accompanied by changes in the rest of the system. We have not supplied systems supports such as food, education, employment, and the like – whereupon the system suffers malign changes ending in breakdown.

The next 40 years
If there have been so many evolutionary jumps in the last 40 years, what will the next 40 bring? A similar series of jumps, only more numerous, intense, and concentrated than before? Likely so. But what will they be? Here our crystal balls fail us, even our imaginations. Surely the most creative speculator will fall far short of what must lie ahead. Who in 1950 could have anticipated even a few of the breakthroughs that are now so widespread and obvious? This warns us not to limit our ideas of what is "realistically" possible. Perhaps the biggest blockage to the future lies not with limitations "out there" but with limitations inside our heads. If we give free rein to our notions of what is possible, we could move through an entire gearbox of vision, creativity, and commitment. Can we learn to see the impossible as an impostor? There are "impossibles" aplenty ahead, most of all the effort to be citizens of the globe and of Gaia. It is a matter of confidence and hope, not of intellect and calculation. So when our nerve fails us, let us recall the outburst of evolutionary jumps of the past 40 years: it will hearten us for the biggest jumps of all.

The information jump
An evolutionary jump is unfolding in information technology, thanks largely to supercomputers and telecommunications. Information is becoming our dominant resource, and already its contribution surpasses past contributions from stone, bronze, soil, metals, energy, and sweat. Information differs from its predecessors by virtue of its capacity to expand as it is used, and because it does not consume other resources. It can be transported at almost the speed of light; and the more it is distributed, the more of it we have, and the more of us have it.

Exponential curves
We have been witnessing change with "accelerating acceleration", as revealed through exponential curves for population growth, energy consumption, and a host of other runaway forms of change. This phenomenon has overturned virtually all our old assumptions. Now we also need to abandon the assumption that the exponential curves can keep on curving. For decades our problems of everfaster growth – terminal threats to grandscale ecosystems, to cite but one example – have not been matched by ever-greater solutions. Must we keep on chasing those curves until they crash? Not that it is easy to sense the danger. At first an exponential curve is little different from a flat line, then it moves on to gradual change, and finally it surges to explosive contrast. If a lily pad doubles in size each day and takes 30 days to cover its pond, it does not reach the halfway point until day 29 – by which time it may be too late to stop its growth. Humankind's activities are spreading like a polluting pad that threatens to suffocate much of the planet's life.

Environmental jumps
Environmental change can feature emphatic jumps. During the past 14,000 years the Sahel has experienced a series of sudden droughts that have coincided with injections of fresh water into the North Atlantic. Decreased salinity leads to anomalies of sea-surface temperature that appear to trigger decreased rainfall in the Sahel. Ice sheets in the northern hemisphere already show signs of melting, possibly as a result of global warming, thus setting up the Sahel for even more frequent and severe droughts than in recent decades. In addition, and again because of the sensitivity of the ocean's salinity to small changes, plus its linkages to temperature, the Gulf Stream's capacity

Types of change
Evolutionary change, for instance steady, gradual change, has generally been the norm throughout the past, together with some cyclical, retrogressive, and occasional "flip" changes. The latter, being less stable forms of change, will become all too familiar to us in a world in turmoil – plus accelerating change, revolutionary change, and catastrophic or "crash" change. Evolutionary change will become the exception.

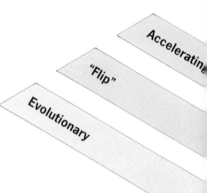

to warm northwestern Europe could be put at risk: within a world growing generally warmer, we could see a sudden and substantial cooling in northwestern Europe. Note, moreover, that sudden changes in the ocean-atmosphere system 10-13,000 years ago led to extreme shifts in the world's climate, including a temperature increase of several degrees C within just half a century – more even than we anticipate through the greenhouse effect as projected. Ironically we are only beginning to learn about the coupling of atmospheric and oceanic systems: climate models are generally not sophisticated enough to include the key factor of feedback.

Retrogressive

Catastrophic

Revolutionary

Cyclical

Accelerating change

For all that most change around us appears gradual, we live in a time of speeded-up change as never before. A leading futurist, John Platt, points out that of the 50 greatest "evolutionary jumps" since the first flickerings of life almost 4 billion years ago, roughly half have arrived since 1950. The development of photosynthesis, the nervous system, tools, thought, speech, and fire all occurred in the prehistoric past. The wheel and the lever, domestication of animals and plants, cities, writing, mathematics and logic, and the use of metal all belong to the first 10,000 years of civilization. Explosives, printing, electricity, the telephone, and disease control all emerged in centuries prior to the present century. But molecular biology, recombinant DNA, nuclear fission, solar power, jets and rockets, space exploration, automation, lasers, television, electronic data processing, feedback control, systems analysis, super-smart computers, and huge-scale design projects all belong, as widespread phenomena, to the last 40 years. The most recent breakthrough of all is our recognition that the planetary ecosystem comprises a single Gaian superorganism that is suffering from human assault of unprecedented scope.

Moreover, and according to Platt's analysis, each of these evolutionary jumps represents an advance indeed. Space travel ranks as the greatest leap into a new habitat since creatures emerged from the seas 500 million years ago. Jet planes and rockets are the most remarkable advances in travel in a new medium since sea-borne ships 5000 years ago. Our advanced tools, notably automated factories and automatic feedback-control systems, could prove to be the single greatest aggregate advance since the first use of tools by the earliest humans 2 billion years ago. Electronics and communications (thanks to radar, lasers, television, fibre optics networks, and satellite relays) allow information and data to be exchanged around the world at the speed of light, marking as great a leap in communications as the emergence of speech and language, writing and printing. We can also reckon with electronic processing, transmissions and storage of data, and giant computers solving problems at speeds millions of times faster than before.

All this amounts to much more than the technological changes that led to the Industrial Revolution 200 years ago. Moreover it has all helped to trigger an onrush of economic and financial unification, the rise of global corporations, the comparative decline of the US, and some pioneering efforts toward political collaboration, even the end of the Cold War. Most significant of all in the long run, it has helped to stimulate the rise of eco-awareness worldwide, leading in turn to such phenomena as eco-nomics.

International crime

A new force is emerging in the international arena with capacity to undermine the very authority of many governments. Like other "jump effects" (see p. 18), its covert approach is difficult to discern. International crime has become a runaway industry of global scope, with participants ranging from cocaine cartels to tax-dodging corporations. Its worth has now topped $1 trillion a year, almost as much as is spent on military activities worldwide. As a result, criminal networks now generate larger sums of money than many national economies. If the recent pattern persists and expands, we shall shortly see the day when international crime can subvert legitimate state authorities throughout sectors of the developing world, thus becoming a major factor in international instability. There is already a list of countries – Colombia, Bolivia, Peru, Panama, Burma, and Laos – where the government is often subordinated to criminal gangs that operate within their borders. Other countries headed in the same direction include Afghanistan, Bangladesh, Thailand, and Kampuchea.

Abrupt change

However much we are programmed to believe that change is steady and predictable, the world is different. It reveals change that can be sudden, erratic, and unexpected – a phenomenon likely to become all too commonplace.

Large-scale ecosystems, for instance, can react in severe and unanticipated manner when subject to disruption of unusual scope. These quantum changes are technically known as threshold responses or breakpoints of irreversible change. They arise when ecosystems, after absorbing stresses over long periods without sign of damage, reach a disruption level at which a "jump effect" takes over. The final factor may be no more than a last-straw affair, some minor extra disturbance that pushes the system into a new state of disorder and instability. Examples include acid rain and ozone-layer depletion, where environmental stresses have built up covertly over extended periods before suddenly revealing themselves in crisis proportions; and species crashes, whether of dinosaurs or whales. What similar upheavals may we be triggering through our multiple, large-scale, and simultaneous interventions in the global environment?

There can be abrupt changes in our economic, political, and social systems too. Recall the economic crash of 1929. The outbreak of war is often the pursuit of political ends by a sudden shift to other means. On a more positive side, the end of the Cold War arose from the final breaking of the dam of repression in Eastern Europe, a process that had been building up for decades before some extra pressure finally persuaded Gorbachev that enough was too much.

We are building up multiple pressures in many systems of our stable-seeming world. "Business as usual" is going to become strictly unusual. We cannot keep on overexploiting the Earth's resources and its environments: we are heading faster than ever toward breakpoint, and one day soon we shall be presented with bills left unpaid for decades. Nor can we persist with gross imbalances of economic and social sort: the average income of the richest 1 billion people is 20 times larger than that of the poorest 1 billion, and the gap is growing. So too the "freedom bug" of Eastern Europe is infecting other regions, such as Southern Africa – perhaps soon China too, even the Middle East?

Both our Earth and our world are ripe with potential for jump effects, as for multiplying changes beyond all experience of humankind. Do we have the parallel potential to cope with them? Better, do we have the vision to exploit them as launch pads for a new future for ourselves – and for all other life on Earth, for Gaia too?

A century of growth

Since 1900 the world's population has increased more than three times, the gross world product 21 times, the consumption of fossil fuels 30 times, and industrial production 50 times. Today the global economy expands every two years by as much as all the economies of South America. Plainly these various forms of momentous growth cannot continue at their breakneck pace, or we shall break more than the neck of the planet's capacity to support our activities. Equally plainly, the world of new thresholds is far from being reflected through new economic systems, new politics, or similar new measures to deal with them.

Chaos and surprise

Unexpected change can arise not only because we humans overdo things. There are "natural" causes too. In fact the entire nonhuman world turns out to be full of chaos and surprise.

This recent discovery represents an about-face from our historic view of the natural order. For centuries scientists have supposed the world runs in accord with the iron laws of traditional physics and mathematics. That is, if we can master all the take-off points of a process, we can work out its entire future course down to the last detail. But this clockwork world is now giving way to a world seen as immeasurably messy. While it still features order within apparent disorder, we shall never understand it all, virtually by definition. Weather remains weather, but it never repeats itself precisely. A difference of one-thousandth of one per cent in initial conditions can lead to entirely different outcomes; or a minor transition in a longer-term process can lead to effects out of all proportion to the cause – the backbreaking straw.

Beyond the physical sciences, we must accept a similar unpatterned pattern within our societies. Human behaviour, while always limited by the supremely imprecise concept of character, is rarely predictable from day to day or even minute to minute. We shall never be able to forecast the stockmarket with accuracy, nor many other features of our economies. Consider too the factor of fashion, which, with billions of dollars at stake each year, remains as unpredictable as ever.

These momentous discoveries have momentous implications for our ideas about the future. All we can be sure of is that we can never be sure of as much as we have supposed. We can never hope, much less plan, for a world on tramlines: all conventional bets are off. We are seeing the break-up of one system after another – our deterministic-world system, our power-politics system, and many another system by which our familiar world has been ordered. A fresh set of systems is undermining them, absorbing them, replacing them. And because of the endemic surprise factor, we must build into our plans an "intrinsic contingency" factor. Just as the best blueprint is amenable to constant modification, so we must learn to make uncertainty our friend in a future of infinite flexibility.

Our responses to a chaotic world
Our new understanding of an intrinsically chaotic world means we must learn to live with more disorder than we normally prefer. It is a world replete with surprise. The more we stick with outmoded images of a world amenable to conventional scientific analysis, the more we shall lay ourselves open to persistent surprise.

Perceptions of chaos

Early humans viewed nature as inherently changeable and unpredictable; even wilful, ruled by fate. In the search for order and security, humans turned first to religion, then to science. Science, it was believed, could unravel the mysteries of nature, and thus learn to predict cause and effect, so much so that it could replace chaos with order, remove all doubt, and make the future, like the past, open to our eyes. But we now know that this mechanistic view of the world is fundamentally off track. We are learning that we must predict limits to our predictions; we must discover how little as well as how much we can anticipate, and how the future will remain the future indefinite. While we may be able to draw broad maps of chaotic systems, we shall never be able to predict their precise workings. Just as this has changed the scientists' view of the world, so it will change the way we choose to cope with it. We shall learn to "manage" while recognizing there is much we shall never manage. Since we shall always encounter chaos in, for example, the behaviour of cars clustering on a highway, we might start to give thought to whether we want so many cars on so many highways.

The future in our hands

All manner of different worlds are on the cards, many of them equally likely or unlikely. Fortunately we still have time, though only just time, to choose those future worlds we believe best suit our needs and opportunities.

The one choice we do not enjoy is to continue with an unchanged world. Change has always been built in to our world, whether our natural world or our human-made world. But today we face change far greater than anything known in the past – and tomorrow will bring far greater change still. *Change will come*, whether we positively pursue it or not, whether it arrives by design or by default.

As long as we fail to anticipate the extent and speed of change ahead, we remain "future blind". This book aims to provide a window into our future, to explore our options. In Part One we look at the mounting pressures that are poised to trigger change in every sphere of our lives, change that stems from a spectrum of sources: technological, scientific, economic, environmental, climatic, social, political, institutional, personal. These pressures are rewriting the entire agenda of our future worlds, however little we recognize them. The better we grow to understand them, the better we shall cope with them – and the more we shall discern the handsome rewards available if we select our futures with informed discretion. But there is no avoiding the pressures. If we do not polish up our crystal balls, we shall be caught with our perceptional pants down.

Part Two moves on to consider the likely impacts of these pressures. Some will be favourable, more will be less positive without swift pre-emptive strikes from us right-away. For sure, certain readers may consider that some of these scenarios are unduly pessimistic: won't technology, for instance, save us? Regrettably that is to view technology in isolation from the capacity of the environment to sustain technology, and from the capacity of our leaders to apply technology judiciously. We must beware the allurements of the easy fix that leaves us in a worse fix. Fortunately the doors on to the bright future have not yet closed: if we recognize the doors and perceive the open landscapes beyond, we can squeeze through the present bottleneck into a future of promise beyond imagining.

Finally Part Three looks at the strategies for us to build the future worlds that we surely desire and are certainly within our grasp. Fortunately, and to reiterate the central themes of this book, we still have time to choose the course we prefer. During the coming decade we shall enjoy a window of opportunity for decisive action. If we miss that window, we shall face a future with walls closing in on us so tightly there will be virtually no escape – or if there is

The personal crisis
In an ever-more complex world, people may come to realize that whatever our capacity for hype-powered technology and other forms of outer advancement, our inner world still depends on an essentially Stone-Age set of faculties for sensitivity, perception, empathy, and ethics. While giants in many respects, we are infants in the one that matters most. Many people may find they cannot bear the strain: for all they can enjoy ten lives within a single lifespan, they can't even cope with one.

The immediate bottleneck
In the next few decades we face an acute bottleneck. It stems from a host of crises – environmental, climatic, technological, economic, social, and political. Beyond a doubt it promises to be the biggest composite crisis that humanity has ever faced. If we do not act promptly and vigorously, we risk an even tighter bottleneck, stretching into the indefinite future. But if we measure up to the challenges ahead, we shall enter on to a future that likewise will far surpass anything humanity has ever known – an indefinite future of promise and plentitude.

Surprise forever?
When we talk about the future, we are really talking about the past. The past is all we know: how can we conceive of anything truly different? So we are programmed to close our eyes to the possibilities ahead. Until we learn to lift our gaze above the parapets of experience, we shall remain predestined to surprises unlimited.

escape, we shall find we have to sweat much more, and with only a fraction as much chance of success as right now. There are little more than 3000 days left until the year 2000, and we lose 1 per cent of our manoeuvring room every four weeks. Through ingenuity, a creative spirit, and above all a clear-sighted view of what is on the cards and what is simply ruled out of court, we can still move toward a future that supplies a home for the best hopes of humankind – and for the ultimate imperatives of Gaia.

The future is waiting to hear from us.

Part One

Pressures and processes

Our world is a-boil with changes that are producing uncontainable pressures. In turn these pressures are generating a torrent of change that is turning our world inside out. More importantly, they are setting the agenda for a far more different world in the future. Part One looks at these pressures together with their processes.

First and foremost is planetary change. We are devegetating the globe, notably through destruction of tropical forests. Our pollution amounts to a poisoning of large-scale ecosystems. We are transforming global climate and depleting the life-protecting ozone layer. We are engaged in a mass extinction of species, set to become the biggest ever. This gross degradation of our biosphere threatens to trigger Gaian-style kickbacks of types we can scarcely guess at: we are simply too ignorant of our world and its Gaian make-up, even though we are interfering with it on a scale unmatched by all except the greatest geologic upheavals.

Much of this is due to excessive consumerism, a responsibility of the rich minority. Equally injurious is the population explosion, which among the impoverished majority of humankind is now entering its most explosive phase. Stemming from the close linkages between both is a series of geopolitical shifts, steadily reordering the mix of global power.

On top of all this comes a foment of new ideas and beliefs, such as holistic endeavours, green consciousness, internationalism, environmental security, renascent cultures, new-age creativity, and keener awareness of selfhood. So too the very foundations of much of our science are being shaken by the recent recognition of chaos as an endemic attribute of our natural world, of much of our human-made world as well. The Gaia hypothesis tells us that the planetary ecosystem works far differently from what we have supposed; and the emergence of holistic concepts teaches us that we need to develop a super-science with contributions from an array of fields.

Combine all these, plus a host of technological triggers, and we have a potent recipe for changes on all sides. But one factor remains little changed as yet, and that is our capacity to recognize the full panoply of change bearing down on us.

Two acts of destruction
A highway (main picture) cuts through devastated Amazonian rainforest, previously lush and impenetrable. A European power station (inset) contributes to global warming.

The shrinking forests

We are changing the face of the planet with all the impact of a geologic upheaval. In times past, the atmosphere has undergone profound changes; species have suffered mass extinctions; forest areas have shrunk and deserts have spread; and climate patterns have altered beyond recognition. But these changes have generally occurred at different times from each other, and they have usually extended over periods of thousands if not millions of years. Now they are all happening at once, and within the space of just a few decades – the flicker of a geological eye.

Yet whatever the changes humanity has wrought to date, they are a pale portent of what is to come within the lifespans of most readers of this book – unless we start to recognize our responsibilities as managers of the planetary ecosystem. By the time today's children are adults, they may be witnessing a disruptive phenomenon unprecedented since the beginnings of the biosphere more than 4 billion years ago.

As a measure of this superscale change, consider the planet's forests. Each year 142,000 sq km of tropical forests are destroyed, and another 150,000 sq km grossly degraded. In total this area is equivalent to the whole of the UK. Outside the tropics we are losing entire tracts of forest to acid rain and overlogging. Globally, forests generally and tropical forests in particular exert a gyroscopic effect on climate (see right), stabilizing atmospheric processes by, for example, absorbing radiant energy from the sun. With tree cover gone, the reflectivity ("shininess", or albedo) of land masses increases and more heat is returned to the atmosphere. The result: disruption of convection currents, wind patterns, and rainfall regimes. In addition forests evapotranspire vast amounts of moisture: when forest cover is eliminated, local moisture stocks often become depleted, whereupon there is a "drying-out" effect, extending even beyond the original forested zone. Moreover deforested lands retain less moisture in their soils, aggravating the desiccatory process.

The forest gyroscope

The Earth's forests serve as a gyroscope for climate functioning. Within their biomass they harbour vast stocks of carbon, and constantly absorb carbon dioxide (CO_2) from the atmosphere. Rather than serving as the "lungs" of the planet, they are a primary factor in regulating the planetary carbon cycle – the balanced flow of carbon between soils, living matter, oceans, and the gaseous atmosphere – a key element in global climate. They likewise serve to stabilize the Earth's water budgets by soaking up rainfall and evapotranspiring it back into the skies. We have yet to understand all their important contributions, and we may well learn of them only through their demise.

O_2

Rate of loss

The Earth's forests are disappearing at ultra-rapid rates. Temperate forests are falling to acid rain; tropical forests to the chainsaw and the matchbox. In 1979 tropical forests lost 75,000 sq km of their expanse; an amount that had risen by 1989 to 142,000 sq km. And the deforestation rate appears to be accelerating still further. (See graph, right, which plots tropical forest losses in millions of sq km, and CO_2 emissions, in billions of tonnes.) The 1989 deforestation means that carbon release has risen from 1.7 billion tonnes in 1980 to 2.4 billion tonnes today, plus increased amounts of other greenhouse gases. Our atlases traditionally feature a vivid green band around the equator denoting the most lush vegetation on Earth. We may soon have to recolour the band a dirty brown to depict the death of the greatest celebration of nature ever to grace the face of the planet.

0.2

1950

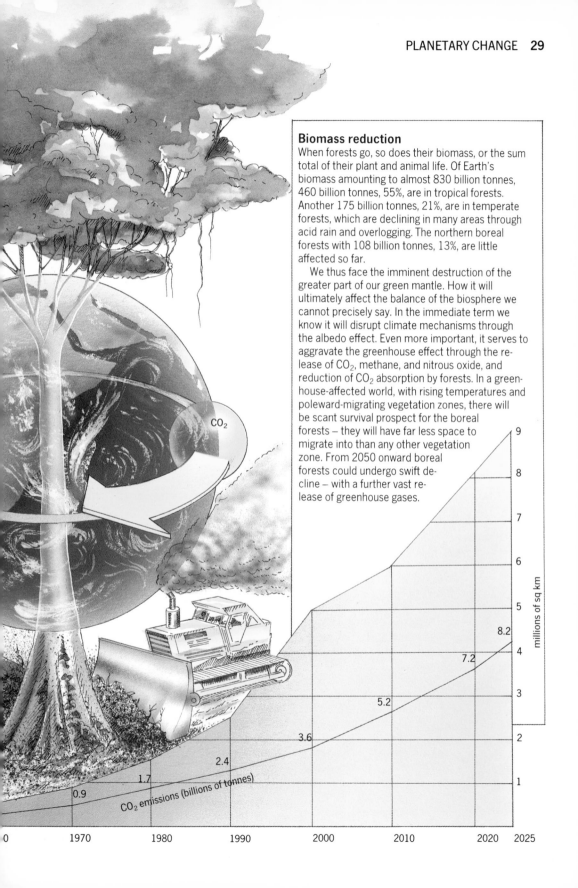

Biomass reduction

When forests go, so does their biomass, or the sum total of their plant and animal life. Of Earth's biomass amounting to almost 830 billion tonnes, 460 billion tonnes, 55%, are in tropical forests. Another 175 billion tonnes, 21%, are in temperate forests, which are declining in many areas through acid rain and overlogging. The northern boreal forests with 108 billion tonnes, 13%, are little affected so far.

We thus face the imminent destruction of the greater part of our green mantle. How it will ultimately affect the balance of the biosphere we cannot precisely say. In the immediate term we know it will disrupt climate mechanisms through the albedo effect. Even more important, it serves to aggravate the greenhouse effect through the release of CO_2, methane, and nitrous oxide, and reduction of CO_2 absorption by forests. In a greenhouse-affected world, with rising temperatures and poleward-migrating vegetation zones, there will be scant survival prospect for the boreal forests – they will have far less space to migrate into than any other vegetation zone. From 2050 onward boreal forests could undergo swift decline – with a further vast release of greenhouse gases.

CO_2

millions of sq km

CO_2 emissions (billions of tonnes)

0.9

1.7

2.4

3.6

5.2

7.2

8.2

9

8

7

6

5

4

3

2

1

1970 1980 1990 2000 2010 2020 2025

0

The poisoned planet

Just 30 years ago there was pollution on all sides. But it was still localized, confined to parts of individual nations. Today it knows no frontiers: acid rain spans entire regions, while ozone-layer depletion and atmospheric warming affect the whole planet.

Industry worldwide now spews into the air and water bodies some 70,000 different chemicals, largely untested for their environmental effects. US factories alone emit 1.2 million tonnes of chemicals annually. Our use of synthetic materials such as plastics entails the release into the environment of highly toxic PCBs; many manufacturing processes lead to emissions of heavy metals with their acute health effects. All reflect our urge for ever-more consumerism and our casual approach to the spill-over impacts of industry and agriculture, based on hosts of chemicals with largely unknown effects.

In particular the skies contain a cocktail of chemicals. Generally it can't be seen or tasted, so it creeps on unnoticed. Most threatening of all are the gases that, by trapping part of the sun's warmth at the Earth's surface, are causing the greenhouse effect: carbon dioxide (CO_2), methane (CH_4), nitrous oxide (N_2O), ozone (O_3), and CFCs (chlorofluorocarbons). Carbon dioxide, which causes almost 50 per cent of the greenhouse effect, stems mostly from the combustion of fossil fuels in power plants, factories, and vehicles. So we are all part of the problem every time we switch on a light, boil a kettle, or travel by car, bus, or train. Over breakfast we all contribute by eating dairy products derived from cows, major producers of methane, and by consuming farm produce that depends on synthetic fertilizers, a source of nitrous oxide.

In sum, our poisoned planet reflects a combination of the world's major challenges: energy demand, food supply, population growth, and land resources. The question to ask, though rarely addressed, is: what further unrecognized chemical cocktails are we producing with capacity to build up steadily before bursting on us with poisonous impact? What will be the future "acid rain" or "greenhouse effect"?

Polluting the biosphere
There are three main sources of biospheric pollution: industry, agriculture, and incidental spillage (as at sea). Many pollutants rise into the sky before being "rained out" on to the land or into the sea. Behind each of these three sources is the hand of the consumer, and to this extent we are all responsible, just as much as the factory owner, the farmer, and the ship's captain.

Atmospheric pollution
Using our skies as a garbage can, we despatch growing numbers of chemicals into the atmosphere. Around 50% of human inputs come from transport, roughly 30% from fuel combustion in stationary sources such as factories, and 10 to 15% from industrial processes. We have already learned, to our acute cost, that one of the most pollutant of all humankind's emissions is harmless-sounding CO_2, the cause of much of the greenhouse effect (see pp. 32-3).

Land pollution

Land is polluted by air contaminants, dumped waste, and agricultural pesticides among many other harmful materials. The prime sources are chemical producers, petroleum refineries, manufacturers, and agriculture. Many of the pollutants are classified as hazardous wastes (for example, corrosive acids and PCBs). The US manufactures about 1.5 tonnes of hazardous wastes per American per year; and each year Western Europe exports 250,000 tonnes of hazardous wastes to Eastern Europe. A more recent form of land pollution is acid rain, affecting lakes, forests, soils, crops, buildings, and human lungs.

Ocean pollution

Oceans are the ultimate sink for much human waste, in the form of urban and agricultural run-off, industrial discharge, atmospheric fallout, effluent from ships, and tanker spills. Part of this total is accidental, much is deliberate: the oceans are viewed as a vast "cost-free" sewer. But we pay a price through fisheries depleted by contamination and declining ecosystems. It is, however, estuaries and other coastal waters that bear the main brunt of pollution – and they are by far the most productive in terms of fish and other life forms. As many as half a million seabirds are killed each year through chronic oil pollution in Western Europe alone.

The chemical cocktail

Each year industry produces another thousand synthetic chemicals. Most of them come into everyday use; and most of them break down only slowly (DDT, plastics), some not at all (mercury, lead, and other toxic items). Worst, at least 80% are inadequately tested for their individual effects on humans and other forms of life, while their combined impacts – the cocktail effect – are barely considered. Because of powerful commercial interests, there seems scant prospect of limitations to our ever-more capable poisoning of the planet.

Climate – the gas cloud

Mark Twain once said that everybody talks about the weather but nobody does anything about it. That remark is now proving to be premature. We are altering the world's climate with far-reaching effect.

As we were warned by the Swedish scientist Svante Arrhenius late last century, we cannot burn fossil fuels without releasing carbon into the atmosphere. There it builds up as CO_2 gas, which exerts a heat-trapping effect, preventing some of the sun's radiation from escaping back into space. For sure, there has generally been a moderate amount of CO_2 in the atmosphere throughout most of the biosphere's history. But during the millennia before the Industrial Revolution began, CO_2 in the atmosphere was about 280 parts per million (ppm). Today the level has risen beyond 350ppm, and is building at 2ppm per year. It is projected to double beyond the 280ppm level by the year 2050, bringing temperature rises of 2–5°C (3.6–9°F).

Other greenhouse gases are increasing too, notably methane, nitrous oxide, ozone, and CFCs. While they are much rarer in the atmosphere than CO_2, they are far more potent. One molecule of methane traps 27 times as much of the sun's warmth as does a molecule of CO_2. Moreover the build-up of methane is proceeding more rapidly than that of CO_2. Something similar also applies to the other greenhouse gases. The overall effect is that the critical CO_2-equivalent doubling level may well arrive by 2030.

CFCs are also ozone destroyers. Whereas the greenhouse effect remains a hypothesized phenomenon, ozone-layer depletion is fact. It was suspected by the early 1970s, and CFCs in aerosols were banned in the US. Despite this, CFCs and other ozone-depleting chemicals have been accumulating and will exact a heavy toll on future generations. Even if CFCs were eliminated immediately, they would remain active and continue their ozone-destroying work for a hundred years or more. So for a lengthy period, the thinning ozone layer will transmit increased ultraviolet radiation (UV-B), causing gross injury to plant and animal life.

1 Total incoming **solar** radiation 2 Reflected by Earth 3 Absorbed by Earth 4 Absorbed by atmosphere 5 Reflected by atmosphere 6 Total reflected solar radiation.

7 **Infrared** radiation emitted by atmosphere 8 Energy from evaporation and thermals 9 Infrared radiation emitted by Earth 10 Absorbed by greenhouse gases 11 Emitted by atmosphere 12 Re-radiated back to Earth 13 Total outgoing infrared radiation.

The greenhouse effect

There are complex processes by which radiant energy from the sun interacts with the atmosphere, the planet, and its life forms to maintain a stable temperature. Basically, and to ensure equilibrium, the amount of energy coming into the system (planet and atmosphere) – to energize climate, winds, currents, and to warm the planet to the level we normally know – must equal the amount of energy leaving it (see above).

But the planet is no passive on-looker, for as well as absorbing energy it also re-radiates it in the form of infrared (IR) heat. This in turn warms atmospheric gases and is re-radiated to the planet. During the process, energy is dissipated as part of the total throughput of energy across the system.

All hinges, therefore, on the amount of heat the atmosphere retains, which in turn depends on its mix of gases. The proportion of these gases is a natural climate regulator, and an increase in greenhouse gases means an increase in average global temperature.

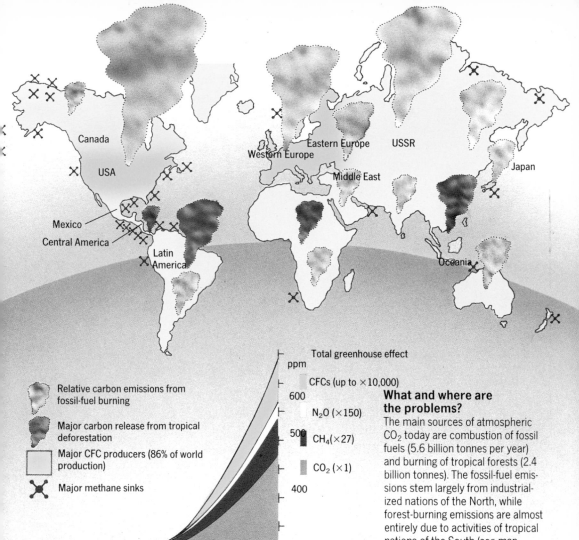

Map labels: Canada · USA · Mexico · Central America · Latin America · Western Europe · Eastern Europe · Middle East · USSR · Japan · Oceania

Relative carbon emissions from fossil-fuel burning

Major carbon release from tropical deforestation

Major CFC producers (86% of world production)

Major methane sinks

Graph labels: Total greenhouse effect · ppm · CFCs (up to ×10,000) · N$_2$O (×150) · CH$_4$ (×27) · CO$_2$ (×1) · 600 · 500 · 400 · 300 · 1800 · 1850 · 1900 · 1950 · 2000 · 2050

The methane Doomsday machine

Imprisoned in frozen tundra and beneath the sea in continental margins is a vast 10-trillion-tonne reservoir of carbon in the form of methane – an amount greater than all known fossil-fuel deposits. As the planet warms, the tundras melt, and methane is liberated to accelerate global warming. Such a methane-driven feedback may become a doomsday machine sometime late next century.

Increase in greenhouse gases

The greenhouse gas receiving most publicity is CO_2. The contribution of other greenhouse gases, although not as great as CO_2, is at least as significant in terms of atmospheric warming. CFC-12, for example, retains 10,000 times more heat, molecule for molecule, than CO_2. The graph above plots the accumulative effect of the major greenhouse gases in terms of their potential for global warming. The actual and projected parts per million (ppm) for CO_2 are given along with the greenhouse values of the other gases as if they too were CO_2.

What and where are the problems?

The main sources of atmospheric CO_2 today are combustion of fossil fuels (5.6 billion tonnes per year) and burning of tropical forests (2.4 billion tonnes). The fossil-fuel emissions stem largely from industrialized nations of the North, while forest-burning emissions are almost entirely due to activities of tropical nations of the South (see map above). But note that developing nations may soon match advanced ones in fossil-fuel burning as they seek to industrialize with all due speed. Consider a situation where India or China were to double its per-capita consumption of commercial energy (as each plans to do by the end of the century or shortly thereafter), albeit to a level that would still be less than one-tenth of what an average American citizen consumes today. Were the US at the same time to take the remarkable step of suspending all further burning of coal (currently providing about 20% of its energy), and to forego burning anything in its stead, the American sacrifice would shortly be swamped by either India or China because of the sheer size of their huge populations.

Disappearing life forms

The assaults on the environment are devastating the habitats and life-support systems of millions of species. Tropical forests are biotically richer than all other biomes, containing between 70 and 95 per cent of Earth's species in just 6 per cent of land area. Yet tropical forests are being destroyed faster than any other biome and may disappear, in all but remote areas, within the next 25 years. Other species-rich biomes, such as coral reefs, wetlands, and Mediterranean-type sectors, are likewise being reduced, with mega-extinctions of species.

Parallel processes can be seen in still other areas. In Britain since 1930, 95 per cent of natural lowland grasslands and 50 per cent of remaining fens have gone; while since 1940 an area of 7000 sq km has disappeared under tarmac and concrete. Britain has also lost 175,000 km of hedgerows since 1950. In the US, wetlands have declined from 870,000 sq km in 1800 to well under 40,000 sq km today, and a further 1200 sq km are drained annually.

The result of habitat loss worldwide is mass extinction. We are losing between 50 and 100 species of animal a day on average, plus one species of plant, and both rates are rapidly accelerating. Within the next few decades, once the tropical forests are gone, we stand to witness the extinction of millions of species – as many as 50 per cent of the total number.

This mass extinction will far surpass the "great dying" of the dinosaurs and associated species 65 million years ago. This time, many more species will be involved, the time span will be far shorter, and there will be much more of an impoverishing impact on the future of evolution. Ironically, this extinction spasm will have been brought about by the activities of just one species – the only one that has ever existed with the power to save other species.

Eventually the process of evolution will generate replacements. But our descendants will look out on a biologically impoverished world for possibly 200,000 generations – ten times longer than since humanity first came into existence.

Speciation

As species disappear, so there is "ecological space" for new ones to emerge – the process of speciation. The natural, or background, rate of extinction before humans arrived was roughly one species a year, with the speciation rate slightly higher. But now that we are losing at least 50 species a day, there is no compensatory outburst of speciation. Whereas extinction can occur virtually overnight, it usually takes hundreds of years for evolution to produce the most rapidly emergent species, such as insects, while vertebrates often require more than a million years.

Habitat loss

Keystone species

The Brazil nut tree is pollinated by a tiny bee, which also pollinates many other plants. In turn, these plants often supply prime sources of food to sundry other insects, which pollinate other plants, and so on. Wasps are obligate pollinators of fig trees, hummingbirds serve a similar function for wild pineapples, and the same for bats, moths, and their host plants such as kapok and balsa trees. The pollinators can be viewed as "mobile links", and the plant species, by virtue of supplying food to extensive associations of mobile links, as "keystone species" (see above).

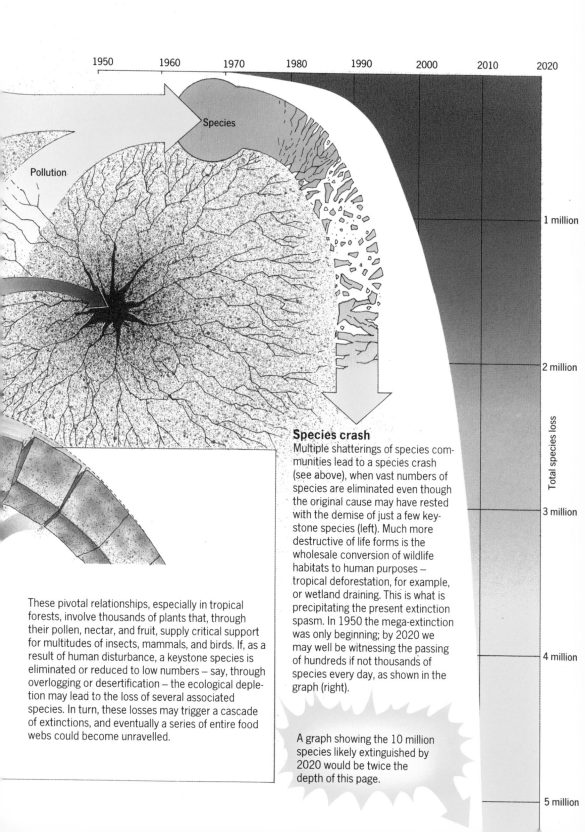

Species crash
Multiple shatterings of species communities lead to a species crash
(see above), when vast numbers of
species are eliminated even though
the original cause may have rested
with the demise of just a few keystone species (left). Much more
destructive of life forms is the
wholesale conversion of wildlife
habitats to human purposes –
tropical deforestation, for example,
or wetland draining. This is what is
precipitating the present extinction
spasm. In 1950 the mega-extinction
was only beginning; by 2020 we
may well be witnessing the passing
of hundreds if not thousands of
species every day, as shown in the
graph (right).

These pivotal relationships, especially in tropical
forests, involve thousands of plants that, through
their pollen, nectar, and fruit, supply critical support
for multitudes of insects, mammals, and birds. If, as a
result of human disturbance, a keystone species is
eliminated or reduced to low numbers – say, through
overlogging or desertification – the ecological depletion may lead to the loss of several associated
species. In turn, these losses may trigger a cascade
of extinctions, and eventually a series of entire food
webs could become unravelled.

A graph showing the 10 million
species likely extinguished by
2020 would be twice the
depth of this page.

Gaia kickbacks

The Earth operates as a self-regulating organism in physical and biological senses combined. In the face of the many assaults we are imposing on the biosphere, we can expect Gaia to respond – perhaps in some unexpected ways.

For instance, there is a little-recognized connection between the greenhouse effect and depletion of the ozone layer. Of all CO_2 released into the skies each year, roughly half seems to be absorbed by the oceans, thanks in part to the photosynthesizing activities of minute plants, phytoplankton, in the surface layers of the seas. Of all organisms susceptible to increased UV-B radiation, phytoplankton probably rank among the most sensitive. Were UV-B to cause a decline in phytoplankton's role as a carbon sink, the greenhouse effect's approach could markedly accelerate.

We can reasonably suppose that there are many such linkages between planetary mechanisms and environmental degradation. We have yet to put our finger on them, let alone to get a scientific grip of them. While seeking out these critical unknowns, we should heed the warnings from the ozone holes, the greenhouse effect, and acid rain, all of which have taken decades to build up unseen before bursting upon us. We should also bear in mind that the biggest change of all, climate change, rarely comes on in a predictably linear fashion. Rather it advances with all kinds of jerks, often making the process faster than we might anticipate. A regular progression is the exception, a surprise-full affair is the norm.

How else is Gaia going to respond to our depredations? What further backlash effects might the unknowns generate through their unsuspected interactions, sometimes visiting a compounded impact upon us? We can be certain that Gaia will not remain indifferent to the assaults of humanity – even though Gaia might be indifferent to the survival of humanity.

Gaia's response to the human assault

Gaia groans under the burden of humanity's reckless overloading of the global ecosystem. The planet's green covering, its oceans, its cycles of key elements, even its climate, are suffering unprecedented damage. The Gaian system can offer no immediate remedy in response: it functions in time spans of millions of years. But meantime it shows sure signs of dis-ease.

Feedback loops

A feedback loop occurs when some factor serves to modify a process by accentuating it (positive feedback) or reducing it (negative feedback). Many species of marine plankton produce large quantities of dimethyl sulphide (DMS), which helps clouds to form over remote oceans, and thus cool the atmosphere. Heating increases the amount of plankton producing DMS; more DMS means more cloud, which brings the temperature back down again. DMS thus serves as a global thermostat. If DMS production were severely reduced, Earth's temperature would rise several degrees. Gaian scientists believe there must be many such feedback processes by which living things regulate climate to their own advantage.

The flip to a new steady state

When an ecosystem is sufficiently disturbed, it can "flip", in other words go through a sudden change to a new state of structure and organization. The new structure may prove so stable that when the original disturbance is lifted, the system may not flip back again to its original state. Such "jump effects" have periodically overtaken the Earth's climate during the geological past. What if our present gross interventions in climate systems were to trigger a flip?

Possible effects

The Gaian system that comprises the biosphere can "kick back" in some unexpected ways – ways that are harmful for humans, while amounting to only an adjustment on the part of the system as a whole. Who would have suspected that the increasing use of aerosol cans in the northern hemisphere could give rise to increasing melanomas in the southern hemisphere? The ozone hole over Antarctica may already be causing a spread of cancers in southern Australia. The evidence is inconclusive as yet, though it could soon become compelling. Similarly the recent polluting "blooms" of algae in the Mediterranean could stem from shifts in the sulphur cycle. We are so far from understanding the Gaian systems of our planet that we cannot possibly anticipate the many kickbacks that could emerge. All we know is that they could be profound and widespread. What, for instance, could be the consequence of eliminating several million species? The ultimate and most serious consequences could be deep-seated breakdowns in the ecological workings of entire broadscope ecosystems. Of course the Gaian system at large will adjust and adapt – but human needs could be grossly set back in ways we cannot even surmise as yet.

Humanity's expulsion from the Garden of Eden

As the Gaian system seeks to find a new equilibrium in the wake of humanity's assaults, it may ultimately cease to tolerate this over-exploitative species. Its responses could lead to the elimination of the disruptive element, after the fashion of an organism's defence system that expels an unwanted foreign body. Gaia's function is to safeguard the health of its system; it does not care about the fate of any individual element.

Human numbers

We are witnessing a population explosion – or more accurately, an implosion. "Explosion" implies that there is space to expand into after the balloon bursts – something that is certainly not the case with the rise in human numbers. Only 60 years ago there were 2 billion of us, a total that had taken 250 million years to attain. Today there are more than 5 billion; by 2000 there will be 6 billion; and by 2025 there could be more than 10 billion. The projection for the final total, when population growth finally tails away late next century, is almost 11 billion (within a range of 8.5 to 14 billion). Thus the main surge in human numbers is still to come.

Even the lower end of the range projected for 2025 (8.5 billion) should be cause for enormous concern. We maintain present numbers thanks only to one technomiracle after another in agriculture, energy, and other key areas of development. Even so, almost 1 billion people are malnourished and we support the present multitude at the cost of the declining capacity of the Earth to sustain us. What if, within another 35 years, there are twice as many people seeking three times as much food and fibre, demanding four times as much energy, and engaging in five times as much economic activity – as is projected if the present trends of meeting our expectations continue unchecked?

So pervasive is the impact of humankind on the planetary ecosystem that our single species is already consuming or otherwise co-opting 40 per cent of worldwide plant growth each year. That means the other 30 million species on Earth have to make do with the remaining 60 per cent. If human numbers double, and the remainder of unco-opted plant growth were reduced toward 20 per cent, where would all species then be – including our own? All the more, a doubling of human numbers seems to be increasingly like a fantasy scenario.

What are the limits?

There is massive reason to suppose that the world is overpopulated. According to the World Hunger Project, if we all ate a vegetarian diet and shared food equally, the biosphere could support about 6 billion people. If diet were upgraded so that 15 or 25% of calories were derived from animal products, feedable totals fall to 4 and 3 billion respectively – figures borne out by today's reality: 5.4 billion people, 1 billion of them hungry. Better agrotechnologies may improve prospects. But the 1988 world harvest was about 5% smaller than in 1985 – while global population had grown by 5%.

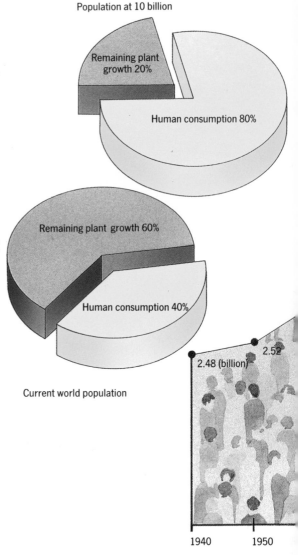

Population at 10 billion

Remaining plant growth 20%

Human consumption 80%

Remaining plant growth 60%

Human consumption 40%

Current world population

2.48 (billion)

2.52

1940   1950

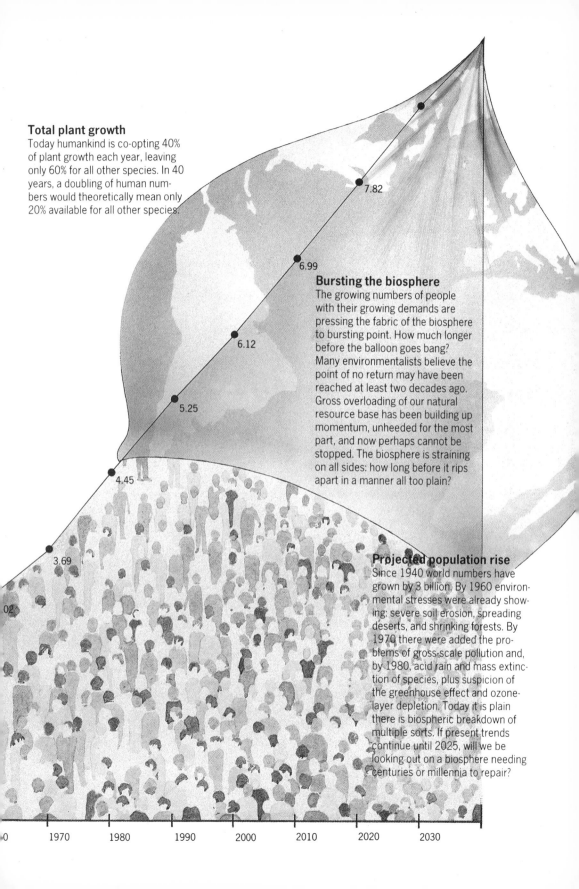

Total plant growth
Today humankind is co-opting 40%
of plant growth each year, leaving
only 60% for all other species. In 40
years, a doubling of human numbers would theoretically mean only
20% available for all other species.

7.82

6.99

6.12

Bursting the biosphere
The growing numbers of people
with their growing demands are
pressing the fabric of the biosphere
to bursting point. How much longer
before the balloon goes bang?
Many environmentalists believe the
point of no return may have been
reached at least two decades ago.
Gross overloading of our natural
resource base has been building up
momentum, unheeded for the most
part, and now perhaps cannot be
stopped. The biosphere is straining
on all sides: how long before it rips
apart in a manner all too plain?

5.25

4.45

3.69

02

Projected population rise
Since 1940 world numbers have
grown by 3 billion. By 1960 environmental stresses were already showing: severe soil erosion, spreading
deserts, and shrinking forests. By
1970 there were added the problems of gross-scale pollution and,
by 1980, acid rain and mass extinction of species, plus suspicion of
the greenhouse effect and ozone-
layer depletion. Today it is plain
there is biospheric breakdown of
multiple sorts. If present trends
continue until 2025, will we be
looking out on a biosphere needing
centuries or millennia to repair?

0 1970 1980 1990 2000 2010 2020 2030

Geopolitical shifts

Of the world's present annual increase of 90 million people, 85 million are in the developing world. But growing numbers of Third Worlders are already making their way to the First World – a trend that will surely accelerate as time passes.

During the past two decades at least 7 million people have migrated from Mexico and Central America to the US, and another 10 million are expected by the year 2000. Today there are more Mexicans in Los Angeles than in any other city except Mexico City; Miami is already half Spanish speaking, which has led to friction with long-standing American minorities. In another few generations, Hispanics, Afro-Caribbeans, and other minorities could outnumber those who have hitherto made up the majority of the US since its founding – white Anglo-Saxon Protestants.

By early next century there could be similar mass migrations into Europe. The countries of the Mediterranean rim from Turkey to Morocco now number over 200 million people, as against almost 400 million living in Western and Central Europe. Within a generation these figures are projected to become 450 and 420 million, reversing the balance. It is also realistic to anticipate parallel spillovers from Indonesia into Australia. Moreover these prognoses derive only from projections of current trends. There will be still greater cause for migrations when the greenhouse effect produces climate upheavals to burden such overpopulated regions as the Indian subcontinent (see pp. 102–3). There could also be some population shift toward the emergent economic powers, such as Brazil.

Within nations, too, there are population changes with powerful political fallout. In Israel, for example, with differentiated family sizes among various sectors of the populace, plus immigration from Asia, by the year 2000 a majority of citizens could well be non-European. This seismic shift in ethnic makeup will have a profound impact on political orientation, as witness the recent move away from Israel's traditional liberalism.

Sub-Saharan movement
This region's present population of 500 million is projected to top 700 million by 2000 and 1.2 billion by 2020. Yet its capacity to support today's multitudes has been declining since 1970. The intervening Sahara notwithstanding, the nearest refuge is Europe.

Across the great divide
The mass migrations we can anticipate in the foreseeable future are driven by both "push" and "pull" factors. The push element is made up of deteriorating means to gain a sustainable livelihood, made up in turn of degraded resource bases compounded in no small measure by population-growth pressures. The pull element comprises mainly the bright hope of a better life, indeed the hope for a decent life at all, in the advanced countries, where there seems to be, in the eyes of the migrants, an endless prospect of material wellbeing.

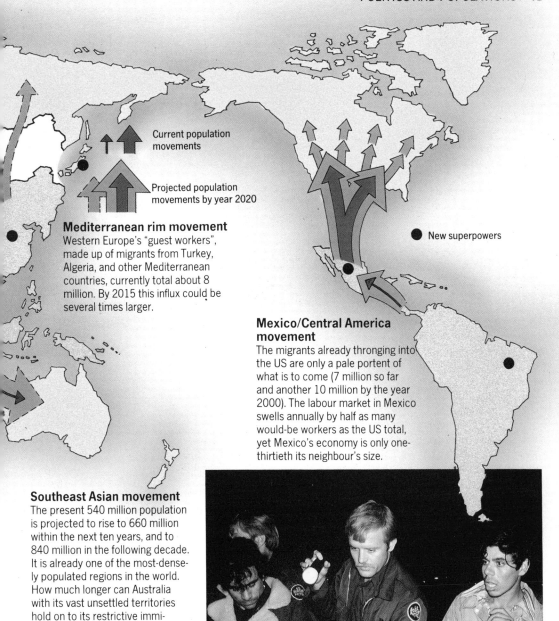

Current population movements

Projected population movements by year 2020

● New superpowers

Mediterranean rim movement

Western Europe's "guest workers", made up of migrants from Turkey, Algeria, and other Mediterranean countries, currently total about 8 million. By 2015 this influx could be several times larger.

Mexico/Central America movement

The migrants already thronging into the US are only a pale portent of what is to come (7 million so far and another 10 million by the year 2000). The labour market in Mexico swells annually by half as many would-be workers as the US total, yet Mexico's economy is only one-thirtieth its neighbour's size.

Southeast Asian movement

The present 540 million population is projected to rise to 660 million within the next ten years, and to 840 million in the following decade. It is already one of the most-densely populated regions in the world. How much longer can Australia with its vast unsettled territories hold on to its restrictive immigration policies?

The human cost

As millions of Mexicans and other Hispanics from overloaded Latin America seek refuge in the US each year, many chance their (illegal) luck with a night-time crossing of the Rio Grande. Often they no sooner set foot on American soil than they encounter the border patrol (right).

Intolerable imbalances

The divide between North and South is becoming ever-more divisive. Since 1960 the developed countries have become richer by an average of $5400 gross national product (GNP) per head, while the developing countries have advanced by only $800. Latin American citizens are on average poorer than they were in 1970. And the poorest of all, the nations of black Africa, must achieve a continuous economic growth rate of 3 per cent per year if they are to return even to their 1970 levels of "wealth" by 2000.

As with the population problem (see pp. 38–41), there are potentially explosive wealth divisions within countries too. For example, the top 10 per cent in Brazil possess a larger share of national wealth and income than all the rest of the population put together. Much the same applies, albeit not so crassly, in many other countries, such as Colombia, Kenya, Ivory Coast, Pakistan, and Philippines. These are all nations where the GNP is forging ahead, yet most of the people are falling behind. The newly rich élites in Nairobi, Bogotá, and Manila have more in common with their counterparts in New York, London, and Tokyo than they have with their fellow citizens a dozen kilometres into the countryside.

Yet other economic entities point up the growing gap. The top ten multinational corporations have a combined annual sales turnover, around $850 billion, that is five times greater than the total GNPs of black Africa (i.e. excluding South Africa); the Shell Corporation alone has a turnover equivalent to the largest economy in black Africa, Nigeria's, which itself is worth almost 40 per cent of all black Africa's GNPs. This gives these corporations enormous leverage in their dealings with host governments.

Thus the deepening divide between the haves and the have-nots must rank as a more potent source of general instability and unsustainable strain than even the pressures stemming from population growth – though the two are closely interconnected.

The growing gap
The gap in the world between the haves and the have-nots is becoming a gulf. Will the so-called Southerners tolerate the absurd imbalances when, to some extent (through inequitable trade terms, for example), they are poor simply because the Northerners are rich – and when many impoverished people among the have-not nations receive less protein per week than a domestic cat in the North?

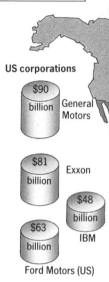

US corporations

$90 billion General Motors

$81 billion Exxon

$48 billion IBM

$63 billion Ford Motors (US)

The rich North
The affluent-world citizen enjoys an average GNP per head of more than $14,000, an amount that increases by $250 each year. More to the point, Americans spend a massive $278 billion each year on gambling alone.

US/Mexico
The US GNP of $4.5 trillion is 30 times Mexico's $150 billion, yet by 2020 Mexico will have at least half as many people as the US. The average Mexican GNP per head is $1900, way below the US official poverty line. At the same time, the share of national income taken by the top 10% in Mexico is a good deal larger than that of the top 10% in the US – and average Mexican income has been declining since 1980, whereas in the US it has been rising.

% below US poverty line

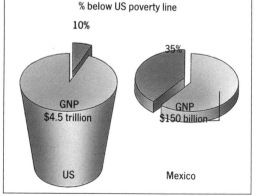

10%

35%

GNP $4.5 trillion

GNP $150 billion

US

Mexico

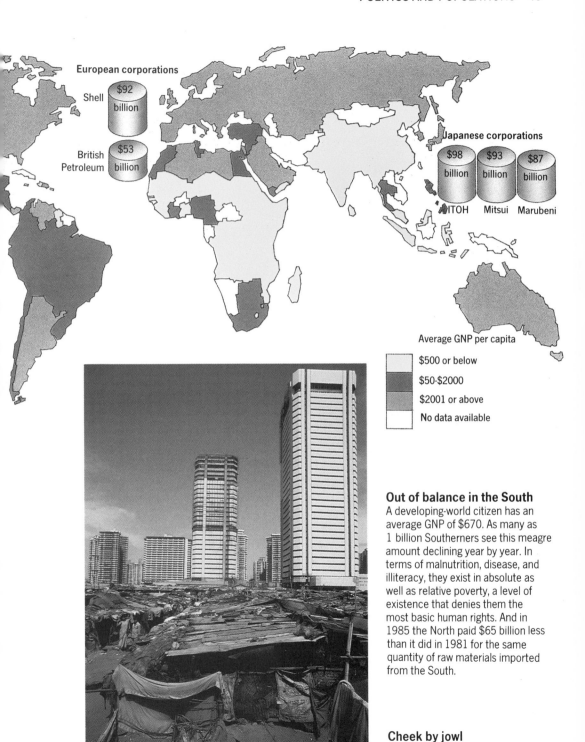

European corporations

Shell $92 billion

British Petroleum $53 billion

Japanese corporations

$98 billion ITOH

$93 billion Mitsui

$87 billion Marubeni

Average GNP per capita

$500 or below

$50-$2000

$2001 or above

No data available

Out of balance in the South
A developing-world citizen has an average GNP of $670. As many as 1 billion Southerners see this meagre amount declining year by year. In terms of malnutrition, disease, and illiteracy, they exist in absolute as well as relative poverty, a level of existence that denies them the most basic human rights. And in 1985 the North paid $65 billion less than it did in 1981 for the same quantity of raw materials imported from the South.

Cheek by jowl
Depressing, insanitary shanty towns crowd beneath towering sky-scrapers, home of the World Trade Centre in Bombay.

The planet

"The Earth does not belong to us – we belong to the Earth." HRH Prince Charles

We are starting to understand that just as we are all part of a single economic system worldwide, so we all share a single planetary ecosystem. We are not only British, American, and Brazilian, we are common citizens of One Earth. More than that, we are one species among 30 million – members of a community with shared rights, shared roles, and a shared future.

This new understanding has been a long time coming. It is more than 20 years since we first viewed the spacecraft photographs of the Blue Planet, and we did not truly grasp what we were looking at. Nationalistic rivalries continued and the ravaging of the biosphere became more energetic than ever. We ignored the astronauts' comment that when they looked back on Spaceship Earth it was all they expected it to be – except that they saw no political boundaries.

At long glorious last we are being pushed by daily evidence of environmental degradation, as of universal energy shortages and debt crises, toward the view that the planet is indeed one, the biosphere is a seamless web, and the Earth is a unitary whole. The image of Gaia – the living Earth – is starting to register as a wholly fresh world view.

As a result there is a sunburst of global awareness. An obvious manifestation is the rise of the Greens. Obscure and derided for more than a decade, they have been steadily building their numbers.

In part this surge of recognition is a reaction to environmental crises. But it also reflects a deeper and longer-standing shift in perceptions and lifestyles. For years there has been ever-widening interest in healthy living and in green consumerism. As a result, conservation is no longer seen as a weekend concern; it has become a central issue for the Monday-morning world.

Local to global view

We are consciously preoccupied with local concerns of our daily lives – whether in the North, with extreme consumerism, or in the South, where the overriding interest is often the next bowl of rice. Yet unconsciously our activities impinge, through economic and environmental interdependence, on the entire planetary ecosystem and its limited capacity to support growing numbers of humans with their growing demands. We need to see both near and far; to see the global with the local. We must develop the sense of vision that matches our status as planetary citizens.

Environmental awareness

Issues concerning the environment – until just a few years ago the sole domain of pressure groups, "worthy" agencies, and non-governmental organizations (NGOs) – are now high on political agendas and are debated as a matter of urgency by world political leaders, bankers, multinational corporations, and financiers. The true import of the issues is still largely misunderstood, but it is on the table to stay.

Opinion polls constantly show that worldwide a full 40% of citizens recognize environmentalism as a major fact of life; in the North 65% are willing to pay higher taxes and risk higher unemployment in order to improve the quality of the environment. In Britain alone, the environmental movement has overtaken the trade union movement in income, and it will soon pass it numerically as the single largest sectional interest in the country.

Environmental security

Partly as a result of green awareness, there is an emergent recognition of the environmental dimension to security issues. The notion of national security can no longer be centred so strongly on simple considerations of military prowess. It increasingly entails key factors of environmental stability that underpin our material welfare – soil, water, forests, grasslands, minerals, and fisheries – all of which are prime components of a nation's natural resource base. If a nation's environmental foundations are depleted, its economy will steadily decline, its social fabric deteriorate, and its political structure become destabilized. The outcome is all too likely to be conflict, whether in the form of internal disorder or hostilities with other nations.

The self

And so to self. Or rather, to the role of "self" that each of us plays out in the planetary scheme of things. There are three prominent aspects at issue: our perception of ourselves as one species among many others; our view of ourselves as members of society; and our recognition of ourselves as individuals. These fast changing images of ourselves are serving as potent triggers of change.

As a species we have long perceived ourselves as lords of all creation. Now Gaian insights tell us that we are not apart from nature but a part of nature – an equal part of a community of species. A distinctive part, but still a part of what is intrinsically a democratic community with shared roles, functions, and rights. This new perception has been reinforced by spacecraft pictures showing the biosphere as a unitary whole. So when we speak of "our planet", "our climate", and the like, we must expand the notion of "our" to embrace our 30 million fellow species.

Next, our growing awareness of our place in society. As we have watched our world wracked by conflict and our planetary eco-system abused on every side, we have become conscious of two profound misgivings. First, that we are in thrall to amorphous forces over which we have scant control; and second, that it must not remain so. We have also witnessed a surging sense that citizens can exercise their freedom and right to stand up against the state with its centralized power. We are learning that the individual's conviction can be matched against the power of overweening authority. We likewise find that we are forging a potent weapon for citizen-inspired change of similar sorts.

Third, and stemming from the other two, is our perception of ourselves, plus our innate yearning to be something more. The assembly line and the corporate structure have taught us to distance ourselves from ourselves. Our bodies have become machine extensions, our minds functions of management, our lives ciphers of society. As a result, we have grown alienated from what we believe should be our real selves.

People power
A Washington peace demonstration (above) shows how people power can face down state power. Sufficient individuals, wanting their individual voices heard, are more than a match for the authority of governments out of touch. These citizen protests are extending around the world, and lie at the heart of sudden changes such as those in Eastern Europe and South Africa where multitudes are realizing that personal conviction must carry over into political commitment. They are assisted by the media, which instantly carries their message on to the world stage. There are no longer local conflicts: thanks to television, any confrontation is brought into the homes of every community on Earth.

Basic values

The Australian Aborigine reflects the capacity of indigenous peoples to remain at one with both their natural world and their spiritual world (below). As Laurens van der Post has written of the Bushmen of the Kalahari, and equally applicable to many indigenous peoples: "The whole of the cosmos was a family. They had an extraordinary feeling of kinship that burned like a flame and kept them on course, that kept them warm and full of meaning . . . In the modern world, we have become so engaged in doing that we have become divorced from the aspect of ourselves which gives us meaning."

Society

The emergence of one-world living leads to pressures for greater co-operation. As the opening sentence of The World Commission on Environment and Development's study, the Brundtland Report, says: "The Earth is one but the world is not." In response to the new realities of interdependence – environmental or economic and political – we have to master a new lesson: that nobody can "win" by dominance, force, or excessive competition. We must co-operate or all will lose. It is a vast step, and we have only half a generation at most to tackle this great challenge. Otherwise the worsening problems will be beyond remedy and may explode into calamitous conflict.

It is a challenge that confronts us at multiple levels. Among the international community each nation increasingly lives in the pockets of others. Whatever nationalistic politicians might assert, there is a steady pooling of sovereignty. With every tick of the clock, sovereignty is penetrated by a host of financial transactions. Yet all too often our response is no more than to go with the flow. We "manage" by default rather than by design.

Our lack of co-operative know-how should not be surprising. We are being overtaken by revolutionary change of unprecedented scope and speed. We grope toward a collaborative future that is baffling as well as inspiring. Yet there is striking evidence of new attitudes: witness the increasingly successful efforts to establish a united and peaceful Europe, first in the West, now in the East, in a continent that has been ravaged by war for centuries.

In cultural senses too there is need *and* opportunity for fresh strategies of sharing. Many people now feel their neighbourhood encompasses localities, regions, and countries. Passport holders that we still are, we are becoming card-carrying citizens of a larger community whose bounds we scarcely grasp but whose promise stretches beyond all known horizons – horizons of geography and of the spirit. Our expanded world is yeasty with potential: can we grow fast enough to savour it to the full?

The crumbling of centralized power

Our old organizational structures have been monolithic affairs, grounded in an outmoded nation-state system with its governments, its military appendages, and the rest of its centralized apparatus. This rigid power apparatus has been reinforced by educational systems, class divisions, and sclerotic cultures that have not kept up with the new "mainstream" trends undermining the whole edifice. Fortunately the crumbling process is now too plain to be ignored. Fortunately, too, there is a host of new actors emerging – just in time.

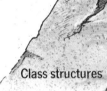

Class structures

Law

New networks

The decay of the old structures has been facilitated by the explosive expansion of financial bodies that once expressed the nation-state in all its economic power. Thanks to an unprecedented growth of international trade and communications since 1960, entrepreneurs, investors, bankers reach out across borders to form global connections (right). Similarly all manner of other innovative networks, within countries and internationally, are springing up in an array of activities – science, technology, environment, development, and peace initiatives among a host of others.

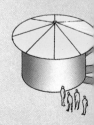

Governments

Financial
institutions

Multinational
corporations

Military

Educational
academies

Mainstream
cultures

The falling fortress
Even if it functioned efficiently, the
nation-state system is now too big
for the small problems and too
small for the big ones. Equally, the
establishment has become too
established to respond fast and
flexibly enough to meet the demands
of a world undergoing tumultuous
change. We don't need more government. We need better governance – a
more direct, flexible, local,
participatory leadership, the type
of contribution best made by NGOs.

GUT reactions

Some aspects of science are undergoing a revolution. They are changing our view of reality, thus of our world, and of ourselves too. Since the 17th century the scientific process has been a cast-iron case of objectivity: scientists must avoid all "contamination" of their enquiries by becoming involved. But we are now learning that far from being the detached observer, the scientist is necessarily a part of every observation and thus affects its outcome.

The classical, or Newtonian, physics postulated a world with "laws" that appeared to drive all physical systems in every last respect. So profound was Newton's analysis, so conclusive did those laws appear, that we came to think of the universe as a mechanical, linear, predictable place. But while we tend to think and act in a linear fashion, we live in a non-linear world. Our best models are but poor approximations of a world seething with disorder.

A manifestation of this new insight lies with advanced physics and its efforts to accept that the long-established linear "rules" of the world, with their absolute "truths", are but part of a larger world where relativity reigns, chaos is pervasive, and uncertainty will ever be with us.

We are also witnessing a process of convergence as the divisions between sciences fade, as those between science, philosophy, the humanities, and art. We are learning that all truths are but different dimensions of a single truth.

Hence the search for a Grand Unified Theory – a GUT reaction to the world and the way we perceive it. And hence, in geophysiology, the Gaia concept – proclaiming that we are all part of the living entity called Earth (see pp. 52-3).

Thus the new physics goes far beyond a better understanding of light, space, energy, and force, and the consequent benefits for our everyday technology. It is centred on a heretical insight: that we are more integrally involved with the world around us than we have supposed. To this revolutionary extent, the new physics probes toward a holistic view of nature and our place within it.

Newton's world machine

In his 1687 book, *Principia*, Newton postulated that the world works in accord with strict mechanical laws. Hence the physicist can eventually persuade it to reveal a single system of mechanistic principles, devoid of variations, universally applicable – a homogeneous world of absolutes. When once we establish all the startpoint details of a phenomenon, we can predict its future course with certitude. But after 200 years of Newton's deterministic world, Einstein's insights revealed the role of relativity.

Einstein's universe

In the early years of this century Albert Einstein initiated two revolutions in scientific thought. His explanation of how light comes in "packets", or "quanta", of radiation became a characteristic of quantum physics – the study of atomic systems. And his theory of relativity established a framework that completed classical physics, but involved drastic changes in the concepts of space and time. These, he suggested, are different aspects of the same "something", fused into a four-dimensional continuum where time has no absolute value. Time and space can be distorted by the presence of objects. This distortion of space provides the "force" of gravity. A consequence of his theory is the famous $E = mc^2$, showing that mass is nothing but a form of energy.

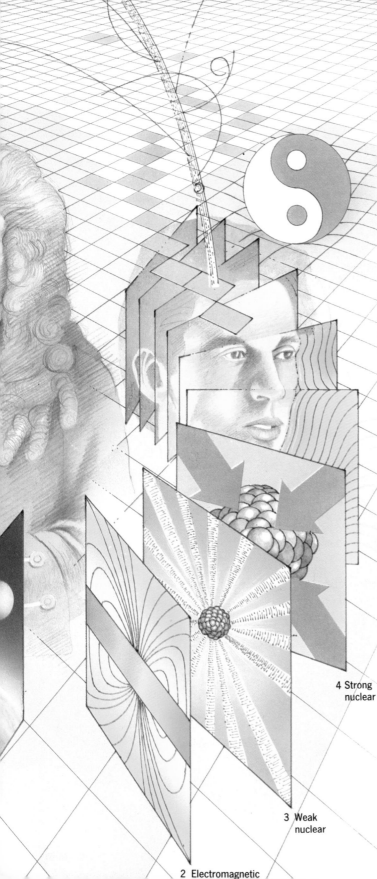

Heisenburg's uncertainty

In the quantum world, objects do not possess separate properties, such as position and momentum; these properties are integrally combined. The more accurately a particle's position is measured, the less accurately can its momentum be defined, a concept expressed by the German physicist Heisenburg's Uncertainty Principle. By our choosing to measure position precisely, a particle is forced to develop more uncertainty in momentum, and vice versa. Thus the observer alters the observed by the act of observation, and the observer becomes the participant.

Quantum physics

The new physics pictures the universe as one indivisible whole, whose parts are interrelated and interacting. Quantum physics tells us that, at the subatomic level, matter does not exist with certainty at definite places. Rather, it shows "tendencies to exist", expressed as mathematical probabilities. More accurately, these are probabilities of interconnections and not of "things". Subatomic particles have no meaning as isolated entities: they can be understood only as interconnections between observation and measurement.

The four fundamental forces: the search for GUT

It is now accepted that the four fundamental forces that drive the universe are: 1 gravity (holds planets and stars together); 2 electromagnetic force (holds atoms and molecules together); 3 "weak" nuclear force, and 4 "strong" nuclear force (which together control the behaviour of particles on the subatomic scale). A "theory of everything", or GUT, is now being sought to show these all to be facets of a single underlying force.

4 Strong nuclear

3 Weak nuclear

2 Electromagnetic

Gaia theory and science

Dr James Lovelock's Gaia hypothesis demands that we rethink our view of the planetary ecosystem and what makes it tick – and how we can help to keep it ticking in a manner that remains supportive of the human enterprise. Scientists have conventionally supposed the Earth to be an inert lump of molten rock populated with an array of organisms; and that the organisms cannot affect or modify their environment to their own systematic advantage. But Lovelock has been struck by the fact that the Earth is profoundly different from what its history in the solar system would predict – and especially different in its capacity to sustain its organisms. Still more important, Lovelock has noted that the organisms apparently modify their physical environments, particularly the atmosphere, in ways that ostensibly optimize their prospects for survival.

As Lovelock postulates: "For this to have happened by chance is as unlikely as for a person to survive unscathed a drive blindfolded through rush-hour traffic." Instead, the biosphere's feedback loops and other control mechanisms are so diverse and interactive that they imply a closely coupled evolutionary response by both biotas and their environments working in constant concert, developing into a kind of supersystem.

In essence, the Gaia hypothesis shows us how the interplay of all the planet's elements produces an outcome greater than the sum of its parts. This is a holistic message that often runs counter to the reductionist minds of conventional scientists.

Earth can be construed as comprising a hypersensitive system with self-regulatory devices so numerous we cannot even begin to comprehend them. Yet instead of treating the mechanism as an extraordinarily advanced and delicate system, to be handled with exceptional care, we are dealing it sledgehammer blows. We tinker with these intricate mechanisms at our extreme peril, even though we casually pollute the planet, sluice away its soil, extirpate its species, and dislocate its climates as if with impunity.

Evolution of a living planet

The first rudimentary specks of life on Earth probably started and died out several times before an enduring toehold was won (see right). Once established, life began to interact with its environment, at first locally and ultimately on a planet-wide scale, as the Gaia system developed. The power of this system is illustrated by the processes of planetary temperature.

The prime source of energy, and of life itself, is the sun. Yet the sun's heat has increased by 30% compared with its temperature at the first start-up of life – far too great a rise for organisms to tolerate. Fortunately, over the aeons, less and less of this solar heat has been retained by the Earth's atmosphere, by virtue of a reverse greenhouse effect – the reduction of atmospheric CO_2 due to the increasing number of plants, land and ocean. These plants, too, appear to be closely involved in the hydrological cycle – the great system that drives water around the planet – as well as in the formation of clouds and even in the return of sulphur from the sea to the land via the air.

Plainly the plants have not planned these interventions, even though they have worked to their enduring advantage. But could the planetary ecosystem have so functioned that in response to its organisms' activities it has tended to maintain a level of conditions that serve to sustain life?

A tale of three planets

We gain an idea of how much life on Earth modifies its environment by comparing this planet with its neighbours. Science knows enough of the history and evolution of the solar system to predict, with fair accuracy, what the composition and pressure of a planet's atmosphere should be, and so its temperature. In the case of both Mars and Venus, evidence from the space programme matches the predictions – that Mars has polar temperatures as cold as $-184°$ C ($-299°$ F), Venus a boiling $450°$ C ($842°$ F), and

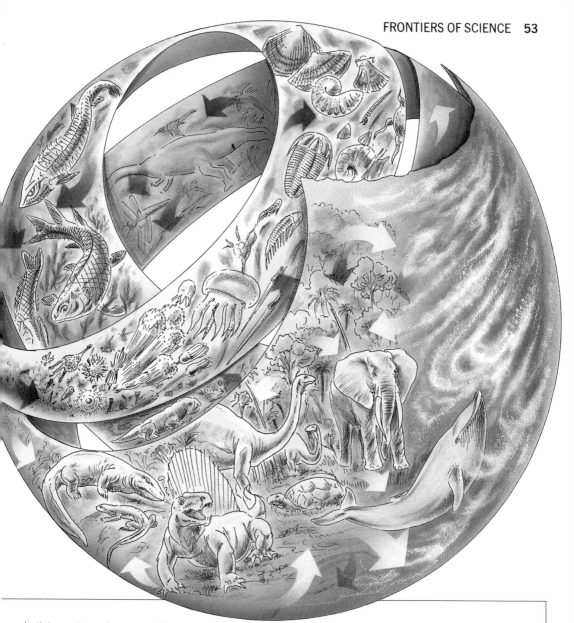

both have atmospheres consisting almost entirely of CO_2. But Earth does not fit the pattern. Our atmosphere should, according to physics, be almost all CO_2, with surface temperatures midway between the other two planets, within a range of 240–344° C (464–650° F). Instead, it has only 0.03% CO_2, 21% oxygen, most of the rest nitrogen, and mild average temperatures of about 13° C (55° F). What makes Earth's environment so especially suitable for life? Life itself, which has slowly fashioned the world we know.

	Venus	Earth (no life)	Mars	Earth (with life)
Carbon dioxide	98%	98%	95%	0.03%
Nitrogen	1.9%	1.9%	2.7%	79%
Oxygen	trace	trace	0.13%	21%
Argon	0.1%	0.1%	2%	1%
Surface temp (°C)	477	240–340	–53	13
Atmospheric pressure	90	60	0.0064	1

Creative chaos

Chaos is a newly emergent science that addresses the global nature of systems – or rather un-systems. Cutting across inter-disciplinary divides, it makes strong claims about the universal behaviour of complexity. It reverses a trend toward the reductionist analysis of systems in terms of their consti-tuent parts, such as quarks, chromosomes, and neurons. Only a new kind of science could begin to cross the gulf between knowl-edge of what one thing does (one water molecule or one cell of heart tissue, for example) and what millions of them do.

Chaos is more than a mathematical theory. It relates to everyday things, such as weather, biological rhythms, economics, art, and even traffic jams. Its insights are already changing the way astronomers look at the solar system, the way businesspeople make decisions, or political theorists con-sider stresses leading to armed conflict.

All depends on tiny differences of input that can quickly become overwhelming dif-ferences in output – known as "sensitive dependence on initial conditions". In weather, for example, this translates into what is referred to as the butterfly effect – the notion that as a butterfly's wings disturb the air today in deepest Amazonia, the per-turbation can, via multiple linkages and com-poundings, trigger a storm next month in distant Europe.

Conventional mathematics has mostly focused on predominant trends as the way to analyse variables. But the key to this strat-egy is that it must eliminate, or at least flatten out, small variations as ignorable nuisances. Yet it is precisely these minute "errors" in mathematical calculations that can become an expanding source of seeming chaos, launching systems toward unpredict-able outcomes.

The very fact that chaos theory is pre-pared to move beyond linear-moded thinking into multi-outcome analysis is a crucial first step. From here on, chaos-ists can start to look for a more expansive sort of system in a universe of un-systems. Turbulence, or chaotic behaviour, contains its own order and rhythm – and the "real world" is both.

The nonlinear universe

Because of the endlessly ramifying consequences of tiny shifts in "triggering variables", we often fail to devise accurate predictions of large-scale phenomena. This has profound implications for human as well as natural systems. Inherent unpredictability demands a basic shift in our approach to planning: we must adapt to expect the unexpected. No wonder the best meteo-rologists working with the best computers cannot yet come up with accurate weather forecasts beyond the next few days. When we recognize we live in a world of endemic uncertainty, we shall learn to cope better with uncertainty – and thereby attain an altogether new form of certainty.

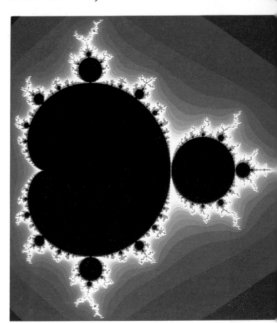

The Mandelbrot set: the mathematics of living things

The Mandelbrot set, a type of public emblem for the new mathematics of chaos and the infinite complexity of nature, is a graphic representation of a set of mathe-matical equations. The equations are simple, the product is complex to extraordinary degree – and beautiful as well (see above). We find that if we zoom in on any particular part of the original graphic and enlarge it, the outcome is a further collection of flower-like designs that always corresponds to the original; and the same again no matter how many times we repeat the process. This is fractal (self-similar) geometry, which has moved be-yond the classic geometry of Euclid with its triangles, squares, circles, and straight lines, to reveal the intricate, dynamic geometry of turbulence, of chaos, of nature.

The Lorenz attractor

Computer analysis of the behaviour of chaotic systems can trace within their disorder a higher level of order. Although a chaotic variable, plotted over time, never repeats or crosses its own path, it remains within a "field shape", held there by an "attractor", such as that first discovered by the American scientist Edward Lorenz. These strange mathematical patterns, often resembling the forms of nature, are key components of the new science of chaos.

Catastrophe theory: the mathematics of change

Catastrophe theory is a branch of mathematics that plots the shape of discontinuity, or, on another level, of sudden jumps in the behaviour of human systems and relationships. It is practically applied in the field of conflict resolution – in business, government, or family life. In the diagram (right), one axis of a situation represents opposed views, the other, energy invested in the confrontation. The greater the energy input, the greater the disruptive impact (the folded line, where the profile cannot surmount the cusp). The process precipitates a catastrophic conflict of irreconcilable views. If, though, energy input is reduced and a new line is plotted, the profile is far shallower and the way is then open for resolution along a continuum of positive options.

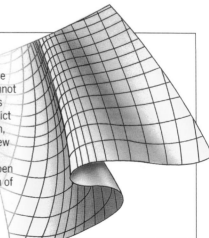

Holistic science

If the 1980s threw up one powerful and original concept, it was the environmental insight of the global ecosystem with its seamless web. An all-embracing idea: all is one, complete and entire.

Yet the idea is not so very original. A full 25 centuries ago Guatama Buddha taught that this world and all it reveals is "a single seamless garment" and that there is no ultimate dividing line between man, the tree, and the mountain. Today, holistic science is starting to grapple with the ages-old notion: could there be an approach that breaks down the boundaries between the various disciplines – and, more radically, one that breaks down the barriers between Eastern holism and Western science? Also between science, art, literature, philosophy, and morality? Holistic science is an expansive form of knowledge encompassing the four "knowings": the *know-what* of scientific enquiry; the *know-how* of technology; the *know-who* of social institutions; and the *know-why* of values.

Thus far we have had but two main manifestations, and they both have to do with health. The first is the Gaian precept of the Earth as a single, interacting system, alive and self-safeguarding. Now that it is sick, Gaia needs the scientist who is equipped to serve as a "planetary doctor", acutely aware of the intrinsic malfunctionings of the system, aware too of the integrative understanding that alone can supply the appropriate therapy.

The second manifestation has to do with the health of the individual person. Human maladies, proclaims holistic medicine, are not disease, rather they are dis-ease – the body/mind system out of balance, to be restored only by "making whole" mind and body in complementary accord.

The same holistic perspective can be applied to the workings, or the malfunctioning, of our economies; to international relations and global governance; to community values and activities; to the root causes of conflict; and to the many other areas where our erstwhile "understanding" is proving to be all too blinkered.

A new world view
Now that we are effectively conducting a vast experiment with the planetary ecosystem itself, science must consider a more integrated view of the world. This needs a new breed of scientist, an interdisciplinary scientist. A good number of scientists believe they already qualify, but they are really multidisciplinary scientists. Worthy as this is, it is far from comprehending the world with its seamless webs of natural and social interactions. The interdisciplinarian appreciates that prime attention should be directed instead to the "grey" areas between disciplines.

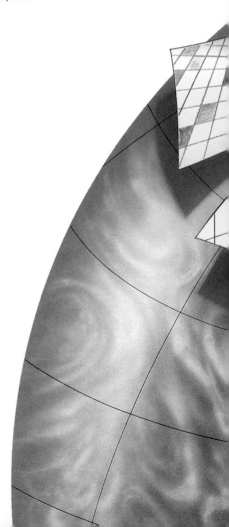

Converging horizons

We see a convergence in modern science between the fast-expanding horizons of New Physics, New Maths, and Gaia. Each postulates that the real world is not a primarily linear affair, deterministic, and predictable when once we know the key factors of start-out information. The orderly world views of Newton and even Einstein are being left behind as we realize the world is not finally knowable. The more we accept its complexity, the more we shall perceive its workings as nevertheless purposive — workings about which we can make probabilistic statements, no more and no less. Furthermore, the Gaian insights reveal the planet as a unitary organism, an entity that regulates itself at higher levels of organization than have ever been supposed. In short, our traditional ways of viewing nature have limited our understanding: scientists have been looking at only a part, probably a small part, of the real world.

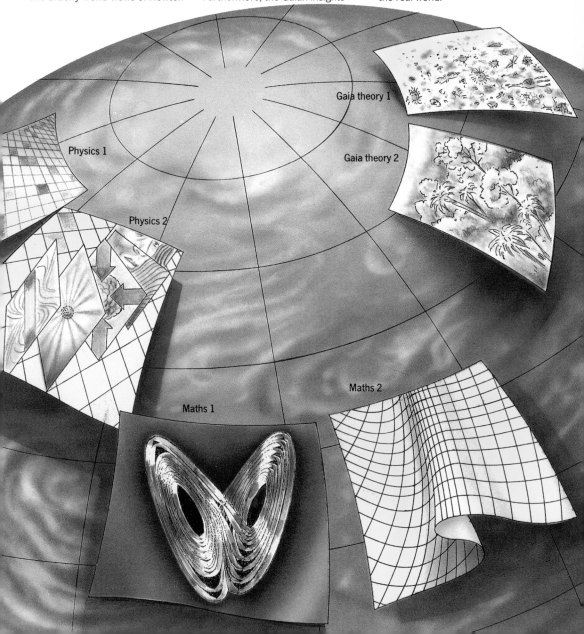

Gaia theory 1

Gaia theory 2

Physics 1

Physics 2

Maths 2

Maths 1

Infotechnology

We are in the midst of an information revolution, the implications of which will spread into every aspect of our lives. This revolution is primarily due to the microchip. The amount of circuitry that can now be etched on to silicon wafers (of which chips are made) is currently 10 million transistors; by the year 2000 it will surpass 1 billion transistors on the same-sized wafer. Moreover, whereas today's chips perform electronic operations as fast as one per four-billionths of a second, by the century's end this is likely to increase to one operation every 200-trillionths of a second, 50,000 times faster than before.

The twin factors of miniaturization and increased speed (plus mass demand) have caused the cost of computing power to drop dramatically between 1970 and 1990, a fall that is expected to continue at an accelerating rate. The result will be machines that can listen to spoken language and translate, others that can "see" and respond to their surroundings, and hyper-capable robots.

Now that the information revolution is under way, computer technologies are multiplying human information-processing capacity by a factor of ten every three years. This means that information has become our dominant resource, playing a role in the developed world equivalent to the historic contributions of stone, bronze, energy, and so on. But information differs from all its predecessors: it expands as it is used. Nor is it hungry for other resources. So a slogan for the information-rich 1990s will not be "The limits to growth" but, instead, "The growth of limits".

The global expansion of information further means the decline of remoteness – not of individuals, but of institutions. All the important markets are now world markets, as markets cease to be places and become networks. There is no longer a New York market or a Zurich market – those notions disappeared on 19 October 1987, the famous Black Monday.

The growth of limits
Consider the shrinking size of a computer with power equivalent to a human brain. In 1950 it would have equalled the space of a major city; in 1960 that of a large concert hall; in 1970 a double-deck bus; in 1980 a taxi; and in 1990 a television set. By 2000 it will be the size of a human brain. Consider, too, the associated cost of "memory". For each 350-word page of information, the cost of a valve/ transistor/chip in 1950 was about $1.6 million; in 1960 $48,000; in 1970 $8000; in 1980 $160; in 1990 less than $1.

The nature of information
Information is not like other resources. It cannot be consumed, rather it is generative. When information is shared it expands, and it cannot be readily destroyed. It can be circulated much more easily, widely, and rapidly than any other resource. It looks set to become the ultimate resource. But let us beware: we could drown in information while being starved of knowledge and distracted from wisdom.

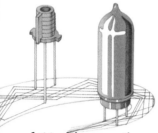

1st to 4th generations

Electronic computers, with their roots in the abacus and other mechanical calculating devices, were developed during World War II. Computer generations refer to the different methods used to store and process "bits" of information. A bit is a single binary number: "1" or "0". Each new generation of memory has dramatically expanded the speed with which computers can process data. The first computers used the thermionic valve (or vacuum tube), each one representing one bit. Transistors replaced valves in the late 1950s (2nd generation), and computers using integrated circuits were introduced in 1964 (3rd generation). The 4th generation of computers uses microprocessors – tiny integrated circuits capable of performing data-processing at incredible speed.

5th generation

The computers of the 1990s are not only more powerful than anything of the past, they are a great deal more intelligent. Today's most powerful computers can think only in one direction at a time, making them ideal for long calculations but poor for creative thinking. In a 5th-generation computer, there are "neural nets" akin to the structure of the human brain, where neurons, while slower than silicon, work in tandem, and hence operate laterally as well as linearly. The breakthrough is due to "parallel processing", rather than serial processing used by the majority of computers. Already experimental neural-network systems are beginning to solve speech and vision problems that have defied attempts using conventional technology.

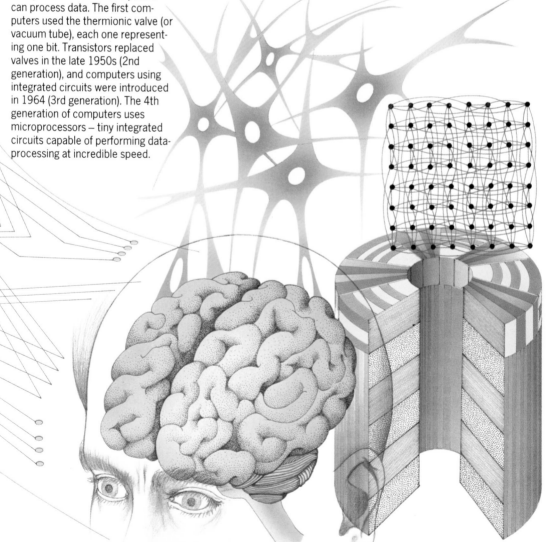

New genes

When the first cultivators started to utilize certain plants and animals in preference to others, they initiated a process of selective breeding. For another 10,000 years the process has steadily advanced and served humankind admirably, though without altering its basic approach. Today we are into the opening phase of another genetic revolution: biotechnology has arrived with a bang.

Already genetic engineering affects our daily lives in myriad ways. Each time we sit down to eat, reach into the medicine cabinet, or use a plastic product, we reap the benefits of a revolution whose impact will shortly be as widespread as any of the great technical revolutions of the past – not only the original domestication of crops, but the harnessing of electricity, the discovery of microbial sources of illness, and the splitting of the atom. Among the products of genetic engineering that can reasonably be predicted by the year 2000 should be, for example, a crop plant with edible leaves, high-protein, bean-like seeds, large, nutritious tubers, and useful fibre from the stalk. Genetic engineering will enable us to devise bugs that degrade environmental pollutants and even help us to extract more minerals from the ground. By digesting and liberating trapped oil in deep wells, they will help us to recover the many billions of barrels of oil that would be left by conventional recovery methods in the North Sea alone.

In short, the new genes offer the possibility of building a sustainable future based on renewable resources. Their potential could well bring us closer to material well-being for all citizens on Earth than has been achieved through human ingenuity throughout the whole of history.

The total market potential for biotechnology could be $100 billion by the end of the century. In Britain alone, the market for pollution-control equipment is already worth $200 million a year; in Western Europe there are 600 companies involved in the development, manufacture, and supply of such equipment.

The genetic resource

We can exploit the genetic resource inherent in biological organisms for the benefit of agriculture, industry and medicine. Instead of using depletable resources, biotechnology employs renewable feedstocks, also waste products, among a wide range of materials not currently exploited. The manufacturing processes require less energy than conventional production methods, they generate fewer toxic byproducts, and they reduce or eliminate the hazards associated with alternative modes of manufacture. In the words of Professor William Brill, University of Wisconsin: "We are entering an age in which genetic wealth . . . until now a relatively inaccessible trust fund, is becoming a currency with high immediate value."

The gene pool's hidden depths

Within species there is much genetic variability, as witness the many breeds of dog and the many specialized types of wheat. The amount of genetic information in the DNA of a mammal such as a mouse would, if transcribed into equivalent terms, fill all 15 editions of Encyclopaedia Britannica published since 1771. As we lose species that would otherwise flourish, we are draining the planetary gene pool in further significant fashion. The plant species maize, for example, exists with trillions of individuals and so is anything but threatened as a species. But its genetic variability is severely depleted as we lose most races of maize. "The loss of a single species is not merely the loss of one volume from the library of nature, but the loss of a loose-leaf book whose individual pages, were the species to survive, would remain available in perpetuity for selective transfer to other species." Professor Thomas Eisner, Cornell University

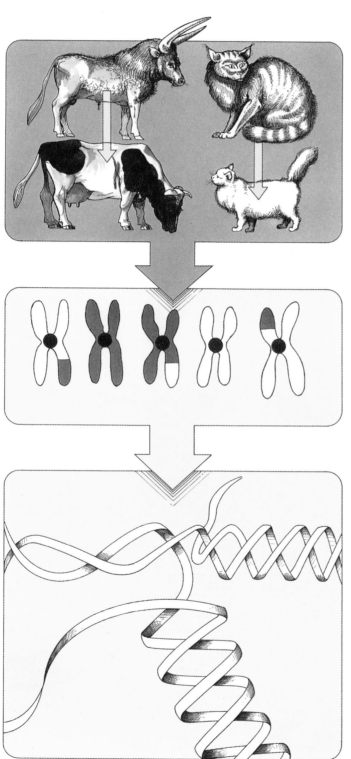

Traditional breeding techniques

For 10,000 years of humankind's history we have worked only with whole organisms. By cross-breeding we have been able to emphasize and enhance favourable characteristics and eliminate undesirable ones. Productive as this process has been, it has remained a slow affair, limited by the generation times of the organisms in question.

Gene manipulation and creation

Using new techniques, the animal or plant breeder can telescope the time needed for trial-and-error experiments by manipulating individual genes. Thanks to the "compressed evolution" that the geneticist can now impose on cell populations through genetic engineering, the process can be reduced to a couple of months, sometimes to just a weekend.

Genetic engineering manipulates the molecular structure of cells in order to alter the genetic constitution of life forms. In turn, this modifies the organism's structure and functions, its growth and adaptability, and so on. By transforming the basic make up of organisms, scientists can claim to be inventing new forms of life.

Genetic pollution

Accidents are inevitable. The difficulty of absolute containment in a laboratory coupled with human fallibility will ensure that one day a genetically engineered organism not intended for release will escape into the environment. And there could be no way to recapture it. An engineered pathogen of this type could wreak havoc with ecosystems, perhaps disrupting natural cycles for the foreseeable future.

New materials and technologies

Three technologies are likely to dominate the future of readers of this book: infotechnology, biotechnology (see pp. 58–9 and 60–1), and the development of new materials. The first two have thus far tended to overshadow the potential of the third, though we may soon find this is the wrong ranking. Examples of new materials and technologies already in use include lasers, high-performance plastics, advanced composites (including some types of fibre), and high-tech ceramics used for superconductors. The value of components produced from these materials in the US alone is projected to grow from the 1988 level of about $2 billion to nearly $20 billion by the year 2000.

One of the most fascinating areas of research into new materials is that of nanotechnology. From the Greek word for dwarf, a nano is a one-billionth part of its entity. A nanometre is one-billionth of a metre, and about ten times the diameter of the smallest atom, hydrogen. The related technology will allow the construction of the smallest, strongest, and fastest devices possible under natural laws as we understand them today. In essence, it will be possible to develop tiny machines with component parts small enough to manipulate molecules. This should shortly lead to solar-electric energy convertors as cheap as glass, diamond-fibre composite materials as inexpensive as wood, ultra-light spacecraft, and molecular correction of most serious diseases, including cancer.

Another new material on the horizon is the biochip, with data stored in organic compounds and manipulated by molecular chemistry. Whereas silicon components are rapidly approaching limitations of size and speed, molecules are smaller and faster. The time may come when we shall have molecular computers for implantation in the brain, where they will interface between external computer circuits and electrochemical circuits inside the brain. Already there have been experiments using implants to bring sight to the blind.

Technology: a Pandora's box?

The new materials revolution offers a wealth of products to perform a multitude of tasks more efficiently and cheaply than conventional materials. Technologists are opening up a box of unprecedented and almost unimaginable opportunities. But like Pandora's box, it may yield products of a less-desirable sort. The US Department of Agriculture alone expects to approve the release of 200 new biomaterials per annum, a number that will surely skyrocket in the early 1990s. If an undesirable outcome is likely to occur once in every 1000 uses of a given technology (a reasonable probability rate), we can realistically anticipate a "downside" result within the nearish future – a result whose manifestations we can only guess at.

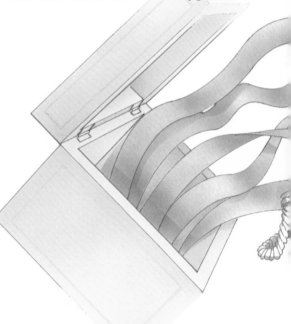

The growing use of new materials

Unaware of it as we may be, we utilize dozens of new-materials products during our daily round. They are feeding into a whole range of economic sectors, including electronics, lasers, optics, communications and information, genetics, alternative energy, ocean science, environmental engineering, and organic agriculture. All reflect the qualitative advance in human knowledge that is now being translated into the everyday economy.

Superconductors

These are particularly important for use in electrical transmissions without the usual loss of power. Immediate applications include specialized microelectronics, magnetically levitated, or Maglev, trains (among other levitated vehicles), wiring to speed the passage of electronic signals in computers, and sensors to detect neurological disorders. In addition, superconductivity could prove to be the marginal factor that makes renewable sources of energy – wind, solar, low-head hydroelectricity – economically feasible.

Biomaterials

By way of illustration of this class of new materials, cows are being "designed" to produce human milk, a product much superior to baby-food formula milk. The technique depends on transferring half a dozen human genes into bovine eggs, whereupon the "transgenic" cows manufacture the relevant human proteins in their milk. In addition, bovine growth hormones are leading to increases in milk production of up to 30%.

Photovoltaics

Inefficient as photovoltaic cells now are (only 10–15%), they are already in widespread use. These cells convert electromagnetic energy, or light, from the sun into electrical current. But because the current produced is small, they need to be connected in large series-parallel arrays in order to give a usable energy output. The development of more efficient types of cell could make solar energy, already nonpolluting and renewable, a major source of energy within the next 15 years or less.

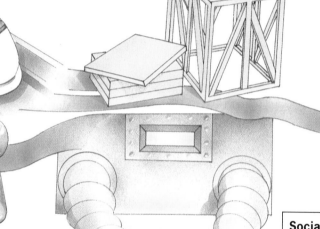

Fibre optics

Fibre optics are revolutionizing the field of information technology by replacing or supplementing traditional copper wires. Thanks to advances in lasers, light-emitting diodes, and digital switches, optical fibres can now transmit billions of bits of information every second – a thousand times greater than is achieved by wires. Because they can handle these huge loads, fibre optics are the lynchpin of new communications networks that already enable people to exchange information by voice, facsimile, and by computer.

Future fusion

Forming an atomic nucleus by the fusion of two other nuclei of lighter mass to liberate energy has considerable lure as an energy source. If the deuterium, an isotope of hydrogen, found in just one cubic metre of seawater were fused, it would liberate the energy equivalent of 2000 barrels of oil. $1 billion a year is spent on fusion research but has only produced minimal gains so far.

Social consequences

While the benefits of new materials and technologies are obvious in a material sense, they may bring certain unfortunate consequences of a social nature. For instance, it is becoming possible to "manufacture" coffee in the laboratory (to produce coffee-drink molecules) without going to the trouble of growing coffee plants. Were this to be taken up on a commercial scale, it would wreak terminal havoc with the entire coffee industry – not only with the packing, distributing, and marketing networks, but with coffee-growing communities in many tropical lands, thus devastating the economies of certain developing countries.

Ecotechnology

Thanks to low-impact technologies, we are learning to do more with less. In one of the biggest shifts since the beginning of civilized communities, we are having to face the fact that there is now no more "West out there" to be won.

A few pioneering enterprises have shown the way. Consider the US Minnesota Mining and Manufacturing (3M) company, with annual sales of more than $8 billion and offices or plants in more than 50 countries. During a recent 14-year period, the corporation saved more than $482 million through pollution prevention, waste recovery, and materials recycling, and eliminated an annual 122,000 tonnes of air contaminants, 400,000 tonnes of solid waste, and 7 billion litres of wastewater. All this has been accomplished within the US alone; elsewhere the corporation has prevented still further pollution.

In the energy sector there is a premium on end-product efficiency (getting more out of each unit of energy) and on conservation (using less energy). Until 1973 conventional wisdom proclaimed there could be no increase in economic output without an equal increase in consumption of energy. Then the oil crises of 1973 and 1979 taught us the true price of oil, whereupon we mobilized a remarkable range of energy technologies that allowed many economies to grow a full 30 per cent by 1984, while actually using less energy overall. Then in 1985 there was a third oil crisis, this one plunging oil prices, and we went back to our prodigal ways. Yet with technologies already available but largely unutilized, and with sufficient political commitment, we could again continue with growing economies *and* declining energy consumption into the indefinite future. All depends on whether we are prepared to venture into the new territories of energy.

Much the same applies to the greening of technology generally. What is needed is, for example, the readiness to see waste as simply bad management of valuable and usable materials.

From "cowboy" to "spaceship" attitudes

We are the first generation to have to face the fact that not all natural resources are endlessly plentiful. Given our rising numbers and our rising demands, we must abandon our traditional "throughput" economies, which consume vast quantities of raw materials and generate vast quantities of wastes as a by-product of production and consumption (see right). We must shift from the cowboy economy (always more "West out there") to the spaceship economy, where we operate with a fixed stock of supplies and nothing is wasted (see below right).

Resources

1 Recycling

Recycling not only offers reduced demand on natural resources, it leads to substantial savings of energy. The US recycles only 10% of its wastes (even though each household produces several tonnes of waste annually), Western Europe on average 30%, Japan more than 50%.

2 Waste as a resource

The British throw out 8 million paper bags a day, yet the national woodpulp bill is over $800 million a year, of which imports account for 70% – adding to an already severe trade deficit. In stark contrast to the rest of Western Europe, more than 90% of household waste is dumped.

3 No-waste technology

Clean technology is the solution to the waste crisis. It reduces or, better still, prevents wastes being created in the first place. One US study projects a potential waste minimization in the US of 90% by the year 2008, but this would be achievable only with the fullest possible economic, legislative, technical, and educational assistance from the government.

The "throughput economy"

This new-age economy depends on endless reuse of crucial raw materials. It need not be a case of endless sacrifice, rather a case of doing more with less and with much more efficiency in our economies. An end to the effluent society will lead to the more affluent society.

4 Energy efficiency

From 1973 to 1984 the world has saved energy worth on average $300 billion a year. While the most profligate consumers of energy are in the industrialized nations (a Bangladeshi consumes 1 barrel of oil a year, an American 55), developing countries could improve energy and consumption practices to the extent of savings of $3 trillion during the period 1990 to 2010.

5 Appropriate-scale technology

Small communities need small-scale technologies. In rural areas, for example, the generation of electricity for domestic use can often most efficiently be done with small wind- or watermills or solar-energy collectors. Central power stations with large-scale distribution grids are inappropriate when they fail to make the best use of local resources.

6 Bioenergy

"Biofuels" comprise any solid, liquid, or gaseous fuel produced directly from plant material (including wood and other biomass), or indirectly from organic wastes from agricultural, forestry, industry, commercial, and domestic sources. In Britain alone 250 million tonnes of collectable organic wastes are generated each year from homes, factories, farms, and forests, with a total energy content equivalent to at least 25 million tonnes of coal, or 8% of energy needs.

New management

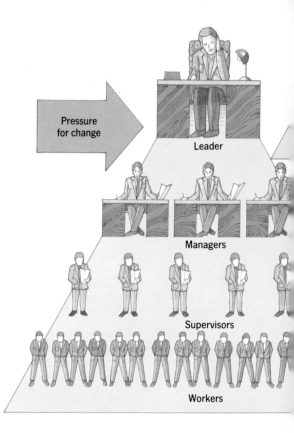

Pressure
for change

In our current management systems – government, business, or agency – there is an emergent revolution in the way enterprises are organized. No longer is the invariable structure a pyramid-like affair (see below right), with instructions, information, and motivation passing down from the management apex to the workforce beneath. The new system tends to be more horizontal in its workings, with far less emphasis placed on hierarchy; its flatter format is facilitated by the free flow of information available via modern technology. In turn this means that the successful executive needs to display abundant flexibility in both attitude and application, in contrast to the autocratic outlook of the traditional "leader". Collaboration and sharing between all those involved, rather than command and control by a few, are the new keys to successful enterprises.

This change has been triggered by change itself. The world no longer runs according to set rules, appropriate to tramline minds. In a time of tumultuous change, where stability has given way to uncertainty and where continuity induces sclerosis, there is a premium on instant adaptability and true teamwork. This applies particularly to business: the corporation that is to remain competitive with the outside world will do so by being more co-operative within its own domain. It will flourish by embracing change: it will learn to exploit chaos as the predominant feature of the day; and bureaucracy will be overtaken by ad-hocracy. Hence the emphasis on a restructured, or destructured, system of working.

When once the rigid lines of "top-down" organizations are removed, there is fresh scope for initiative, imagination, and autonomy. Energies can be concentrated on the task in hand, instead of being dissipated on maintaining status, while time is spent on creative endeavour rather than on protecting power and position.

The old and the new
A pyramid of power is good at implementing a given set of rules, far less capable of responding to the unpredictable. It militates against the kinds of cutting-edge thought and "risk preference" that generate the most productive advances in a knowledge-based society. In the new systems, the pyramid is replaced by cellular modes of organization. Far from being the type of structure that can be reduced to a diagram, it is a mosaic of ever-shifting components that regulate themselves. Above all, these systems encourage participants to think the unthinkable – and this is the arch-attribute of success in a world where old rules and regimented attitudes are failing us.

Pressure
for change

Leader

Managers

Supervisors

Workers

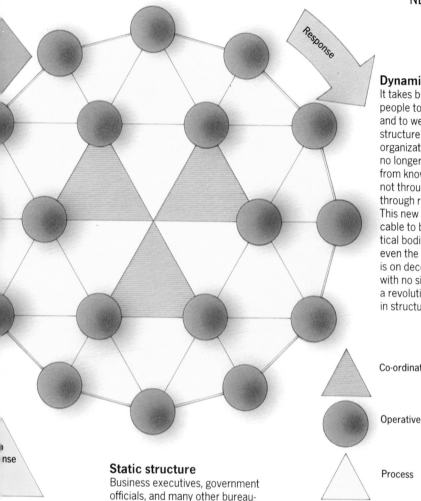

Dynamic structure

It takes brave (or cool-headed) people to thrive in fluid situations, and to welcome the weak power structure that is the hallmark of new organizational systems. Authority no longer derives from position, but from knowledge. Control is exerted not through ordering workers but through reprogramming software. This new strategy is equally applicable to business corporations, political bodies, national planning, and even the nation-state. The emphasis is on decentralized organization with no single point of leadership – a revolution in attitude as well as in structure.

Co-ordination

Operative

Process

Static structure

Business executives, government officials, and many other bureaucrats are expert at straight-line extrapolation. In fields as diverse as commerce, economics, technology, and resource energy, they identify trends in today's world and then simply extend them into the future. They thereby postulate that whatever processes are at work today will continue to operate tomorrow, with changes that are less than crucial. This "business as usual" approach is unimaginative: however much it may seem safe and scientific, it is usually neither – and riven with risk. Working well in periods of stability, it is critically unsuited to a period of revolutionary upheaval such as exists today.

New management in a new world

The mass media is being overtaken by direct-broadcast satellite, cable, cassette, ad-hoc networks, and small-circulation media for every conceivable part of the community, with information flooding in from every part of the world. This new age is not dependent on centralized data banks, but on personal computers in every home, linked up with ever-widening and ever-changing networks. It all adds up to a nightmare for old-style management with its emphasis on centralized planning.

Chance or choice?

This part of the book has shown we face a great transition. We are being propelled into a future that will be as different from today as today is from the start of the century. Through multiple pressures and triggers of change piled upon change, we are poised at a great divide, even as a new world struggles to be born.

The build-up has revealed a host of stresses and strains. Our biosphere groans and rends under its burden; the nation-state is undergoing greater change than since its emergence 400 years ago; and new modes of governance are springing up on every side, though with little cohesive structure to meet the unprecedented challenges of one-world living. Economies are surging in some areas, failing in others, even as they integrate in ways almost beyond comprehension by virtue of the microchip and the tele-communications revolution. Our scientific perception of the planet and its workings is being transformed, as is our grasp of the wider, indeed universe-wide, processes revealed through the new physics and maths. So too is the perception of our planetary home springing to life as we encounter one fresh horizon after another, and as we all grope toward sustainable lifestyles. And there is a realization in many individuals of a greater selfhood and an assertion of more enduring values.

Thus we see one revolution after another after another – an uproar of change. Only one thing seems little different, and that is our grasp of the world around us. Herein lies the chief source of stress and strain. We still hanker for a ride into the future while looking through the rearview mirror. But while we face new choices – creative and enriching choices without number – we do not always recognize that one option is no longer open to us: business as usual. The future cannot be an extension of the past: that prospect has been foreclosing for decades.

The crunch question is, will we determine our future by choice, or allow it to impose itself on us by chance? Will the future arrive by design or by default?

Perceiving the changes

Each day as we venture outside our doors we witness a world undergoing greater climate change than for tens of thousands of years, and experiencing a mass extinction of species greater than for millions of years. If environmental change were like a heart attack, we would rush our ecosystems into intensive care. But it is like a cancer, working away under the surface until it finally makes itself undeniably known. Much the same applies to other forms of change – social, technological, scientific, and even personal. As the late Barbara Ward put it: "The door of the future is opening on to a crisis more sudden, more global, more inescapable, more bewildering than any other encountered by the human species."

Tides in the affairs of humanity

Certainly there are tides that "taken at the flood, lead on to fortune; omitted, all the voyage of their life is bound with shallows and in miseries" (William Shakespeare). We are being swept along by the greatest single tide ever, proffering a future of untold richness of material wellbeing, intellectual enhancement, social and spiritual awareness. But behind the tide come waves of tumultuous change that could throw our societies on to the rocks.

Green investment

A noted manifestation of the rise of "greenery" is the offering of investment in companies that reflect environmental values. In Britain there is the Merlin Ecology Fund, which shuns businesses that are considered to be intrinsically polluting, such as oil industries. In the US there is New Alternatives, a fund that invests primarily in companies developing alternative-ecology and pollution-control technologies. Green investment trusts usually require signatories to: make compensation for environmental damages; disclose incidents of such damage; have at least one environmentalist on the board; and publish annually an independent environmental audit.

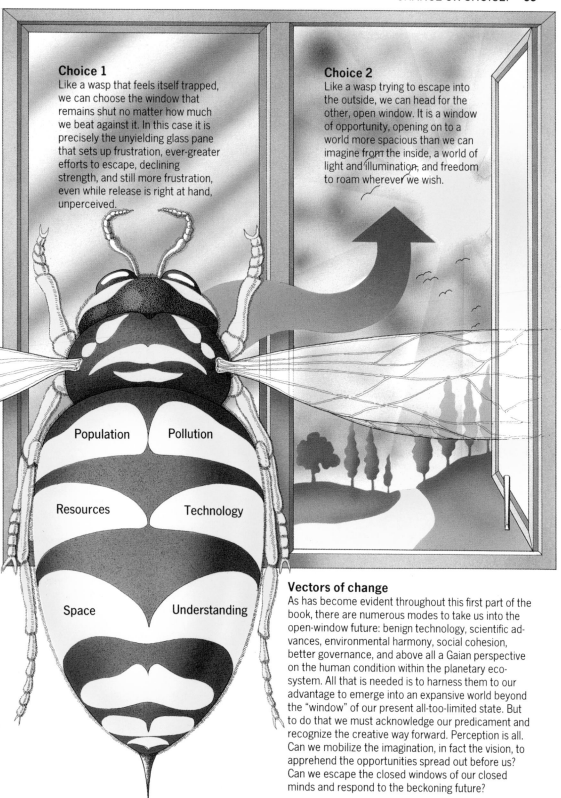

Choice 1

Like a wasp that feels itself trapped, we can choose the window that remains shut no matter how much we beat against it. In this case it is precisely the unyielding glass pane that sets up frustration, ever-greater efforts to escape, declining strength, and still more frustration, even while release is right at hand, unperceived.

Choice 2

Like a wasp trying to escape into the outside, we can head for the other, open window. It is a window of opportunity, opening on to a world more spacious than we can imagine from the inside, a world of light and illumination, and freedom to roam wherever we wish.

Population   Pollution

Resources   Technology

Space   Understanding

Vectors of change

As has become evident throughout this first part of the book, there are numerous modes to take us into the open-window future: benign technology, scientific advances, environmental harmony, social cohesion, better governance, and above all a Gaian perspective on the human condition within the planetary eco-system. All that is needed is to harness them to our advantage to emerge into an expansive world beyond the "window" of our present all-too-limited state. But to do that we must acknowledge our predicament and recognize the creative way forward. Perception is all. Can we mobilize the imagination, in fact the vision, to apprehend the opportunities spread out before us? Can we escape the closed windows of our closed minds and respond to the beckoning future?

Impacts and outcomes

The pressures and processes of Part One are generating a host of impacts and outcomes. As never before, things are flying apart and the old centres cannot hold. Moreover, however taxing it is to recognize the triggers of change, it is even more difficult to discern their consequences. They work away beneath the surface of everyday life, with potential to affect all our lives to come.

Part Two starts by looking at climate impacts, and what they will do to all aspects of our future worlds. In particular we look beyond the immediate repercussions of the greenhouse effect in terms of general warming, regional droughts, and coastal flooding. We consider the knock-on effects that could prove still more disruptive, such as mass migrations of environmental refugees, hundreds of millions of them within a few decades.

It is these second- and even third-order effects that are an underlying theme of the rest of Part Two. The information revolution will not only benefit everybody, it will confer undue advantage – technological, financial, economic, and hence political advantage – on those few nations that are way ahead of the field. Photovoltaics will not only transform our energy scene, they could give a sizeable boost to tropical nations with year-round sunshine. We shall see a continuing shift in the proportion of animal biomass represented by humans and livestock, from one-twentieth of the total at the start of this century to around one-third within just a few decades – with all that implies for the rest of animal life on Earth. We shall see deep-seated changes in regional entities, such as greater Europe, the Soviet Disunion, and the Muslim world, entraining shock-wave effects for the entire global community; and the rise of the Pacific-rim nations could prove so powerful that they could eventually make the rest of the world seem like the real rim. All these knock-on effects will boost the biggest knock-on of all, the pressure toward global governance.

It is the compounded impacts that tend to catch us unawares. So Part Two contains three Surprise spreads. The first looks at how climate change could become much more changeable, even apocalyptic, if we do not give urgent attention to long-range outcomes that are gaining hold already. The second considers the night-and-day changes of Eastern Europe, which in effect have occupied a few moments of recent history: how did we overlook the portents? The third considers AIDS, which gave abundant warning of its arrival, yet found us altogether unready to tackle it in its early stages. So is surprise largely in the eye of the beholder?

Two aspects of Africa
Hardship prevails in an Ethiopian refugee camp (main picture) while a radiocassette player entertains people in Niger (inset).

Changing lands

The greenhouse effect will alter the face of the planet more widely than for hundreds of thousands of years. On average, by the mid-2000s, global temperature is predicted to rise by an estimated 3-5°C (5.4-9°F) above the level prevailing in recent centuries – a change to be compared with the 4° C (7.2° F) in the other direction that was enough to trigger the onset of an ice age. But while the tropics are likely to see a little increase, the temperate zones may well witness a rise of 5-7° C (9-12.6° F), and the poles a vast 6-12° C (10.8-21.6° F).

As temperature bands shift away from the equator, vegetation bands will try to follow. For agricultural crops we may, through heroic efforts, and if other things remain equal (a highly unlikely prospect), be able to shift our food-growing regions to follow suit; or simply grow other crops in warmer lands. As for wild plants, they will need to migrate at ten times the speed they have ever achieved – a prospect they are simply not adapted for. Entire communities of plants will all but die out, as will their associated communities of animals (see pp. 34-5).

At the same time, sea levels will rise by 0.5 to 1.5m, not due to the melting of glaciers and ice caps (this will come later with far larger sea-level rises) but because warmer temperatures will cause the upper layers of the ocean to expand. Coastal megacities, such as Shanghai, Calcutta, and Lagos, will start to disappear under the waves: the same too for London, Tokyo, New York, Rotterdam, and many others. Worse, entire regions and some nations will be at risk of submersion.

Drought and flooding combined could well lead to 400 million people becoming environmental refugees, predominantly in the developing world. These countries will protest their new straits are not of their own making, having been mainly caused by the fossil-fuel profligates of the industrialized countries, and may seek help on a vast scale as well as reparations. All this in a world where disaffected communities can practise nuclear terrorism.

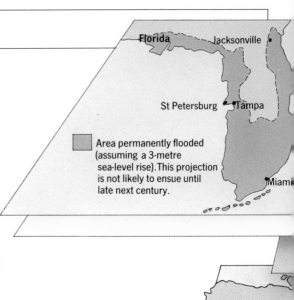

Area permanently flooded (assuming a 3-metre sea-level rise). This projection is not likely to ensue until late next century.

Global effects

The greenhouse effect will cause radical changes. The North American grain belt may start to become unbuckled, while the USSR will have plenty of space to move its wheat belt and perhaps grow tropical crops on present-day wheat lands. Thus the USSR may become the world's bread basket. Moreover global warming will put territories such as southern Florida in the US and East Anglia in the UK at risk of drowning. One-third of Bangladesh is likely to be inundated forever. Estuaries such as the Chao Phraya, Salween, Irrawaddy, Mekong, and Yangtze will suffer similarly. Nations such as the 1200 islands of the Maldives will disappear.

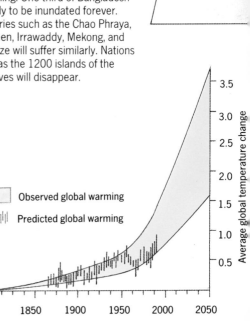

Observed global warming

Predicted global warming

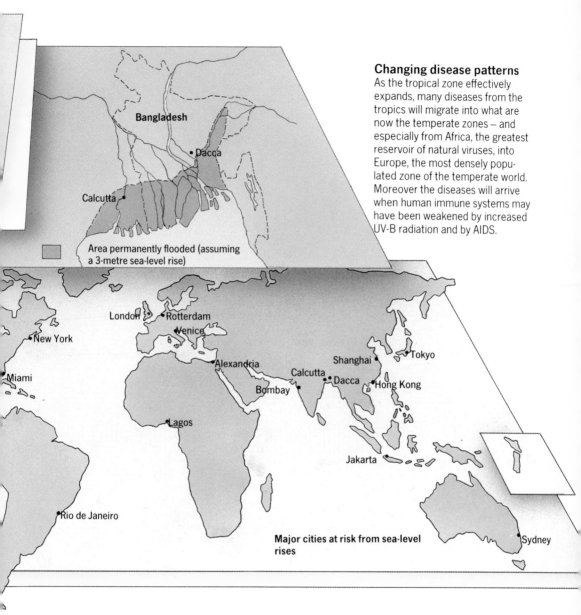

Bangladesh

• Dacca

Calcutta •

Area permanently flooded (assuming a 3-metre sea-level rise)

London • Rotterdam
Venice
• New York

Miami

Alexandria

Shanghai • Tokyo

Calcutta
• Dacca
Bombay •   • Hong Kong

Lagos

Jakarta

• Rio de Janeiro

Major cities at risk from sea-level rises

Sydney

Changing disease patterns

As the tropical zone effectively expands, many diseases from the tropics will migrate into what are now the temperate zones – and especially from Africa, the greatest reservoir of natural viruses, into Europe, the most densely populated zone of the temperate world. Moreover the diseases will arrive when human immune systems may have been weakened by increased UV-B radiation and by AIDS.

Population effects

Florida stands to lose one-quarter of its land area. Of course Florida could always build extensive dykes to hold back the sea; or it could simply "move" Miami and other coastal communities inland over a period of decades. A US Environmental Protection Agency (EPA) study projects that to protect the US from a 1-metre sea-level rise would cost up to $111 billion (at 1988 prices) – and there would still be a loss equivalent in area to Massachusetts. No such solution is available to Bangladesh, which lacks the space, finance, and the skills to respond. Many other developing-country areas – notably the Nile Valley, China's eastern seaboard, and parts of Indonesia – look likely to encounter uniquely destructive flooding, leading eventually to hundreds of millions of environmental refugees.

Surprise – climatic dice

The changed map of a greenhouse-affected world will be shock enough for us given only the expected shifts in climate and vegetation, and the realignment of coastlines. But there could be bigger changes in store.

One possible scenario is a shift in the direction of ocean currents, such as the Gulf Stream turning southward in the northeastern Atlantic, just as it did several thousand years ago when climate systems were undergoing one upheaval after another. This would mean that northwestern Europe would cease to enjoy its present temperate climate, and instead would have conditions something nearer to what Iceland presently "enjoys", including frozen rivers, estuaries, and seaports. Another predicted scenario is greatly increased storminess and disrupted climate patterns worldwide – from hurricanes to failing monsoons. More significant still, nearly all greenhouse models fail to look at truly doomsday scenarios. What if global warming were to speed up due to sudden shifts in ocean/atmosphere mechanisms? Still more drastic, what if the greenhouse effect were to become grossly compounded by the warming-induced death of boreal forests and other biotas, with *several times* more greenhouse effect than is presently projected? Or suppose the world were to continue with "business as usual, only much more so", until by 2035 carbon emissions from 9 billion people were to average the level of North America today? In each case, the eventual warming would inflict such damage on our lifestyles that civilization would come to a swift end.

The surprise element does not lie with the climatic outcomes, it lies with our capacity to lay ourselves open to cataclysmic surprise. For it is in the area of dynamic interplay between components of climatic systems that we are critically ignorant. So powerful are these synergistic interactions that the result can be a whole order of magnitude higher than the sum of their individual effects. Add in the reinforcing effects of economic, social, and political systems, and we have a recipe for surprise supreme.

Jump effects

Large-scale ecosystems can react in an extreme and unanticipated manner when subject to disturbance of exceptional scope. These quantum changes are known as threshold responses or breakpoints of irreversible change. They arise when ecosystems, after absorbing stresses over long periods without much outward sign of damage, reach a disruption level at which a "jump effect" takes over.

Among large-scale ecosystems that seem especially susceptible to synergistic disruption are tropical forests, coral reefs, wetlands, estuaries, and montane environments. But the one that may eventually reveal the greatest environmental discontinuity, with greatest harm to human purpose, comprises the oceans. A sudden reorganization of the ocean-atmosphere system some 10–13,000 years ago led to extreme shifts in the world's climate, including a temperature rise of several degrees within just half a century. What similar upheavals might we be setting up thanks to our multiple, grand-scale, and simultaneous interventions in the workings of the biosphere? Remarkably enough, climate models do not generally include the key factor of feedback. They simply are not sophisticated enough.

Eroded gene base

In the wake of the greenhouse effect many agricultural regions look likely to experience sharply changed climate conditions: higher temperatures with dry regions becoming drier, wet ones wetter, and stormy ones stormier. Yet most of our agricultural crops are finely tuned to present climate regimes. Hence there is a need to expand the genetic underpinnings of our crops in order to enhance their adaptability. This places a premium on germplasm variability to build up drought resistance. The same applies to genetic adaptations for crop plants and domestic animals to counter new pests and diseases. Yet we are permitting their gene reservoirs to be depleted at rapid rates. So while genetic erosion is already serious, it will become much more so when compounded by the greenhouse effect. Conversely, too, greenhouse-affected crops will be in much deeper trouble if their adaptability cannot

Desertification

Global warming

Ice age

Our grand-scale ignorance

In large part we are ignorant of synergisms because we simply do not know enough about the discrete factors, let alone their interactions. Consider UV-B and its impact on plants. So far researchers have investigated only a handful of crop species from this standpoint. They have hardly made a start on the trees, shrubs, and grasses that account for 90% of the planet's plant growth, and no more than cursory attention has been given to four out of ten major types of terrestrial ecosystem, with no studies at all of tropical forests, savannahs, and wetlands. We have some way to go before looking at the impact of UV-B in compounded conjunction with such things as acid rain, rising temperature, and reduced rainfall.

The Pluto syndrome

A Berkeley biologist, Professor John Harte, and his colleagues have run a survey of 285 articles in four consecutive issues of four prominent ecological journals dealing with wildlife. Not only have they found that the articles all but ignore the influence of wildlife on soil, water, air, and climate, but more significantly not a single one mentions the interactions of these factors. The Berkeley group terms this the "Pluto syndrome", meaning that much ecological research could be conducted just as well on the planet Pluto, since it overlooks a host of physical and chemical factors that characterize the planet Earth.

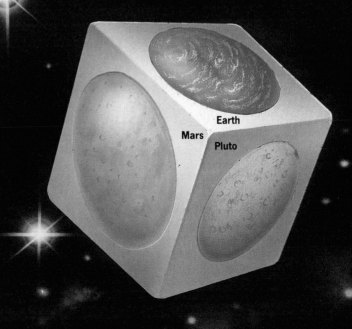

Earth

Mars

Pluto

New rich/new poor

Our future world, already unfolding, will feature many changes in who is rich and who is poor. Since 1973 we have recognized the huge economic power, followed by political might, that can be gained by those nations endowed with oil reserves. What new "resource surprises" lie ahead for us over the coming decades?

First will be energy, but in new forms. As we seek to move beyond a fossil-fuel-based world (if only for reasons of climate change), there will be a premium on nonpolluting sources of energy. Nations with abundant stocks of the most widely available form of energy, solar energy, will be well placed. Thus tropical nations could rank among the world's new rich. So could those countries with moderate sunshine but immoderate means to exploit it through technology – Japan, for example.

Another new form of wealth will be food, especially in a world demanding three times as much to eat if we are to accommodate growing numbers of people and meet nutritional needs. The great grain belt of North America, which now provides food surpluses to a hundred nations, could turn into a dust bowl under the impact of the greenhouse effect, whereupon the US, perhaps Canada too, would find it hard to keep up with domestic demand. The new food-rich could well include the Soviet Union with its fertile Siberian soils waiting to be farmed as the greenhouse effect pushes food-growing zones northward. Other leading food producers, benefiting from improved climate, could include Australia, Mexico, and certain countries of South America.

What other resources will confer unexpected wealth? Among possible candidates are information, natural-world resources (biodiversity, for example), and even government knowhow or institutional flexibility. Plainly we shall need to revise our ideas of what constitutes wealth and who possesses it – with all that implies too for the new poor of the world.

Winners and losers

As well as successes on the world stage, there will be newly poor countries too. Not only is North America likely to lose ground because of its agricultural problems, but in an energy-efficient world losers could include those nations that are now pre-eminent in oil. And non-tropical states with their relatively impoverished biotas will find themselves at a disadvantage *vis-à-vis* "natural-world" winners.

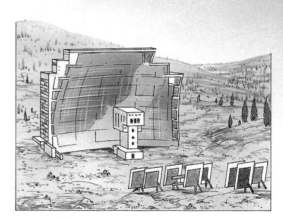

The energy rich

If global energy needs ever depend primarily on the vast amounts of that most abundant natural energy, sunlight, the nations to benefit most could well be those best endowed with year-round sunshine – which broadly means today's developing nations. But they will be heavily dependent, at first at least, on technology from the developed nations.

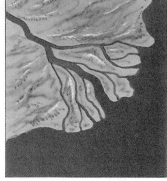

The food rich
As temperature belts and rainfall patterns shift due to the influence of the greenhouse effect, today's great food-producing nations could give way to a new set of bread-basket countries. "Winners" could conceivably include Mexico, Argentina, some nations of the Sahel and the Middle East, India, and Australia – provided of course that they have the agrotechnologies to exploit their newly favourable conditions.

The information rich
The electronics revolution and communications technology could lead to the emergence of an unprecedented cadre of information-rich nations. Leaders could well include Japan, the US, and the European Community. In turn, information could prove to be the basis for several other forms of new wealth, such as energy and agriculture: information appears set to become the resource *par excellence*.

Natural world wealth
Biological wealth is not yet widely perceived as a vital resource. But as we better learn how to value nature's endowments in, for example, tropical forests and wildlife species, and to tap them sustainably, so we may come to esteem those peoples with abundant stocks of natural wealth and the folkloric wisdom to draw on Earth's bounty with respect and restraint, in perpetuity. These peoples include the tribal people, who today number only a few tens of millions, but who could eventually emerge as contributors to a sustainable future.

Other communities

The useful species that comprise our agriculture are heavily outnumbered by a panoply of pests and weeds. There is also a vast community of other camp followers that result from our activities – rats, rabbits, sparrows, flies, cockroaches, diseases, and the like that have proliferated in the wake of our spread around the Earth. What new communities of unwanted species will accompany our advance into the future if we continue to disrupt natural biotas and impoverish ecosystems?

This is not to discount those species that have supported the human cause. Since the onset of agriculture 10,000 years ago, together with the start of sizeable human settlements, we have drawn abundant benefit from a few dozen animal species, including cattle, goats, pigs, sheep, and buffaloes. Even more important are our main sources of food in the form of wheat, maize, rice, barley, and a couple of dozen other kinds of food plants.

Domestication has come at a price. As soon as we had grain fields, we had rats and mice; as soon as we had houses we had flies and cockroaches. Our efforts to combat pests – for example by the use of pesticides – merely lead to resistant strains that proliferate worse than ever. Thus we convert pests into plagues, as miracle grains foster miracle rats and weeds.

Equally damaging for our future prospects is the depletion of crop species' gene pools. Crop breeding for sheer productivity is geared to genetic uniformity, planting a single variety in millions of hectares, often in lands where other varieties then become squeezed into oblivion.

All this bodes ill for our future unless we switch to a less simplified agriculture, and give heed to more efficient ways of dealing with pests. Much the same applies to our simplified lifestyles, which are a boon to cockroaches and other unwelcome guests of our human settlements. Unless we shift to a more ecological approach, we can confidently expect that our increasing camp followers will find that the future represents a field day.

The camp followers

Remarkable as are today's congeries of camp followers, it is only a small part of the potential that awaits us if we lift the lid and delve beyond what is essentially a Neolithic spectrum of species. Very few domestications have occurred since the first ones, and they have been mostly extremely recent arrivals, such as the Kiwi fruit, unknown in our supermarkets until a decade ago. Some promising candidates for the future include amaranth grain, pomelo fruit, and beefalo, being a cross between the cow and buffalo. Were we to mobilize even a small fraction of plants and animals that could serve our cause, we would surely witness an array totalling hundreds if not thousands of species. In New Guinea alone there are 200 forest fruits that have proven acceptable to the human palate, yet have not come into use beyond local level.

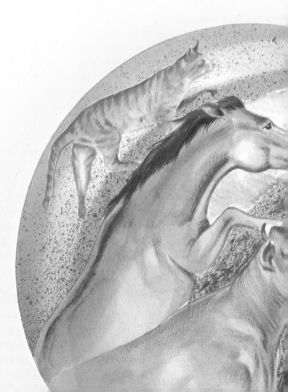

Hand in glove

Many other creatures benefit from human society apart from domesticates. As the number of people increases, human garbage too, so there is a surge in population of less desirable animals, such as flies, rats, and cockroaches – also, though less obviously, of human-disease bacteria. It seems as if we cannot have one without the other. When once we accept the company in society of certain members of the wild and tame them to our purposes, the "genie bottle" releases all manner of unwanted congeners. Pollute and generally corrupt the environment as they might, they don't destroy it. They merely feed on humankind's presence and rejoice at the folly of its proliferance.

Implosion of the wild

A number of wild species are expanding their ranges, exploiting the thrown-out food stocks of urban communities and enjoying habitats with few wild competitors. We have long been familiar with pigeons and sparrows; now they are being joined by foxes in Europe and coyotes in North America, occasionally appearing even in city centres. We can expect a continuing implosion of the wild as rural areas become ever more intensely farmed.

The pet industry

Americans spend well over $5 billion a year on dog and cat foods, or seven times more than on baby foods. Products for cats now include food treats as well as weight-reducing diet foods, and health-care services, such as diagnostic tests and medical insurance. So successfully do domestic animals flourish that, in the UK alone, some 300,000 cats and more than 370,000 dogs have to be killed annually by animal-welfare groups.

Global village

In 1950 Winston Churchill declared that he had got on well enough in his life without knowing much about Cambodia, and he saw little reason to change his point of view. A few years later came the Vietnam War, and we all had good cause to learn about Cambodia – as indeed the Cambodians and Vietnamese had to learn about Americans, Russians, Australians, and others who impinged on their lives. Marshall McLuhan's concept of the global village was becoming fact, until today there seems to be a Timbuktu around every corner.

The village-ization of our global community is due to a range of interrelated factors. Partly it is a case of the fast-growing network of economic and hence political relationships worldwide, spawned by the explosive growth of international trade and investment; in turn these foster networks of social and cultural liaisons as business leaders and government officials roam far and wide, pursued by the media circus.

Partly too this coming together of a global community is a result of the extraordinary advances in communications technologies with their instant rapport. Political encounters, moon walks, Sahel famines, the Olympic Games, and Live Aid concerts, all are beamed around the world and hence touch everybody's lives. If we are to live in everybody's pockets, it is in our best interests to get to know them; there is now a greater intrinsic interest in the lifestyles of the Smiths and Jones in their billions. And with tourism so much a part of the developed world, there is every opportunity to travel to their countries and see them where they live. Just 50 years ago few people travelled more than 50 km from their homes; now for millions of people it is commonplace to climb on board a plane for a 5000-km flight.

Almost without realizing it, we have become world neighbours. But the essence of global-village life will be what we villagers find we really have to say to each other.

Elements of the village
Every second of our daily round we reach out to fellow villagers around the world through instant communications, primarily via electronic networks, such as the telephone system, but also through a host of other linkages. These world-shrinking processes foster a host of relationships – economic, social, cultural, educational – that bind us ever-more closely into a single, coherent global community.

Removing social distance
Through the international telephone system it is possible to speak across the world with any one of nearly 1.8 billion people. To this extent distance has not so much shrunk as evaporated.

Immediate response
We can now speak with people in remote sectors of countries on the far side of the globe, and do so with virtually zero delay. The telephone, telex, and fax are making us all neighbours, sharing a common back-garden fence.

Remote sensing
The eye in the sky of Landsat and SPOT satellites allows us to peer into everybody's backyard – and they into ours. Of course, that is not the prime purpose of remote sensing; rather it is to map and detail the principal changes taking place in the biosphere.

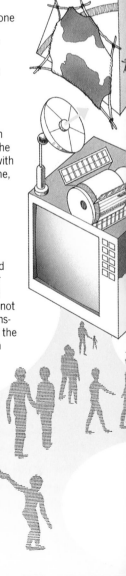

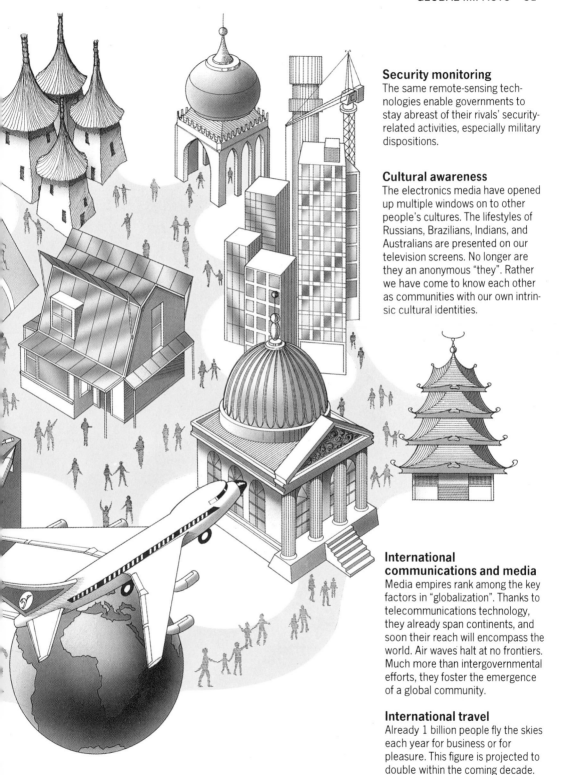

Security monitoring
The same remote-sensing technologies enable governments to stay abreast of their rivals' security-related activities, especially military dispositions.

Cultural awareness
The electronics media have opened up multiple windows on to other people's cultures. The lifestyles of Russians, Brazilians, Indians, and Australians are presented on our television screens. No longer are they an anonymous "they". Rather we have come to know each other as communities with our own intrinsic cultural identities.

International communications and media
Media empires rank among the key factors in "globalization". Thanks to telecommunications technology, they already span continents, and soon their reach will encompass the world. Air waves halt at no frontiers. Much more than intergovernmental efforts, they foster the emergence of a global community.

International travel
Already 1 billion people fly the skies each year for business or for pleasure. This figure is projected to double within the coming decade.

Supercities

Our world remains mostly rural. Within another ten years it will become mostly urban. This will be one of the most profound shifts since people first started to congregate in villages.

Equally striking is the tendency for certain cities to become supercities. In 1980 one of the largest cities was Los Angeles, with almost 10 million inhabitants. By the mid-1990s there are likely to be 22 larger cities, headed by Mexico City and Sao Paulo, with about 25 million each.

This means that many cities will be larger than many nations. It will also bestow on them a status that, in some senses at least, is likely to enable them to operate as nations. Already Los Angeles engages in its own relations with the Japanese government.

Their unwieldy size will also bestow on supercities a superset of problems. They will have grown too fast to build up the support systems and general infrastructure required to work as liveable communities. It took New York 150 years to reach a population of 8 million, but it will take Mexico City only 15 years to add another 8 million to its present throngs.

Nor are the supercities' problems confined to the cities themselves. They suck in resources from a vast support region: they become parasitic on their hinterlands. In Kenya, for example, the major cause of deforestation is not villagers' use of wood for fuel, which can be sustainable; it is the widespread conversion of wood to charcoal for sale to urbanites.

Nobody as yet has found an acceptable way to stem the runaway growth of supercities. There is a fast-growing reservoir of would-be migrants waiting in the countryside, and there is not enough investment in rural development to keep people on the farms. Thus the acute problems – *and* the lost opportunities – of supercities reflect the failures of development overall. The outcome is tragic, since the explosive arrival of these mega-experiments in collective living could have been one of the most adventurous of all human endeavours.

Two sides of a single city
Within New York live individuals with business holdings equal to the aggregate wealth of a town with 50,000 people. Also in New York live individuals with no homes at all. In New Delhi a handful of millionaires consume more material goods every three months than many fellow citizens consume in their lifetimes. In many other cities – Los Angeles, Miami, Rio de Janeiro, Lagos, Nairobi, Johannesburg, and Manila – some of the richest people on Earth live within a kilometre of the poorest of the poor.

The polyglot city

Many city communities, such as Notting Hill (above) in London, feature people of all sorts and conditions. The social, ethnic, and cultural mix makes for a polyglot city with greater diversity within a single locality than has been found in entire cities of the past. But diversity can also breed conflict if minorities feel threatened by "majority swamping", and rioting (left) becomes an all too frequent scene when distinctively different groups rub shoulders too closely with each other.

The termite queen

Many a modern city is the ultimate "ant heap" of humanity, with tens of thousands of people to every square kilometre, the highest density ever known on Earth. But this mass of humanity is also like a termite queen, attracting workers and other dependants from far and wide. Cairo and Mexico City each harbours around one-quarter of their country's populace; indeed each has more people than dozens of individual nations (and Cairo has more cars than all of China). To this extent a modern metropolis lives as a parasite, feeding off the support of its hinterland, drawing in labour, skills, food, water, and other raw materials.

International governance

For 400 years the nation-state system has dominated international relations. Not that it has been much of a "system". Rather it has been a free for all, with many governments inclined to make up their own rules as they have gone their independent ways.

What convulsive changes these last 40 years have wrought. International manufacturing trade has increased seven times, and there have been manyfold increases in investment and capital flows. There have been similarly revolutionary increases in air travel, telecommunications, and myriad other forms of communication, such as letter and parcel post. And still the pace quickens.

This all means that a nation's borders are increasingly porous affairs. What a government decides in its economic policy can be blocked or even overturned by the actions of other nations or their institutions.

Thus the new name of the game is economic interdependence and, by implication, political interdependence. At the same time we are experiencing environmental interdependence, as witness acid rain, marine pollution, and the greenhouse effect. Still other interdependencies arise in regard to terrorism and drug trafficking.

Yet our capacity to organize these proliferative international relationships is primitive in comparison with our needs. We have all too few institutions that do more than peck at problems. Our very understanding of the new complexities reflects a simpler and gone-forever era: politicians prate about sovereign jurisdiction even as they exalt the financial processes that proclaim independence is dead.

Fortunately we can exploit new means of one-world living. These comprise international networks or corporations, banks, scientific communities, religious bodies, the media, and a host of nongovernmental organizations (NGOs). These new networks are adept at working in arenas beyond the purview of governments. Even though they may not have heard the term, they are experts at the new form of international relations, governance.

Who is running the roundabout?

Governments think they run the world. Until recently they were largely right. But today the business of governance is undertaken by business as much as by governments. The banking community can resist and even reverse the economic policy proposed by a government. Finance networks can transfer inflation across national boundaries; global corporations can export unemployment; armament manufacturers can stoke up bush-fire conflicts in many parts of the world; media can inflame communities beyond government control; crime rings can display contempt for national and international sanctions; and religious extremists can foster revolt in neighbouring countries. True, governments still have their role to play, but they must share power with a host of other purveyors of governance.

The driving force

Beneath the charade of all-powerful governments at the top of the governance system lies a complex machinery that does much, if not most, of the work. The world's top ten banks have individual holdings greater than the GNPs of many entire nations. The international arms trade, worth in excess of $50 billion a year, is twice as great as the GNP of New Zealand. International crime controls funds equal to the annual income of the poorest half of humanity. These potent interests, often dominated by a few individuals and generally answerable to no electorate, exert vast influence over our world's future – and their influence is expanding ever-more rapidly.

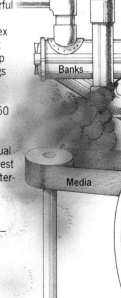

Banks

Media

Arts

Humanities

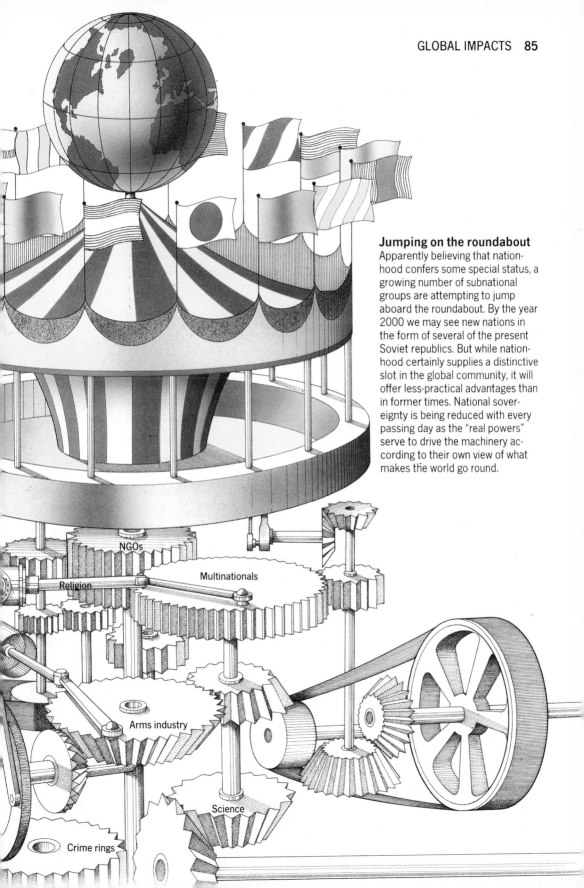

Jumping on the roundabout

Apparently believing that nationhood confers some special status, a growing number of subnational groups are attempting to jump aboard the roundabout. By the year 2000 we may see new nations in the form of several of the present Soviet republics. But while nationhood certainly supplies a distinctive slot in the global community, it will offer less-practical advantages than in former times. National sovereignty is being reduced with every passing day as the "real powers" serve to drive the machinery according to their own view of what makes the world go round.

NGOs

Multinationals

Religion

Arms industry

Science

Crime rings

Local power

As if to counterbalance the new interest in global governance, there has been an increased emphasis on localized activities. Partly it is a case of "Think globally, act locally". Partly the emphasis reflects a general urge toward decentralization of power. Partly, too, it stems from an outburst of cultural awareness, or the "new tribalism", as demonstrated by the nationalism of such groups as the Scots, Bretons, Basques, Karens, Kurds, and Inuits.

The process is largely stimulated by information technology and accessible communications, both of which enable local groups to "plug in" easily and cheaply to nation-wide networks. Thanks to ultra-rapid computers and communications satellites, there has been an outburst of decentralized networks of common-interest citizens. These "new networkers" know the best way to make the most efficient use of cheap teleconferencing, data-transmission techniques, on-line roundtables, resource-sharing collectives, volunteer-talent pools, and a dozen other powerful and innovative forms of intellectual outreach.

Even more important than their modes of operation, these networkers share a vision of the future where individuals and organizations communicate directly, bypassing bureaucracies. The upshot should be a light-year's advance in participatory organization – and thus the revolution in information technology is spawning another revolution, the emergent politics of super-participation. It serves to create societies with masses of informed people, leading to a diffusion of power. Hence the twin processes serve to promote egalitarian decision-making bolstered by exceptional feedback capacities.

In short, communication networks are becoming an increasingly important force for social and political change. They offer much scope, and hope, to lower the barriers within and between the world's nations and their peoples.

Unifying the image

The polyglot array of local activists, pressure groups, and NGOs may present a bewildering spectacle to the observer. Where is the pattern, where the cohesive structure? But it is precisely in the unstructured formation of local-power bodies that their strength lies. Because they do not work along formal procedural pathways, they can remain instantly adaptable and flexible, able to put into effect "bottom-up" initiatives by contrast with the rigid autocracies of "top-down" government. In Kenya, for example, local initiatives resulted in the planting of more trees in a single year than the government had managed in the previous ten. To some degree there is a meshing of both levels, but it needs to be a kind of organic growth, self-generative, and autonomous – thus reinforcing the creative attributes of local power.

Significant trends

While the principal manifestations of local power are too numerous to list, consider the implications of the following illustrative examples. The green movement in the developed world, now extending into the developing world; the planet-wide campaign to plant new trees, from the Green Belt Movement in Kenya, Indonesia, and Colombia, to President Bush's project to plant a billion trees a year; the measures of slum dwellers to take their fate into their own hands, as witness the efforts of people in Chicago, Lusaka, Calcutta, and south London; the antipollution lobby, as backed worldwide by nearly 4 million supporters of Greenpeace alone. Each area of local activity is significant; each forms a segment of a much wider, indeed a global picture.

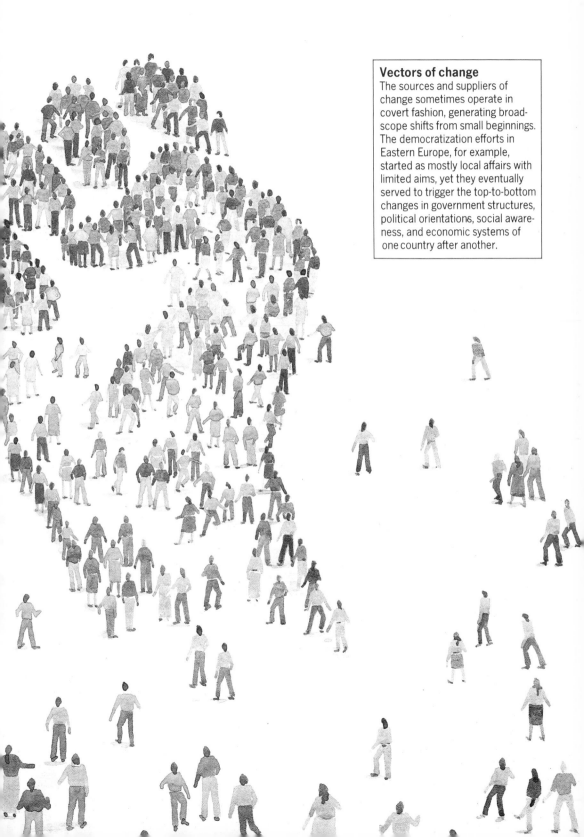

Vectors of change
The sources and suppliers of
change sometimes operate in
covert fashion, generating broadscope shifts from small beginnings.
The democratization efforts in
Eastern Europe, for example,
started as mostly local affairs with
limited aims, yet they eventually
served to trigger the top-to-bottom
changes in government structures,
political orientations, social awareness, and economic systems of
one country after another.

North America

The biggest economy, the biggest military, the biggest technology, the biggest stock of key natural resources – how can the US do other than go from strength to super-strength? All too easily. It has the biggest deficits in budget and trade, the biggest drugs problem, the biggest AIDS epidemic outside Africa, and the biggest influx of illegal migrants. Plus it has the prospect of faring unusually badly through the green-house effect; and perhaps the biggest dose of complacency about the future.

In addition, its west-coast states are increasingly drawn toward the Pacific-rim arena, global epicentre of 21st-century action. Californians are finding there is another West out there to be challenged. With stresses and strains such as these – some of them, it is true, capable of being seen as creative tensions – what outlook for the country that would lead the world?

No outlook if it still wants to be leader. In a multipolar world there is room for co-operators rather than pace setters. Just as the Soviet Union cannot control Lithuania, the US cannot control the Philippines. In any case, the US may find itself preoccupied with problems within its own borders if immigrants continue to flood in from Mexico and Central America (see pp. 40-1).

Further turmoil may ensue as the green-house effect starts to take a grip. With heat-wave weather starting to be common rather than rare in more states than not, and with the great grain lands suffering from dust-bowl droughts without respite, there may be a drive to migrate northward. And what if countries such as Egypt and Bangladesh, with tens of millions of greenhouse refu-gees, were to look to the US for relief or sanctuary – on the grounds that it had been the US's prodigious consumption of fossil fuels that had principally triggered global warming? Yet the US remains liberty's flag-bearer. With its open society, citizen partici-pation, freedom of speech and information, and capacity for ideas and inventiveness, the US may weather its future storms.

The Divided States of America

While the idea of a geographical break-up of the US is an absurd prospect, the country faces greater social strains than it seems aware of. Ethnic divisions will soon become more divisive than ever (see below). The drugs problem, with already at least 25 million regular users, shows every sign of growing worse fast. The economy is giving hordes of hostages to tomorrow. Each of these problems will be sorely aggravated by the greenhouse effect, which looks likely to affect America more severely than all but a dozen countries. The overall result could well be a set of pressures that will eventually stress the fabric of American society far more profoundly than any crisis of the past.

US ethnic composition

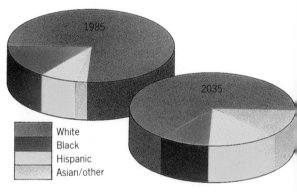

White
Black
Hispanic
Asian/other

Underfed, underpaid, and over here

In the past two decades at least 5 million Mexicans, plus perhaps another 2 million from south of the border, have made their way into the US. If recent migration trends continue to accelerate, there could be another 10 million Hispanics crossing the Rio Grande by the year 2000, and it is not unrealistic to envisage 25 to 30 million in all within a further ten years. The new entrants tend to be impoverished as compared with Americans, and have no option but to take poor-paying jobs. At the same time, their family size is often twice that of Americans, so their numbers are growing proportionately all the time. But signifi-cantly, they are the first arrivals who seem disinclined to go through the melting-pot process. Far from be-coming "proud Americans", they prefer to remain Mexicans, Guatemalans, and so on, living in a foreign land, thus engendering additional social strains (see pp. 40-1). Most significant of all, it is estimated that whites will be in the minority by 2050.

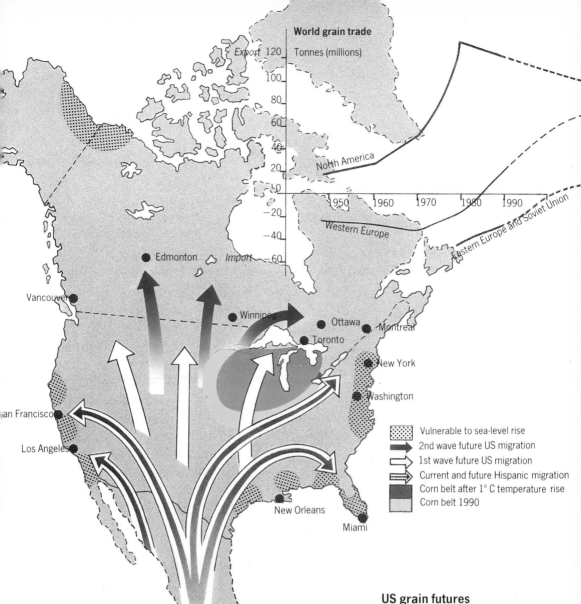

World grain trade

Tonnes (millions)

Export

North America

Western Europe

Eastern Europe and Soviet Union

Vulnerable to sea-level rise
2nd wave future US migration
1st wave future US migration
Current and future Hispanic migration
Corn belt after 1° C temperature rise
Corn belt 1990

Edmonton, Vancouver, Winnipeg, Ottawa, Montreal, Toronto, New York, Washington, San Francisco, Los Angeles, New Orleans, Miami, Import

Population shifts northward

By courtesy of the greenhouse effect, the number of days per year when the temperature rises to "intolerable" levels (37° C/100° F) in Miami, New Orleans, Dallas, and other southern cities may shortly increase from a few dozen to well over a hundred. Coupled to this is the prospect of the great grain lands suffering dust-bowl droughts without respite. The result might be a drive for Americans to migrate northward, even into Canada. Could the US relocate itself, just like that – even if the Canadians held wide the door?

Canada's expanding horizons

Canada could find its prospects transformed. Global warming will mean the country no longer needs to be, in effect, an inhabited strip 7000 km long by 100 km wide. Much more of the north will become climatically agreeable. As the Arctic ice melts and the sea passage becomes a year-round affair, there could be far more economic activity in the polar sector. The most telling change could be the arrival of multitudes of Americans fleeing their overheating country – if indeed Canada wants to be Americanized in that further fashion.

US grain futures

The 1988 drought, with only a 15% decline in soil moisture, caused a 30% fall-off in the US grain harvest. Americans in that year actually consumed more food than they produced. What if, in the light of climate change, there is a drought twice or even three times as severe – and persisting year after year? Instead of exporting in excess of 86 million tonnes of food grain per year, as it has been doing on average since 1985, the US could find itself having to import food instead – even, as a consequence of the greenhouse effect, from what might be the newly productive wheat lands of Siberia.

Latin America

The people of southern Brazil and central Mexico enjoy a level of living comparable with those of southern Europe; Bolivians and Paraguayans are as impoverished as many Indians and Africans. Which groups offer the most probable future portent?

The region is the only one bordering a developed country, the US. As was seen on pages 40–1, this has already triggered waves of migrants into the US, a country that now faces a dilemma. If it allows the migrant throngs to continue, they will transform American society. But if it closes off the safety-valve border, it could well precipitate enough social tensions in Mexico to engender revolution.

Fortunately, certain countries in the region – notably Brazil and Argentina – show promise of enough productive capacity to enable them soon to enjoy many of the benefits of electronics technology. This, plus their fast-growing industrial muscle, could bring them economic advancement until they become newly affluent countries by early next century. Of course much depends on how soon the region can emerge from beneath its debt burden – an average of over $1000 per citizen. Much depends too on how long the region continues to be a prime source of narcotics.

The region's future is overshadowed by environmental problems. If Amazonia continues to burn there will eventually be a mini-spasm of species extinctions that itself will match all but the greatest mass extinctions of the prehistoric past. More immediately, gross deforestation could ravage the rainfall regimes in southern Brazil's breadbasket farmlands. Argentina and Chile, by virtue of their southerly location, could be among the first nations to experience enhanced ultraviolet radiation via Antarctica's worsening "hole" in the ozone layer.

With a long history of political volatility, the region shows plenty of scope for strife and confrontation as nations jostle for advantage if not outright leadership. Moreover Brazil and Argentina possess the ability to "go nuclear".

The American poor relation

With a combined GNP of $700 billion, or one-seventh that of the US, Latin America feels distinctly disadvantaged. Although Brazil and conceivably Argentina could become "almost great powers" within a few decades, and most countries have a per-capita GNP of more than $1000, several of the Andean nations are going backward economically. Overall the regional outlook is far from bright, dominated as it is by five key concerns: demography, debt, drugs, deforestation, and democracy. What the region needs is more investment and technological support from its giant neighbour to the north, as well as from Japan and Europe: will it get it?

Rest of developing world

Total developing world debt (1988 – $1156 billion)

Cocaine cash crop

About 25 million US citizens use illegal drugs at a cost of $150 billion annually. This is roughly equal to the combined GNPs of Colombia, Peru, and Bolivia, the countries that produce 98% of the coca leaves processed into cocaine for the international market. The coca-cocaine economy has played a vital role in cushioning the economic crises facing these countries with their huge foreign debts. Bolivia's debt is an extraordinary 115% of GNP. Although most profits are taken by drug traders out of the region, cocaine is a cash crop that has helped hundreds of thousands of farmers and hired labourers. A conservative estimate puts the combined income from cocaine to Bolivia, Colombia, and Peru at more than $1 billion. Even so, the total debt of these countries is only one-quarter what US citizens spend on illegal drugs in a year.

Mexico City

To North America

The future of Amazonia

The nine nations that share the 5-million-sq-km region should halt deforestation for their own emphatic good, as well as to reduce the greenhouse effect. But fearful of climate change, the developed nations now need the tropical-forest nations as never before. And these latter nations have a potent lever in the form of their forests to bargain for fairer terms of trade, debt relief, and development measures. Until an equitable bargain is reached, however, Amazonia is likely to continue going up in smoke, with the loss of millions of species.

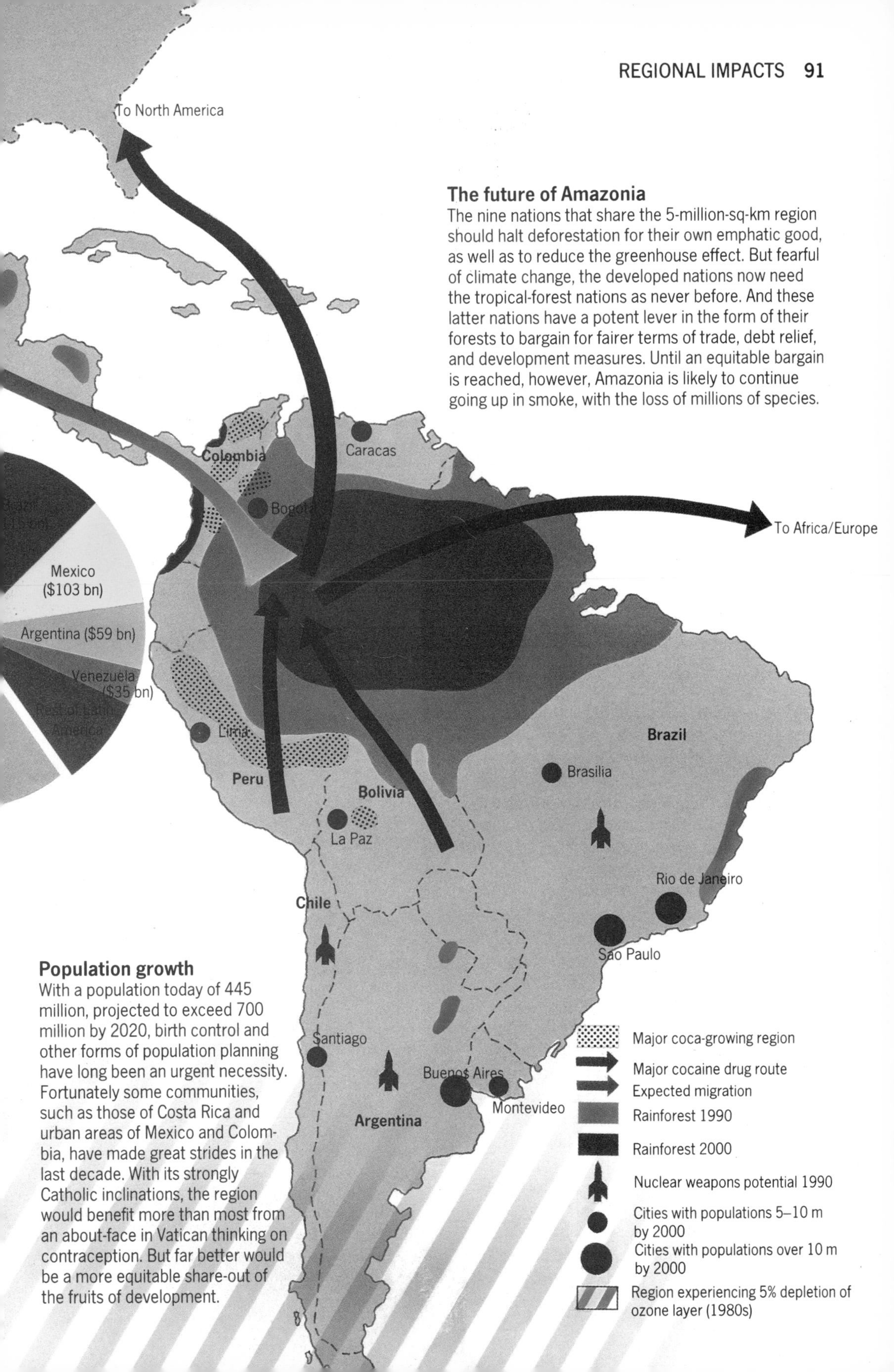

To Africa/Europe

Colombia

Caracas

Bogotá

Brazil
($115 bn)

Mexico
($103 bn)

Argentina ($59 bn)

Venezuela
($35 bn)

Rest of Latin
America

Lima

Brazil

Brasília

Peru

Bolivia

La Paz

Rio de Janeiro

Chile

São Paulo

Population growth

With a population today of 445 million, projected to exceed 700 million by 2020, birth control and other forms of population planning have long been an urgent necessity. Fortunately some communities, such as those of Costa Rica and urban areas of Mexico and Colombia, have made great strides in the last decade. With its strongly Catholic inclinations, the region would benefit more than most from an about-face in Vatican thinking on contraception. But far better would be a more equitable share-out of the fruits of development.

Santiago

Buenos Aires

Montevideo

Argentina

	Major coca-growing region
➡	Major cocaine drug route
➡	Expected migration
	Rainforest 1990
	Rainforest 2000
	Nuclear weapons potential 1990
●	Cities with populations 5–10 m by 2000
●	Cities with populations over 10 m by 2000
	Region experiencing 5% depletion of ozone layer (1980s)

Europe – East and West

A maelstrom of change in the final months of the 1980s means that Europe could soon grow to become a giant on the world stage. Equally possible, too, it could decline into endless internal bickering and turmoil. Or it could likewise go several other ways. No other region in the world presents such scope for change and surprise.

Much depends on how Europe is defined. If, in the expansive Gorbachev spirit, it is to be the home for all who call themselves Europeans, then Europe extends from the Atlantic to the Urals. What if Russia itself were to assert that it is also an East European state? If it swapped communism for a market economy, became a prosperous and democratic community, and divested itself of its unruly Asian empire, who could deny that Moscow and Leningrad are as European as London and Madrid?

The main consequence of 1989's upheavals in Eastern Europe was not the economic failure of communism. Rather it was the removal of the Iron Curtain, ushering in a "rejoin-the-world" era for nations that are as European as Ireland or Portugal. The political possibilities are immense, placing a premium on a truly Europe-scale entity emerging as a new superstate. Could we witness, in just the next decade or two, the arrival of that overarching community that fired the ambitions of Charlemagne, Napoleon, and Hitler, while offering freedom and prosperity on a scale beyond the dreams of visionaries?

Could the new Europe even become a state that exemplifies the best of its historic past – Ancient Athens, Renaissance Italy, Elizabethan England, and Belle-Epoche France – with a flourishing of the human spirit in its most sophisticated cultures? Could Europe regain the leading position in the world it enjoyed from the 16th to the 19th centuries?

Europe – a leader again?

Europe could well regain its predominant position in the world. Were the European Community's 325 million people to be joined in some associate form by the 32 million of Western and Central Europe not presently Community members, and by the 110 million people of Eastern Europe outside the Soviet Union, this enlarged "European Economic Space", with its 467 million people, would feature an aggregate gross domestic product (GDP) of around $6 trillion, a good deal larger than the US's $5.1 trillion or Japan's $3.1 trillion (1990 figures). In turn this enlarged Europe could supply a marvellous locomotive to draw along much of the global economy toward expanding prosperity. But it could also take on a Fortress Europe mentality, indifferent to the unfortunates beyond its gates.

The drive North

As climate change compounds the upheavals already underway in Africa, there could be multitudes seeking sanctuary in Europe. Already there are 8 million official "outsiders" within this haven (a migration almost as large as the mass movement of people at the close of World War II), plus perhaps half as many again illicit immigrants. The annual European intake is now larger than that of the US, Canada, and Australia combined; in several European countries the proportion of people born abroad is 10–15%, compared with 6% in the US. The recent arrivals have come mostly from Turkey, North Africa, and other adjoining lands; there are 3.3 million in West Germany, making up about 5.4% of the population and causing some ethnic tension. Within another decade there will surely be many times more people seeking sanctuary from North Africa, with its 150 million people suffering the impact of the greenhouse effect.

Within the more distant future there could be yet more multitudes from still farther afield: it is not an impossible prospect that entire armadas of new boat people will eventually attempt the journey from sub-Saharan Africa to this promising land.

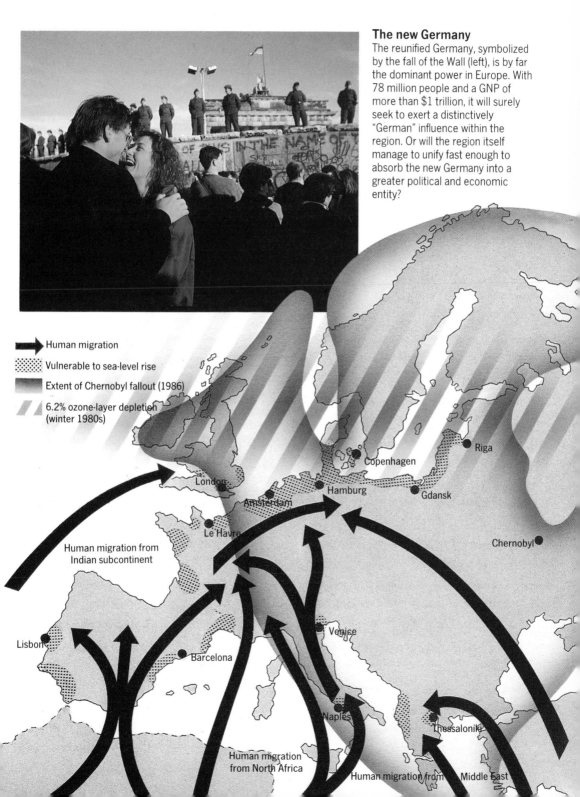

The new Germany
The reunified Germany, symbolized by the fall of the Wall (left), is by far the dominant power in Europe. With 78 million people and a GNP of more than $1 trillion, it will surely seek to exert a distinctively "German" influence within the region. Or will the region itself manage to unify fast enough to absorb the new Germany into a greater political and economic entity?

Legend:
- Human migration
- Vulnerable to sea-level rise
- Extent of Chernobyl fallout (1986)
- 6.2% ozone-layer depletion (winter 1980s)

Human migration from Indian subcontinent

Human migration from North Africa

Human migration from Middle East

Riga
Copenhagen
London
Hamburg
Gdansk
Amsterdam
Le Havre
Chernobyl
Lisbon
Barcelona
Venice
Naples
Thessaloniki

Soviet Asia

The question is not whether the Soviet Union breaks up, but how far and how fast. First, the three Baltic states will surely break away, probably by a "salami" process of constantly slicing away more of their liaison with the Russian empire. Then some of the secessionist southern republics will insist on ever-greater degrees of autonomy. These could be followed by the Ukraine, Byelorussia, Georgia, and who knows what others, until finally the Russians are left more or less alone.

Russia, however, may decide to leave the others more or less on their own by electing to join a "European home" community of nations. Historically this holds appeal for Russians, who, Europeans as they see themselves, don't altogether care for intimate union with a host of Asiatic societies, except as a measure of protecting their backs from invaders from Central Asia. If Russian security were to be assured through some other means, such as growing integration with a European superpower system, wouldn't Russians emerge from their historical (and somewhat justified) fear of attack by Mongol hordes, albeit in latter-day guise?

An impossible scenario? Well, is it any more impossible than the Russian bear relaxing its grip on Eastern Europe – for the very reason that the *cordon sanitaire* of Eastern Europe was either no longer necessary or too costly to maintain? Moreover an economically revived and technologically revamped Russia, with its 155 million people, would still be a force to be reckoned with – to be worked with too – rather than confronted and contained. Recall too that in a greenhouse-affected world, Russian Siberia could become a breadbasket for much of the outside world.

And what of the fates of the Soviet appendages once stripped away from the greater Union? The Muslim states might well look southward for kindred states (see pp. 100–1); the Mongol states to China (see pp. 96–7).

Soviet disunion
The strains that emerged in the late 1980s presage an effective break-up of the Soviet Union during the 1990s as nationalisms reassert themselves. More broadly, the Asiatic peoples with scant affinity for the European Slavs, especially the Russians, will want to go their own way. The Muslim population has been growing four times faster than the Russian population. In 1960 Muslims totalled only 25 million, but they are projected to reach about 70 million by 2000, whereas Russians will have increased from 129 million to 140 million. So the Muslim to Russian ratio will grow from 1:5 to 1:2.

Estonia
Latvia
Lithuania
Byelorussia
Chernobyl
Ukraine
Georgia
Armenia
Azerb
Caspian

Leningrad •Arkhangelsk

Russian Federation

Yenisey

oscow

•Chapayevsk • Nizhnity Tagil

West Siberian Plain

Magnitogorsk • Kyshtym (nuclear disaster)

•Krasnoyarsk

strakhan **Kazakhstan** Novosibirsk

Lake Baikal

Aral Sea Semipalatinsk
—1960
—2000

Uzbekistan

Turkmenistan

Region with serious ecological damage

Major hydroelectric project

Potential break-away states

Major industrial region

Ecodisasters

It took a disaster on the scale of Chernobyl in 1986 (see pp. 92–3) to awaken the Soviet people to the extent of the environmental destruction of their country. Radioactive contamination has rendered vast areas of agricultural land unusable and hydroelectric dams have flooded more land than the total area of The Netherlands, with more land lost to salinization. The total area of cultivable land is declining by 1000 sq km a year, and all this in a country gripped by food shortages. As well, the Aral Sea was once the fourth largest lake in the world, but the withdrawal of water for irrigation has shrunk its surface area by 40%, leaving behind a 30,000 sq km salt desert (see left). Now millions of tonnes of salt contaminate the region, and the lake's gradual disappearance has had a disastrous effect on local climate, with warmer summers and colder winters.

A new bread basket for the world?

In theory at least, Soviet Asia could prosper under the greenhouse effect by virtue of the agricultural lands it could open up. Warmer temperatures and possibly increased rainfall could boost crop yields and could enable farmers to move their great grain-growing territories several hundred kilometres northward to take advantage of the fertile soils in northern Russia, especially in Siberia. Conceivably it could become a bread basket for other nations, with all the economic and political leverage that would generate. But much depends on whether Russia will be able to make plans and put them to work in a more productive manner than has been the case to date.

China

For the last ten years China's economy has been growing at an average of 10 per cent a year, thus doubling every seven years. If China can maintain this exceptional record, and if it does not fall prey to gross pollution, it could well boom for the foreseeable future. By the late 1990s the Chinese economy could surpass that of Britain, and by early next century it could soar past that of Germany. By the year 2020 it could be worth over $5 trillion (in 1980 constant dollars), or as large as the combined expected GNPs of Britain, France, and Germany. This is all the more on the cards if China makes common cause with Japan, benefiting from the latter's technology and investment while supplying the workforce and raw materials.

China feeds 22 per cent of the world's population on only 7 per cent of the world's cultivable land. It has boosted food production by the use of irrigation and fertilizers, though grain production peaked in 1984.

But looming large over this outlook are several profound problems. First and foremost is the population issue, recognized as an acute problem 20 years ago. Not only is the environmental-resource base severely overburdened in this respect, it also supports an economy heavily dependent on natural resources – soil, water, vegetation, atmosphere, and climate. Despite a remarkable family-planning effort, there are projected to be at least one-quarter as many people again in China within 30 years.

With 1.5 billion people in the year 2020, moreover, China may be suffering the greenhouse effect, with disruption of the monsoon system that underpins its rice-based agriculture. Its coastal plain is the most densely settled large territory on Earth, leaving it all the more vulnerable to the knock-on effects of sea-level rise.

What if a combination of these problems were to induce China to look over its northern border toward the vast and little-occupied lands of Siberia?

Industry and the environment

China possesses a full one-third of the world's coal stocks, an unusually polluting variety at that. Though it now derives three-quarters of its energy from coal (industrialized nations only 20–30%), China's per-capita energy consumption is still very low, only 7% of that of the US. So China plans to burn ever-larger amounts of coal to fuel its development. Given the size of China's population, this adds up to vast quantities of CO_2 for the global atmosphere. Were the US to abandon its use of coal, and to burn nothing as a replacement, the gain for the greenhouse effect would be swamped by China's plans. Similarly China plans to produce 100 million refrigerators for its citizens by 2000, which, if employing CFCs, will cause huge depletion of the ozone layer. The solution must be for the outside world to provide massive assistance, both technological and financial, for China to utilize alternative materials.

Mounting social strains

Can China stay aloof from the democratization processes that are sweeping across Eastern Europe, the Soviet Union, and South Africa? Can the government maintain its authoritarian grip across a country as large as the US and twice the size of Europe? Presumably not without stifling the entrepreneurial spirit it sorely needs to sustain its economic advancement. So could China decline into a despotic backwater? Or will it not rather accept the liberalizing changes that are transforming much of the world elsewhere?

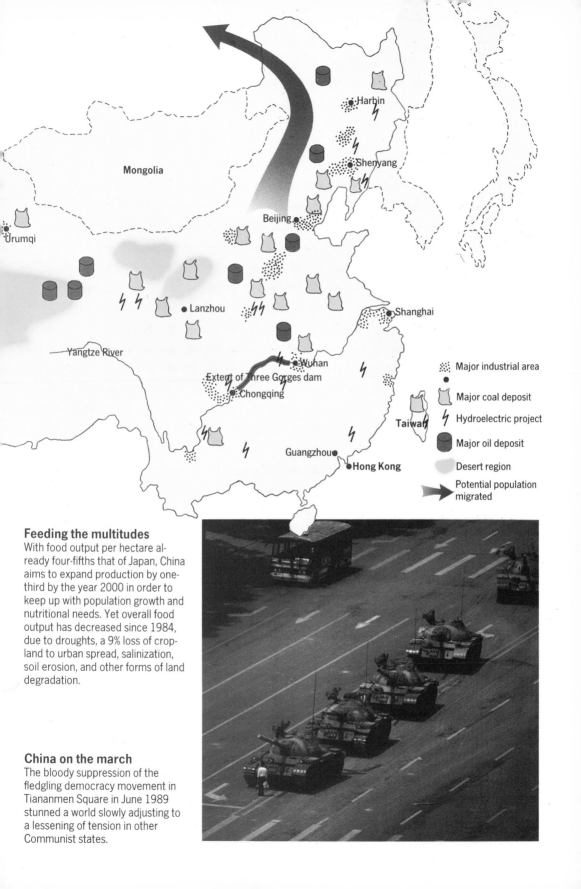

Mongolia

●Harbin

●Shenyang

Urumqi

Beijing●

●Lanzhou

Shanghai●

Yangtze River

●Wuhan

Extent of Three Gorges dam

●Chongqing

Taiwan

Guangzhou●

●Hong Kong

Major industrial area

● Major coal deposit

Hydroelectric project

Major oil deposit

Desert region

Potential population migrated

Feeding the multitudes

With food output per hectare already four-fifths that of Japan, China aims to expand production by one-third by the year 2000 in order to keep up with population growth and nutritional needs. Yet overall food output has decreased since 1984, due to droughts, a 9% loss of cropland to urban spread, salinization, soil erosion, and other forms of land degradation.

China on the march

The bloody suppression of the fledgling democracy movement in Tiananmen Square in June 1989 stunned a world slowly adjusting to a lessening of tension in other Communist states.

Sub-Saharan Africa

It is difficult to be hopeful about sub-Saharan Africa. The most impoverished region on Earth, its people are mostly hungrier than they were in 1960.

Problems abound. It is naturally drier than any other developing region, and the greenhouse effect could rapidly make this worse; all too easily, sub-Saharan Africa becomes Saharan Africa. It has enjoyed almost no Green Revolution and all too few agrotechnology breakthroughs adapted to its unpromising conditions; the numbers of people who suffer outright starvation are projected to rise from their 1985 levels of 30 million to 130 million by 2000.

Alone among developing regions its population growth rate is still rising (a reflection of its pervasive poverty), and average families total between 6 and 7 children; its 1990 total of 520 million is projected to reach 1.3 billion by 2025, and finally level out at 2.5 billion early in the 22nd century. It suffers from numerous wars and features a higher rate of increase in military spending than any other region. Nor are its problems all of its own making; it experiences more adverse terms of trade with the rich world than any other region – a coffee farmer must now sell five times as many bags as in 1965 to afford a tractor. In 1985 for every $1 affluent nations gave to famine-stricken Africa, they took back $2 in debt repayments. In that same year, 40 per cent of US aid to Ethiopia was military. And the region endures more AIDS than any other.

Africa's fragile economies cannot take the strain. To quote General Olusegun Obasanjo, the former head of state of Nigeria, speaking in 1987: "Africa may be the major area of conflict in the 21st century. We have the possibility of real, serious catastrophe – in terms of human suffering, in terms of violent conflict and in terms of a retrogression in development. But these factors can be reversed if the world can collectively take care of resource distribution, population control, and saving the environment. Otherwise Africa will become a destabilizing factor in the equation of international peace and security."

Permanent problem or great challenge?

After 30 years of development efforts, most African countries are worse off than when they started out on independence. Moreover their outlook is distinctly unpromising. But not all is gloom. The proportion of Zimbabwe's couples practising contraception, for example, has increased by 171% during the period 1982–7, one of the most remarkable achievements of its type anywhere in the world. During the same period the country has switched from being a food importer to a food exporter. Kenya has mounted one of the finest soil-conservation programmes anywhere; its women's groups and schoolchildren (see below right) planted more trees in their first year of grass-roots operations than the government managed in ten years. Canada and France have recently cancelled much outstanding debt. No doubt about it, a joint effort by the region and the outside world could still transform an unusually dismal prospect into an unexpectedly successful future.

What if...?

What if the region were to remain impoverished, declining into ever-worsening deprivation and degradation, all suffered by fast-growing multitudes without hope? How would that fit into the world of the future? Why should the rest of the global community become sufficiently concerned to do more to assist beyond its paltry efforts of the past? Simply, humanitarian factors should impel us to do more than just watch from afar. But to adopt the cold-eyed approach of the politician, we might also consider that a region of growing destitution would drive many millions of Africans to seek refuge elsewhere, however hazardous the attempt. And it would supply vast scope for military adventurism on the part of future Gadaffis.

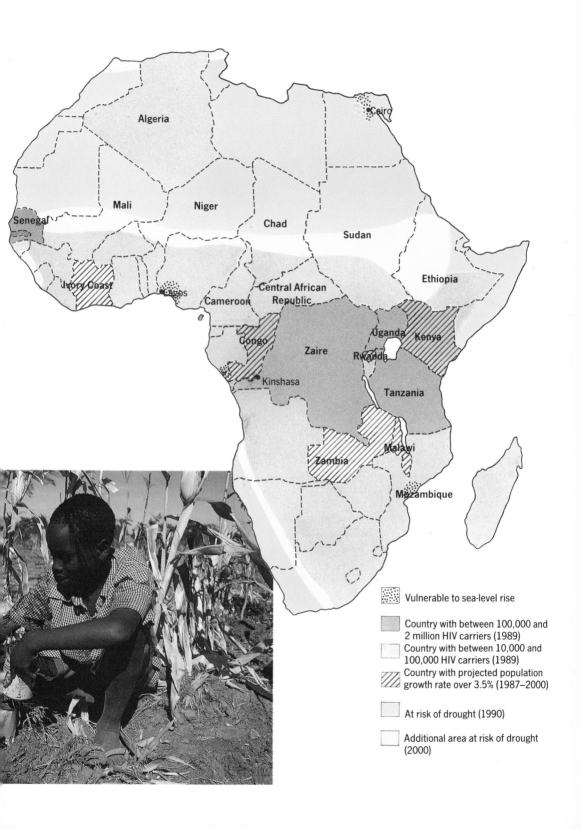

Algeria

Mali

Niger

Chad

Sudan

Senegal

Cairo

Ethiopia

Ivory Coast

Lagos

Cameroon

Central African Republic

Congo

Zaire

Uganda

Kenya

Rwanda

Kinshasa

Tanzania

Malawi

Zambia

Mozambique

Vulnerable to sea-level rise

Country with between 100,000 and 2 million HIV carriers (1989)

Country with between 10,000 and 100,000 HIV carriers (1989)

Country with projected population growth rate over 3.5% (1987–2000)

At risk of drought (1990)

Additional area at risk of drought (2000)

The Muslim world

The world's fastest-growing religious group, Islam, now encompasses more than 1 billion people. Every fifth person on Earth is a Muslim: that could become every fourth by the year 2020. There are more Muslims in Asia and Africa than in the Arab nations.

More than 90 per cent of Muslims live in Saudi Arabia, Iran, Pakistan, Bangladesh, Indonesia, Egypt, Turkey, and Algeria. Yet in 40-plus other nations, Muslims make up between 50 and 100 per cent of the population. There are tens of millions of Muslims in India, China, Malaysia, and Nigeria. In the USSR there are more than 55 million, growing fast enough in numbers to be over one-quarter of Soviet citizens by early next century – and often feeling as much affinity for their fellow believers in Pakistan or Iran as for their European overlords in atheistic Moscow.

Even in Western Europe Islam is in the ascendant, with 7 million adherents. In the early 1970s France had only a dozen mosques. Today, thanks to an influx of migrants from North Africa and Turkey, there are more than one thousand.

Islam spreads in part through the prose-lytizing fervour of its practitioners. On one front after another, and especially in sub-Saharan Africa, it is making inroads into the realms of its "competitor" religions.

A world with a greater voice for Islam will tend to be a world with more laws based on the stringent Koran. Repressive in certain respects, many Muslims are also becoming more liberal as they enjoy the benefits of development. Fortunately most Muslims are Sunnis, more moderate than the fundamentalist Shias. The liberalization of Islam may bring some shocks to the monolithic nature of Muslim societies. What will happen as more Muslim women become educated: will they still accept the veil over their faces and their outlook? What if the structure of Saudi Arabia were to be undermined by creeping egalitarianism – would the Saudi hierarchy start to crumble, with all that would entail for stability in the Middle East?

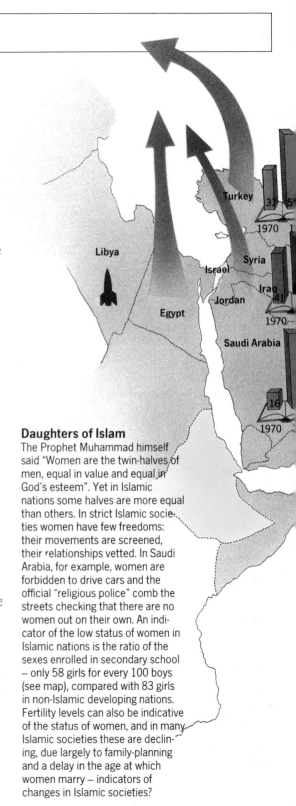

Daughters of Islam
The Prophet Muhammad himself said "Women are the twin-halves of men, equal in value and equal in God's esteem". Yet in Islamic nations some halves are more equal than others. In strict Islamic societies women have few freedoms: their movements are screened, their relationships vetted. In Saudi Arabia, for example, women are forbidden to drive cars and the official "religious police" comb the streets checking that there are no women out on their own. An indicator of the low status of women in Islamic nations is the ratio of the sexes enrolled in secondary school – only 58 girls for every 100 boys (see map), compared with 83 girls in non-Islamic developing nations. Fertility levels can also be indicative of the status of women, and in many Islamic societies these are declining, due largely to family-planning and a delay in the age at which women marry – indicators of changes in Islamic societies?

Islamic fervour

Ayatollah Khomeini's doctrine of Islamic fundamentalism found whole-hearted support among the Iranian population (right), even with women, often the most disadvantaged segment of society in the Islamic republic.

49 67
1970 1986

16 49
1970 1986

Iran

Afghanistan

25 38
1970 1986

Pakistan

Bangladesh

30 45
1970 1986

India

Malaysia

Maldives

64 73
1970 1986

Indonesia

Population growth

Islam increases its impact through sheer growth in human numbers as well as through proselytization. Whereas the average-sized developing world family is around 4.4 children, it is more than 7 in Algeria, Saudi Arabia, and Jordan, and more than 5 in a handful of other leading Muslim countries. This is not so much because of the Muslim religion, rather it is due to the patriarchal, traditionalist nature of Muslim communities, often with a meagre degree of economic advancement and with low status for women.

Muslims in Europe

There are already 8 million Muslims in Europe, including 2 million in each of France and Germany, 1.3 million in Britain, and 500,000 in Spain. Many more are on their way, quietly infiltrating through the porous frontiers of southern Europe, coming from the workless communities of North Africa, the Middle East, and southern Asia. Failing to integrate into their new homelands, they often show signs of becoming a dissident and vociferous minority.

☐ Country with 50% or more Muslim population

☐ Country with 25–49% Muslim population

⚐ Nuclear weapons potential/capability suspected

⚒ Nuclear reactors ordered/operating

◼ Women in secondary education per 100 men

➡ Migrations to Europe

The Indian subcontinent

The three main countries of the region, Pakistan, India, and Bangladesh, together with Nepal, Bhutan, and Sri Lanka, form a population colossus. Today's total of 1.1 billion people is projected to reach 1.9 billion by 2025 and 2.5 billion by the time population growth finally levels out late next century. This will mean almost one-quarter of humanity crammed into one-thirtieth of the Earth's habitable surface. Each year the regional population expands by half as many people as there are in Britain.

Already the population burden is imposing unsustainable strains. Despite exceptional feats in Green-Revolution agriculture – India has transformed itself from a food-deficit nation in 1960 to a feed-itself one today – there has been scant increase in per-head food output since the early 1980s. Soil erosion is severe, forests will soon become a matter of history, and water shortages cause conflict between India and both its neighbours. Farming families that are near or outright landless already comprise as many people as there are in the US.

Still other upheavals will stem from climate change. The greenhouse effect (see pp. 32–3 and 72–3) appears likely to disrupt monsoon patterns – and India receives 70 per cent of its rainfall from the monsoons. With most of the 1196 islands of the Maldives barely above sea level, the President referred to his country as an "endangered nation" in the face of sea-level rise. Bangladesh will suffer severely from sea-level rise, losing a projected one-third of its territory (see photograph right). In the past 20 years flooding and storm surges have killed hundreds of thousands and made homeless millions, yet these disasters will seem paltry in comparison with what lies ahead. We may soon witness more refugees from Bangladesh than the global total today.

Perhaps most significant of all, Pakistan and India, inveterate foes, are nuclear powers. Shall we one day wake to find the region has become an irradiated wasteland?

Population and climate change: the pincer grip

The region's present 1.1 billion people are projected to reach an eventual 2.5 billion within the next hundred years. Yet after the remarkable advances in agriculture between 1955 and 1980, enabling the subcontinent to become largely self-sufficient in rice and wheat, food output per head has stagnated during the past decade, and there is scant hope for further breakthroughs in agrotechnologies. Worse is the prospect of climate change. Were the greenhouse effect to cause dislocations in the monsoon system, the prospect for agriculture would indeed be grim – fully 70% of India's irrigation water comes from monsoon rains.

India, an economic power?

With the seventh-largest industrial base in the world, India's economy is now worth around $300 billion. If it maintains recent growth rates – and it is a very big "if", since population pressures plus climate change could wreck its prospects – it could pass $2 trillion by 2020. It would then be twice as large as the expected economies of Britain and Italy combined.

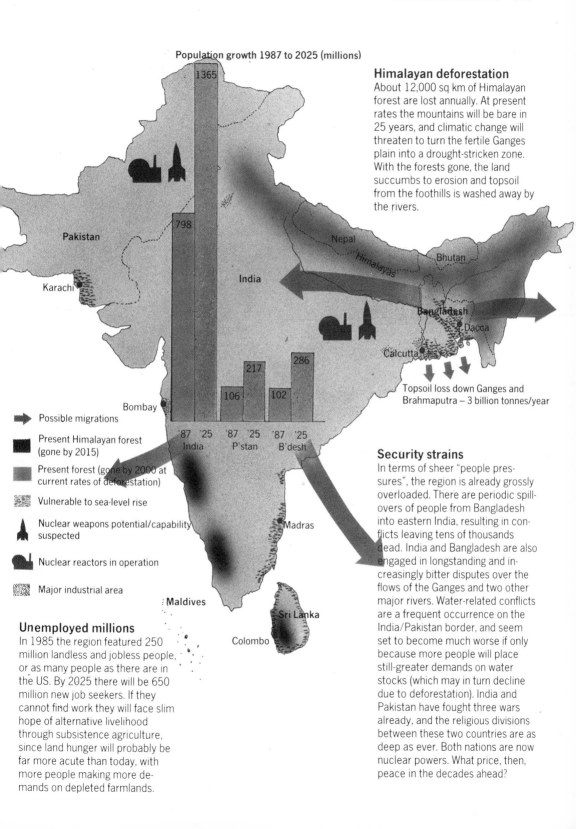

Population growth 1987 to 2025 (millions)

Himalayan deforestation
About 12,000 sq km of Himalayan forest are lost annually. At present rates the mountains will be bare in 25 years, and climatic change will threaten to turn the fertile Ganges plain into a drought-stricken zone. With the forests gone, the land succumbs to erosion and topsoil from the foothills is washed away by the rivers.

Topsoil loss down Ganges and Brahmaputra – 3 billion tonnes/year

Possible migrations

Present Himalayan forest (gone by 2015)

Present forest (gone by 2000 at current rates of deforestation)

Vulnerable to sea-level rise

Nuclear weapons potential/capability suspected

Nuclear reactors in operation

Major industrial area

Security strains
In terms of sheer "people pressures", the region is already grossly overloaded. There are periodic spillovers of people from Bangladesh into eastern India, resulting in conflicts leaving tens of thousands dead. India and Bangladesh are also engaged in longstanding and increasingly bitter disputes over the flows of the Ganges and two other major rivers. Water-related conflicts are a frequent occurrence on the India/Pakistan border, and seem set to become much worse if only because more people will place still-greater demands on water stocks (which may in turn decline due to deforestation). India and Pakistan have fought three wars already, and the religious divisions between these two countries are as deep as ever. Both nations are now nuclear powers. What price, then, peace in the decades ahead?

Unemployed millions
In 1985 the region featured 250 million landless and jobless people, or as many people as there are in the US. By 2025 there will be 650 million new job seekers. If they cannot find work they will face slim hope of alternative livelihood through subsistence agriculture, since land hunger will probably be far more acute than today, with more people making more demands on depleted farmlands.

The Pacific rim

Five hundred years ago the focus of world trade shifted from the Mediterranean to the Atlantic. Today an even more momentous move is under way, this time to the Pacific, and the Atlantic cities of London, Paris, and New York will have to give ground to Tokyo, Hong Kong, Shanghai, Singapore, Sydney, Los Angeles, and Vancouver.

This shift to the Pacific-rim nations is likely to continue for decades if only because the region's development is so broadly based. In turn this is due not only to the economic powerhouse of Japan, but to the swiftly changing giant of China and the newly industrializing countries (NICs) of South Korea, Taiwan, Hong Kong, and Singapore (perhaps soon to include Malaysia and Thailand, and eventually, though more doubtfully, Indonesia and the Philippines). By extension the region includes the Pacific states of the US, notably California; the western provinces of Canada; the nations of Australia and New Zealand; and Mexico and other Pacific-bordering nations of Latin America.

Economic growth in this vast region has been stimulated by a happy combination of three factors. First is the spectacular rise in industrial productivity by export-oriented societies, in turn leading to greater increases in foreign trade, shipping, and financial services. Second is a marked move into the latest technologies as well as into cheaper and labour-intensive manufacturing. Third is an immensely successful effort to increase agricultural output (especially of grains and livestock) faster than total population growth. Each success has beneficially interacted with the others to produce a rate of economic expansion that has far eclipsed that of traditional Western powers in recent years. The centre of gravity of world economic power is indeed shifting to the Pacific-region nations, where economic expansion overall is now proceeding five times faster than in Europe and North America during the heyday of the Industrial Revolution.

The region to beat the rest
The dynamism of the Pacific Basin has been felt in the shifting economic balances within the US itself. American trade with Asia and the Pacific was only 48% of that with Europe in 1960, but had risen to 122% by 1983 – a change that has been accompanied by redistribution of both population and income within the US in the direction of the Pacific. Equally to the point, the fast-rising numbers of new Americans from Latin America and Asia mean that the US is changing from a European offshoot to a multiracial nation anchored on the Pacific.

Monte Bello

California on the rim
The Golden State's economy is bettered only by the total of the other 49 states of the US, Japan, Germany, the Soviet Union, and France. It features nine Japanese-affiliated banks with assets of more than $10 billion, plus 750 subsidiaries of Japanese enterprises. Through its ports flows trade that has increased 17 times since 1970, 80% of it directed toward Pacific-rim countries; the state's trade with Japan is worth half that of the other 49 states combined.

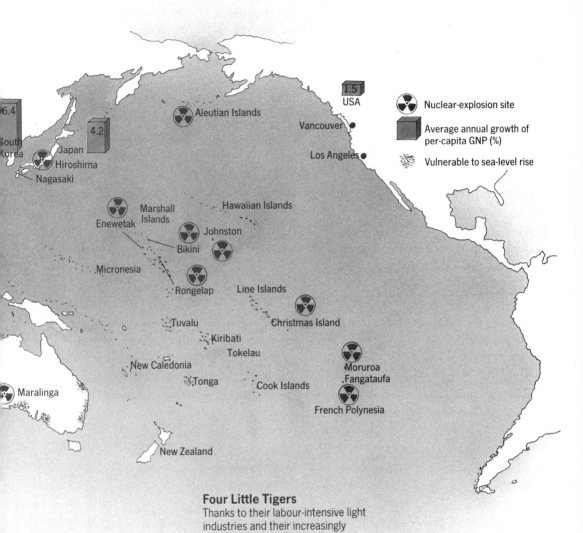

Nuclear-explosion site

Average annual growth of per-capita GNP (%)

Vulnerable to sea-level rise

Map labels: USA 1.5, Aleutian Islands, Vancouver, Los Angeles, 6.4, South Korea, Japan 4.2, Hiroshima, Nagasaki, Marshall Islands, Enewetak, Hawaiian Islands, Johnston, Bikini, Micronesia, Rongelap, Line Islands, Tuvalu, Christmas Island, Kiribati, Tokelau, New Caledonia, Tonga, Cook Islands, Moruroa, Fangataufa, French Polynesia, Maralinga, New Zealand

Four Little Tigers

Thanks to their labour-intensive light industries and their increasingly skilled, highly motivated labour forces, the newly industrializing countries (the "Four Little Tigers") of South Korea, Taiwan, Hong Kong, and Singapore are fast catching up with the more advanced world. South Korea's per-capita GNP has now exceeded $2700 and Singapore's $8000, and during the 1990s they will probably surpass the per-capita GNPs of Britain and Italy. If they maintain their recent high growth rates – as is eminently feasible, with foreign exchange reserves now totalling $100 billion, or more than Japan's – their per-capita incomes will expand by the year 2005 to $15-20,000.

Growing economic muscle

In 1960 the combined GDP of the Asian-Pacific countries (excluding the US) was a mere 7.8% of world GDP. By 1982 it had soared to 16.4%, and since then the region's growth rates have exceeded those of Europe, the US, and the Soviet Union by even wider margins. Come the millennium, it is likely to contain more than 20% of world GDP, or the equal of Europe or the US. If the "Alaska to California" component is added in, the total GDP could reach 30% plus by the year 2000.

Nuclear-free Pacific

Since the devastation of Hiroshima and Nagasaki by atomic weapons in 1945, the Pacific and its peoples have borne much of the brunt of the nuclear age: weapons and missile testing, uranium mining, radioactive waste dumping, and confrontation between nuclear-armed navies. The South Pacific Nuclear Free Zone was created by the Pacific peoples and antinuclear policies are implemented by such nations as Belau and New Zealand.

Japan

Japan is already an economic and technological superpower, achieving the status with only 3 per cent of the world population in 0.3 per cent of its habitable land. How will the nation deploy its exceptional might, growing ever mightier, in the global arena of the future?

Today Japan is the largest creditor nation, with the rest of the world owing it $500 billion, a figure likely to double as soon as 1995. Not surprisingly, the world's ten leading banks (in terms of assets) are all Japanese. Moreover during the 1990s Japan seems set to become the leading nation, or at worst the second nation, in computers, robotics, telecommunications, automobiles, shipbuilding, biotechnology, and even aerospace. In several of these fields it has already gained a chokehold on innovative technologies and major markets. In each of the years 1988, 1989, and 1990 Japan has been investing more than 20 per cent of its GNP in new plants and equipment – a larger proportion than any other nation has ever invested. This remarkable feat is the economic equivalent of an athlete running three marathons in a row, and setting a world record each time.

But there could be problems ahead. Due to the greying of its population, by 2010 Japan will have the lowest ratio of working-age people among the leading industrial nations. This will require high social-security outlays and could lead to a loss of dynamism. On the climate front, the Tokyo Bay metropolis could be among the most vulnerable conurbations anywhere as sea levels rise; the economic dislocations could be severe in such a crowded country. Probably most important of all, Japan feels that despite its favourable position in the global economic and power-political order, its critical dependence on foreign sources of raw materials leaves it in a vulnerable position that could be badly deranged through international upheavals. To this extent Japan seeks, through eternal compromise, to slow down or deflect many of the pressures for change – inappropriate as this strategy will surely prove to be in a world of unstoppable change.

The factors of success

The country's success is due in large measure to a social ethos that favours several key factors: entrepreneurship, hard work, and company loyalty. While gaining hardly any international awards such as the Nobel Prize, Japan produces more engineers than any other advanced nation – a full 50% more than the US. Its army of research and development workers is greater than that of Britain, France, and Germany combined. The military share of total Japanese research and development amounts to just 0.7%; in the US, the military accounts for up to 40%. By keeping a tight rein on military spending, Japan, and other countries like it, are the only winners of the arms race.

Recycling and efficiency

As a leading importer of natural resources worldwide (99% of its oil, 92% of its iron, and 100% of its copper), Japan makes exceptionally efficient use of its materials. It recycles more than 50% of its garbage, as compared with West Germany's 30%, and the US's 10%. From 100,000 tonnes of typical Japanese garbage comes enough woodpulp to make a roll of paper that would wrap around the planet ten times.

Japan consumed 6% less energy in 1988 than in 1973, even though its GDP grew by 46%. As a result of the low amount of energy needed to produce economic growth, Japan's exports are much cheaper than those of America. Japanese industries often out-perform their competitors in part because they use only half as much energy.

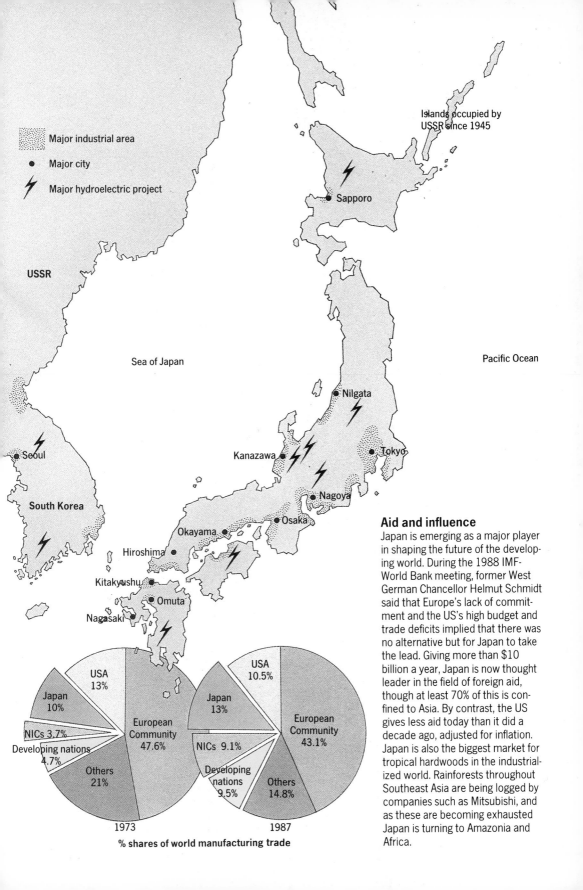

Major industrial area

Major city

Major hydroelectric project

USSR

Sea of Japan

Pacific Ocean

Islands occupied by USSR since 1945

● Sapporo

● Nilgata

Kanazawa ●

● Tokyo

● Nagoya

● Osaka

Okayama ●

Hiroshima ●

Kitakyushu ●

● Omuta

Nagasaki ●

● Seoul

South Korea

Aid and influence

Japan is emerging as a major player in shaping the future of the developing world. During the 1988 IMF-World Bank meeting, former West German Chancellor Helmut Schmidt said that Europe's lack of commitment and the US's high budget and trade deficits implied that there was no alternative but for Japan to take the lead. Giving more than $10 billion a year, Japan is now thought leader in the field of foreign aid, though at least 70% of this is confined to Asia. By contrast, the US gives less aid today than it did a decade ago, adjusted for inflation. Japan is also the biggest market for tropical hardwoods in the industrialized world. Rainforests throughout Southeast Asia are being logged by companies such as Mitsubishi, and as these are becoming exhausted Japan is turning to Amazonia and Africa.

USA 13%

Japan 10%

NICs 3.7%

Developing nations 4.7%

European Community 47.6%

Others 21%

1973

USA 10.5%

Japan 13%

NICs 9.1%

Developing nations 9.5%

European Community 43.1%

Others 14.8%

1987

% shares of world manufacturing trade

Surprise – the changing face of Europe

Among all the sudden changes of the past two decades, including the rise of OPEC, the fall of the Shah of Persia and the rise of Islamic fundamentalism, Black Monday, and the rise of the South American drug barons, none has taken us more unaware than the events in Eastern Europe in late 1989. But why should we have been so surprised? Could we not have anticipated them? What was there in the situation, or in us, that caused it to be such a shock?

We constantly proclaim that in a fast-changing world there is a premium on looking ahead ever-more carefully and clearly. Indeed there are now thousands of "futurist experts" whose task it is to expect the unexpected, to discern the sudden turnings in the road ahead. Yet in 1989 our best crystal balls completely failed us. What went wrong? It is illuminating to pause here, to take Eastern Europe as an example, and to ask ourselves why we were so inept at reading the world around us.

In point of fact, certain signs had been there for some time, but the experts had systematically overlooked them. It was the accumulating speed of change that hood-winked them. Whereas Poland took ten years to work itself into a position for a new start, Hungary took ten months, East Germany ten weeks, and Czechoslovakia and Romania ten days each. True, behind all these events was the catalytic hand of Mikhail Gorbachev. But could we not have foreseen that he too was being pushed by unstoppable – and all too apparent – pressures to make abrupt changes in Eastern Europe? Had not the Soviet economy been showing steadily mounting signs of not only creaking under the strain of military spending burdens, but actually cracking? Was not a basic shift becoming inevitable and, therefore, foreseeable? Yet the best seers, the finest economic analysts, the foremost readers of the political tea leaves, were all taken by surprise. What can we learn from this phenomenon in order to do a better job next time? Where will the next "Eastern Europe" be?

Gorbachevs of the future
President Gorbachev's main contribution has been that he understands the past cannot continue into the future. Either he had to make a radical departure, or the situation would have done it for him. Where are the new human vectors of change who can look over the brow of the hill, who can envisage the horizons ahead? We can all don the prophet's mantle, peer into our crystal balls, and try to spot the leaders of imagination as well as intellect. Could they be in the Middle East, or the new Europe, or the Pacific rim, or the emergent powers of China, India, and Brazil?

Subversive airwaves

One of the key factors in the upheavals in Eastern Europe was the
penetration of the Iron Curtain by
telecommunications. Russians in
Leningrad could tune into Helsinki
television, East Germans could do
likewise from West Berlin, Hun-
garians the same from Vienna. They
learned there were other and more
desirable ways of running their
countries and living their lives. Until
the mid-1980s photocopiers were
virtually unknown in Eastern
Europe, since they could be used to
foster an underground press. But
eventually too many machines
found their way in, and the damage
was swiftly done.

The unexpected fallout

What surprising spin-offs stem from
the surprise of Eastern Europe? One
is that the espionage business has
fallen on hard times. More important is the realignment of the power
structures of both NATO and the
Warsaw Pact, and the far-reaching
ramifications this will have not only
for Europe but the rest of the world.
How the cards will eventually fall is
up for grabs. So why not match
yourself against the pundits who
failed so miserably to predict the
upheaval, and try to anticipate
those mini-surprises in store?

Our limited perceptions

Perhaps we missed the build-up to
the seismic shifts in Eastern Europe
because we were stuck with our
traditional views of history and geography – both of which are undergoing one momentous upheaval
after another in all parts of the
Earth as we enter a radically different world. Eastern Europe has
tended to be perceived by Britons,
Germans, and others as marginal to
the main-action scene of Western
Europe: what a limited outlook!
Could our blinkers be stopping us
from anticipating new hot-spot
areas in, for example, the Arabian
peninsula, the Himalayas, the Carib-
bean basin? Even today, which of us
can name all the states of Central
Asia – let alone draw a map of the
region or summarize its recent
history?

Agribusiness and petrochemical industries

If we are to feed more people more adequately, we shall have to produce almost half as much food again within another 15 years. Within another 35 to 40 years, if global population surges to well over 10 billion, we shall have to produce food on a scale equal to all cultivated lands being farmed as intensively as East Anglia's or Iowa's best grain fields today, or about three times the current world average. Yet since the early 1980s there have been few improvements in agricultural productivity, and today there is a levelling off in Green-Revolution advances in both developed and developing lands. What will be the response of some of the leading protagonists in agriculture/agribusiness corporations, and of another enterprise sector that is increasingly allied – the petrochemical industries?

Hitherto agribusinesses have been practising industrialized agriculture, which is so heavily dependent on synthetic fertilizers and pesticides and capital-intensive machinery that consumers have in effect been eating oil. This resource-based agriculture must now shift toward a science-based agriculture, exploiting the Gene Revolution (see pp. 60–1) and other forms of eco-agriculture. In addition, and much more importantly for the long run, agriculture needs to become far more adaptable if it is to cope with the upheavals of global warming and ozone-layer depletion. All in all, agriculture faces as big a transformation within the next 50 years as any since the dawn of agriculture 10,000 years ago.

All this ties in with the changes overtaking petrochemical industries. Due to the massive contributions of fossil fuels to recent agriculture, many leading petrochemical concerns have been infiltrating agribusiness in order to promote agrotechnology packages that strengthen the dependence on oil-based inputs. Plainly this must change, if only because of the short-term life of known oil supplies.

Organic farming

Conventional agriculture is a high-input/high-output affair, which levies a high toll in degradation of the soil and other factors of agro-ecosystems. New-age agriculture will switch to low-input/moderate-output practices, with less support from chemical fertilizers, pesticides, and energy, and emphasis on biological recycling of nutrients and energy, and primary reliance on naturally occurring pest control.

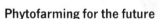

Phytofarming for the future

A few experimental farms in the US are engaging in "controlled-environment" agriculture. Entirely enclosed within factories, they utilize artificial soil and electric light, hence they produce vegetables the year round. A typical factory can produce in a single hectare as much food as 10 hectares of greenhouse or 100 hectares of farmland. True, agro-factories are heavily dependent on fossil-fuel energy. If, however, the electricity were supplied by photo-voltaic cells, small-scale hydro-power, or some other environmentally benign source of energy, this style of farming could face a dazzling future.

Foods for the future

A mere 20 plants provide 90% of our food, even though 70,000 plants are edible. We still depend on the same stock of plants domesticated by the first farmers: our agriculture is essentially a Stone-Age affair. But American supermarkets now commonly feature more than a hundred plant products, mostly new fruits and vegetables, from Asia and Latin America. The kiwi fruit, unknown a decade ago, enjoys a market worth $22 million a year in the US alone. Within a decade we could be shopping from an array of hundreds of new "kiwi fruits".

King car

The city where the car has been king, Los Angeles, aims to phase it out from much of the landscape by the year 2000, mainly to reduce the incidence of killer smogs. Air pollution alone causes $13 billion in damages every year. Car pooling is becoming mandatory for many businesses, with $25,000-a-day fines for laggards. All fleet vehicles will shortly have to switch to methanol or other clean-burning fuels. By 2000 all new cars will have to use alternative fuels, and within 17 years there will be a complete ban on petrol and diesel engines. America's two largest carmakers, Ford and General Motors, have anticipated the clean-fuel era and aim to have 10,000 nonpetrol cars on the road by 1993. Two leading oil companies, Arco and Chevron, are setting up dozens of methanol stations. As the Los Angeles blueprint becomes more widely applied, Americans will have to overcome their fixation with the fast lane.

A carbon tax on fuels

If petrol prices reflected their true costs, including such environmental costs as acid rain and global warming, we would be paying at least twice as much as now. A hefty carbon tax on petroleum, as on coal and natural gas, will be with us soon. This will prompt us to abandon our love affair with the car, and next century will see an outburst in building train tracks rather than motorways – even perhaps a landscape networked with cycle tracks.

Military-industrial complexes

Fortunately we may be witnessing a decline in the spending spree enjoyed by the military-industrial complexes, a bonanza that has been absorbing $1 trillion a year. Two-thirds of all countries spend more on the means of killing people than on keeping their citizens fit and healthy. Both the present world superpowers seem agreed that it is time for peace to break out. But what of the unforeseen tensions of an overcrowded world with too little food, fuel, and other resources? Still, for the first time in 31 years, 1989 witnessed no new outbreak of war.

As for other major players on the world stage, Japan and China seem content to pursue economic might – recognizing perhaps that military prowess, by virtue of its phenomenal expense, is incompatible with any other sort of significant status. Japan's yens are securing a stake in America more surely and securely than military conflict ever could hope to achieve. India may wish to seek regional hegemony, especially in light of its naval aspirations linked with its nuclear capacity. Among other members of the nuclear club – whether actual, implicit, or potential members – are South Africa, Pakistan, Iran, Iraq, Israel, Libya, Brazil, Argentina, and Chile.

Recall however that the developing world, while accounting for only 10 per cent of all military spending, has been boosting its outlays more rapidly than the superpowers. The outbreak of peace in the North may not be matched by peace in the South. Indeed the arms manufacturers will now feel they must avidly seek new markets among developing countries, encouraging those with belligerent self-images to sample their wares. In addition there could be an increase in "low-intensity" conflicts, especially on the part of guerrilla groups and other disaffected bodies. By the year 2000 such organizations could be armed with missiles carrying chemical, biological, or even nuclear, weapons.

The economics of swords into ploughshares

The military-industrial complex is a drain on economies. The production of the hardware of destruction makes no contribution either to ordinary consumption or to the main means of economic output. Worse, the civilian economy overall is deprived of funds for investment, research and development, and infrastructure. For the cost of the Stealth bomber programme, $80 billion, the US could cover 80% of its clean-water budget to the year 2000. The Soviet Union is already pressing ahead with a conversion programme – a Volgograd factory, for example, has switched production from missiles to washing machines. But the military-industrial complex will not readily go down to defeat. Precisely to counter such an eventuality, the US Defense Department, which has been handing out no fewer than 56,000 contracts each working day, has made sure that in each of the 50 states there is big money and many jobs at stake.

The superpowers sheath their swords

If *détente* extends into outright peace, both superpowers could cut their military budgets by at least 30% to 50% by the mid-1990s. This would release $220 to $330 billion per year. What if the superpowers were to make amends for their militaristic savaging of much of the world's economy (let alone its peace prospects) over a period of 40 years, by diverting, say, $100 billion of savings a year to global peace? This sum would be enough to save the world from the worst ravages of the greenhouse effect. As Mikhail Gorbachev repeatedly asserts, the greatest threat is no longer missiles from the sky, but global warming from the skies.

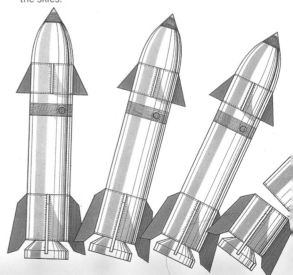

The arms bazaar

The death business continues to flourish. In 1990 it was worth $65 billion worldwide. It is dominated by just six countries – the US, the Soviet Union, France, Britain, Germany, and China – which account for 90% of international trade in weaponry. While they claim it helps their economies, they underestimate its spin-off "benefits", such as the boost to the funeral trade in 150 other countries.

Nuclear terrorism

By the year 2000 nuclear-power-reactor countries will produce a total of 1600 tonnes of plutonium. One-quarter of this will be commercially separated from the reactor-fuel elements, whereupon the plutonium will generally be returned to its original owners. This means that huge quantities of plutonium will be transported worldwide by all the main transportation systems – road, rail, sea, and air. It is when plutonium is being transported that it is most vulnerable to theft. Only 8kg of reactor-produced plutonium (an amount about the size of a small grapefruit) are needed for a nuclear explosive roughly equivalent in power to the Nagasaki bomb. Even a crude device would have enough explosive power to destroy the centre of a large city, thus providing a fine blackmail weapon for terrorists. But with thousands of nuclear scientists available, there is no reason for the device to be crude.

Ugandan soldiers respond to a new call for arms.

Space industries

Despite setbacks and delays, it seems likely that our incursions into space will continue into the foreseeable future, culminating in the establishment of a permanently staffed base on the moon within another two or three decades. This base will act in many capacities: as a launch pad for far more extensive probes toward neighbouring planets in our solar system and into "deep" space; as a laboratory workshop for many gravity-free technological manufacturing processes; and as final confirmation that we are indeed committed to a space-era future with new frontiers of myriad sorts.

It is thanks to satellite astronomy, for example, that we can now begin to comprehend the nature of the universe itself, as well as come to an understanding of the mechanisms and forces that maintain our own planetary system, as seen through the eyes of orbiting satellites, such as Landsat (see far right). Better data on the planet's natural systems are essential if we are to respond to the consequences of the changes that human activity has already induced. Earth-based telescopes are severely limited by the atmosphere, which either distorts or diminishes many important types of electromagnetic radiation (such as x-rays, gamma rays, infrared, ultraviolet, and so on) emitted by stellar objects, galaxies, and other sources. Observations from satellite stations above our blanket of atmosphere are bound by no such distorting constraints.

In addition, our exploration of space should serve to enhance and refine our sense of common history and shared destiny. The Outer Space Treaty and the Moon Treaty have been the first steps in that direction, encompassing such important concepts as space as a global commons not subject to national appropriation, collective management, shared benefits, peaceful use, and conservation, both present and future. Space science and satellites must be used for the benefit of the planet and its entire human community. The challenge is to ensure that "planet management" does not become a tool for technocrats and corporations to overcommercialize space.

The double-edged sword

Our ventures into space, which should become a thoroughly multinational enterprise, will spawn a host of space technologies. Many will be of direct benefit in ensuring the habitability of the Earth; others could turn out to be more questionable. By reaching into space we may be unwittingly opening yet another Pandora's box.

On the plus side, space-based technologies will enable us to gain a much more comprehensive understanding of our own world. Remote sensing through Landsat and SPOT satellites (see right) already permits us to document our geosphere and biosphere in more systematic detail than can otherwise be accomplished; it gives us synoptic insights into the spread of deserts, the decline of forests, the erosion of topsoil, and the changes in climate among other paramount processes. Remote-sensing ventures offer huge scope for international co-operation, while spy-in-the-sky satellites monitor military activities and disarmament.

Equally important, the INTELSAT system of communications satellites, with services to more than 150 countries, constitutes a global communications network that can send the information equivalent of the Encyclopaedia Britannica three times every second. The potential of space communications for the next century is even more awesome, including global television, library access, telecommuting, and rural communications for developing countries. Satellites will be pivotal in enabling the global family to operate within a single global household.

Conversely, the space age has facilitated the absurd Star Wars approach to so-called defence; and, various treaties notwithstanding, it has encouraged nationalistic notions about "who controls space?" among other forms of a space-grab mentality. In similar style it fosters confidence in fix-it technology, and the spirit that believes techno-ingenuity can master challenges of whatever sort and scale. Above all, space exploration consumes vast amounts of funding that could be better spent on such activities as improved agriculture, energy efficiency, conservation of species, and elimination of disease.

The big banks

At the close of the 1980s, 11 of the world's top 12 banks were Japanese, the exception being the American conglomerate Citicorp. In banking terms, the change-around has been virtually instantaneous: only a quarter of a century ago seven of the top ten banks were American, whereas Citicorp is now the only American bank in the leading 25.

With their banks holding 35 per cent of all international banking assets, the Japanese are firmly ensconced as the banking giants of the future. Indeed global banking is likely to be dominated by a maximum of 15 mega-corporations, offering a full range of financial services that extends way beyond traditional banking interests, and including multiple-type investment and trade support. The global leaders will be backed by capital assets of unprecedented scope. They will operate in all the main financial centres, notably Tokyo, New York, and London, and they will have offices in thousands of shopping streets. It will become commonplace for Americans and Britons, Germans and Brazilians, French and Australians to use Japanese systems.

The emergence of banking giants is due primarily to new information technology, which supplies an electronic nervous system of worldwide extent. In turn, this network enables bankers to conduct immediate business with colleagues in any part of the globe.

Still more advanced technologies, such as voice recognition by computer, will soon allow customers to do all their banking by phone. By the year 2000 we shall find that cash is used for only the most trivial purposes; banks will inform us that cash has become too costly for them to handle except in extreme instances. Instead of cash we shall use plastic banking cards, which will finally become fraud proof once electronic security systems learn to identify the owner's fingerprints, eyes, and voice.

The financial house of cards

For all the growth upon unprecedented growth of the global economy during the course of the last four decades, the achievement has been built on all-too-shaky foundations. Now the global economy is far too lop-sided to maintain stability, with huge financial surpluses in Japan and Germany misbalanced by vast deficits in the US, France, Britain, and other leading countries. The Western banking system, especially that of America, is also at risk from the developing-world debt crisis. The global nature of the system ensures that the removal of one major prop would bring the whole house crashing down.

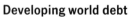

Developing world debt

Debtor countries in the developing world today owe Western governments and banks more than $1 trillion, and rising. Many of them have committed a third to a half of their foreign currency earnings to pay the interest and principal, and it is not enough. All the major debtors, especially Brazil, Argentina, Mexico, Venezuela, Peru, Chile, and South Africa, are in default and have had to reschedule their repayments. For the big Western banks this means that the loans outstanding, which they account for as assets, are grossly underperforming and are unlikely ever to be repaid profitably, let alone in full.

Thus far the banks have been able to stave off collapse through a blend of official initiatives to ease

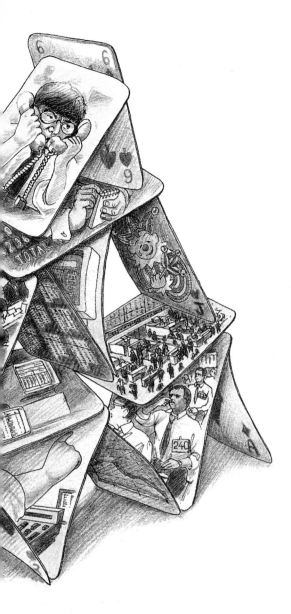

Trends in outstanding bank loans to developing countries $bn

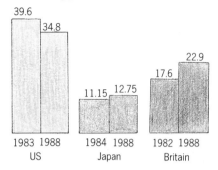

39.6	34.8				22.9
1983	1988	1984	1988	1982	1988
US		Japan		Britain	

Assets of major banks by region $bn

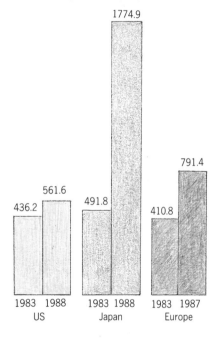

436.2	561.6	491.8	1774.9	410.8	791.4
1983	1988	1983	1988	1983	1987
US		Japan		Europe	

the burden of the poorest countries, lending even riskier new money to allow a paper settlement of some outstanding debt. Central financial institutions have assisted the big banks to avoid disaster.

New plans by governments of developed nations to ease the debt liability of developing-world debtors are continually being unveiled. The urgency of these efforts reflects to some extent the importance these governments place on international financial stability and the lives of the world's poor. But for the large part it reflects the danger the big banks – and therefore the Western world's financial system – are still facing.

While European banks are vulnerable to developing-world debt, their domestic markets are generally less unsettled than those of the US. Their governments and banks are likewise working hard to prevent a banking crisis, through much the same means as US leaders and bankers.

It will be the banks of Japan and the oil-rich countries that benefit most from the debt crisis. They have enormous resources from their domestic industries and customer base, without the insecurity of massive bad debt. These countries will be in a strong position to take advantage of any loss in confidence in other Western banks.

Action groups

This is the age of the nongovernmental organization (NGO). Hardly a slogan to stir them in the streets – yet the rise of the NGO is one of the most revolutionary phenomena of our times. And as problems grow more numerous and complex, lending themselves to responses by grassroots initiatives, we can expect to become increasingly aware of, and more involved in, the multifaceted roles of NGOs.

Their unprepossessing title tells us what they are not, without saying precisely what they are. They are usually professional activists in support of such causes as the environment, development, population planning, and child welfare. Notable examples include Greenpeace, Oxfam, Friends of the Earth, Population Concern, the Worldwide Fund for Nature (WWF), and the Save the Children Fund. By rousing public opinion about specific projects and raising public funds they serve as public watchdogs, coordinating closely through their worldwide networks to bring pressure to bear on governments and official agencies. Above all, they take care of a host of activities that lie beyond the purview of nationally rooted governments because of a lack of imagination, of capacity, or of will.

Thus they increasingly take on an array of functions that used to rest with governments but now lie with the nongovernmental sector. Whereas governments are slow and unresponsive, NGOs, by virtue of being smaller and more streamlined, can move swiftly and sensitively. In response to huge problems they provide a multitude of mini-solutions. And they can reflect public opinion readily: Band Aid's London concert in 1985, for example, raised far more for Ethiopia than the British government deemed appropriate to pay from its coffers. It is not that NGOs seek to usurp national or international authorities, rather they prefer to work in complementary accord with governments after they have been goaded into action.

The age of the NGO

As recently as 1960 there were little more than a thousand NGOs, also known as Public Voluntary Organizations, around the world. Today there are more than 5000, and their numbers continue to surge. These proliferating bodies represent one of our best portents for the future. By their very popularity they reflect the views of the citizenry at large; and through their worldwide organizations they transcend the restricted structures of national governments. Above all, they show no signs of suffering from a hardening of categories, in contrast with the bureaucratic inertia, vested interests, and sheer lack of vision displayed by many governments.

Friends of the Earth

In 1980 FoE had 14,000 members in Britain. Ten years later it had 180,000, and a total budget that has soared from $320,000 to nearly $9 million. Worldwide there are now almost 40 FoE organizations, including ones in Poland and Estonia, with a membership of more than 450,000.

Friends of the Earth

Oxfam

Oxfam now operates through organizations in the US, Canada, Australia, Italy, Belgium, and Hong Kong, as well as Britain, working with groups in 71 developing countries. The British body spent $18 million in 1980 and more than $70 million in 1990, with 30% going to relief activities (famines and other disasters) and, more importantly, 50% going to longer-term development programmes.

The overwhelming wave

We should be wary of supposing that NGOs will supply our total salvation. Even as they grow more capable of reaching out to stragglers in the rising waters, they are themselves threatened with being overwhelmed by a tidal wave of still-greater problems. Can they mobilize more and bigger lifeboats fast enough to save us?

Rotary International

Within its ranks Rotary International has almost 23,000 clubs with more than 1 million members worldwide, drawn from many professional and business fields. Its PoliPlus Campaign has raised $230 million to provide polio vaccines for the WHO Polio-Eradication-by-2000 goal. What if the 7000 RI clubs in North America alone were to be encouraged by environmental NGOs to engage in co-operative activity with the 8700 clubs in developing countries to promote such projects as soil conservation, safe water supplies, or wildlife protection?

Light at the end of the tunnel

Haiti is environmentally and economically bankrupt, the government hardly functions outside the capital city, and its forests are a matter of history. All efforts at tree planting failed – until an Agroforestry Outreach project, supported by Oxfam USA, Catholic Relief Services, and the Cooperative for American Relief Everywhere, started work in close collaboration with Haitian NGOs. Result: in just two years local farmers planted 3 million trees.

Health in the North

The World Health Organization (WHO) has adopted the goal of Health for All by the Year 2000: all people shall attain a level of health that will enable them to lead socially and economically productive lives. WHO and member governments have formulated global, regional, and national strategies, based on comprehensive primary-health-care programmes. The parties involved may indeed achieve their target but run the risk of falling well short of true health for all without a better understanding of "health".

While there are plenty of ways to be sick, there are only a few ways to be healthy. Health is far more than the absence of disease: it amounts to the capacity to live, work, and enjoy leisure to one's full potential for as long as possible. Thus it encompasses not only physical wellbeing but mental, emotional, and spiritual health as well. The aim should be not only to add years to life, but life to years.

Within this approach, health extends to the countering of dis-ease – whatever disorder on whatever level that arises within the entire person. Both psyche and soma should work in close accord, since their harmony underlies the only true form of all-round health. Similarly a dislocation of their hand-in-hand functioning contributes to the origin of sickness – as it does to treatment too. To this degree all healing is, to some extent at least, self-healing. By our very attitudes to health, indeed by our approach to our lives as a whole, we help to engender and stimulate disease – and likewise to trigger cures and to maintain health afterward. Those who doubt this view might reflect on the emerging evidence that certain cancers appear to be associated with long-term anxiety and other forms of stress, and that a positive attitude, bent on fighting cancer, often seems to be a central factor in the restoration of health.

The growing awareness that health is primarily a case of personal responsibility means that health is now too important to be left to doctors.

Head of population per physician 1984

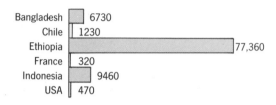

Bangladesh	6730
Chile	1230
Ethiopia	77,360
France	320
Indonesia	9460
USA	470

Daily calorie supply per head of population 1986

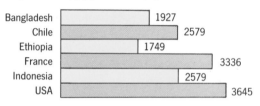

Bangladesh	1927
Chile	2579
Ethiopia	1749
France	3336
Indonesia	2579
USA	3645

Life expectancy at birth 1987

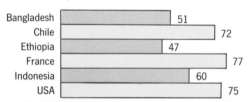

Bangladesh	51
Chile	72
Ethiopia	47
France	77
Indonesia	60
USA	75

Stress and lifestyle

In the developed Northern world the two greatest killers are circulatory-system diseases and cancer – both strongly linked to lifestyle and high-stress environments (left). In other words, there seems to be a correlation between the very symbols of success and at least 70% of all deaths. Can the developing world learn from the North and avoid paying the same price in the future? Spending on tranquillizers alone in the North exceeds the combined public-health expenditure budgets of more than 60 of the world's poorest countries. And the poor of the Northern world suffer a higher incidence of diseases than the better-off.

The greying of the population

A major health and socioeconomic challenge of the future is caring for the elderly – the many more elderly as a percentage of population who will soon become an unprecedentedly prominent feature of Northern societies. In 1950 there were only 214 million people aged 60 years or more, but by the year 2025 there will be a projected 1 billion, or one person in eight of world population. During the same period the number of people aged 80 years or more is expected to rise even more proportionately, from 15 million to 111 million. This will pose many challenges to healthcare and social services – the cost to these sectors per head for those aged 75 or over is, for example, six times higher than for those under the age of 65.

The fitness boom

In Britain an estimated 2 million people now rank as regular joggers (left), and another 2 million engage in other forms of vigorous exercise, such as squash, swimming, or aerobics. So about one in ten of active-age adults is attempting to ensure a longer, fitter lifespan. By the year 2000 this could rise to one in five.

Health in the South

In most Southern communities there is 30 times more prospect of dying from malnutrition and preventable diseases than of dying from war. The leading challenges for the year 2000 will be coping with the 1-billion-plus people who will be underfed and supplying basic health care for 5 billion people altogether. Whereas a typical developed nation assigns 10 per cent of its national budget to health services, in the South the figure is more likely to be 2 per cent or less – a mere $10 per head.

Worse, most developing countries have yet to come to the idea that health is better achieved through preventative rather than curative medicine. Many Southern capitals may feature a grandiose hospital, so well equipped that it consumes a full one-quarter of national health budgets. Yet it may be effectively costing thousands of deaths a year in its hinterland, where the funds could be better spent on supplying domestic-water facilities. The world's greatest health problem is lack of clean water. A full 80 per cent of illness in the South is directly or indirectly attributable to poor water supply and sanitation. To provide the prerequisites of water, sanitation, malaria control, multiple immunization, basic drugs, and suitably trained personnel can generally be achieved for about $15 per person per year.

To close the gap and provide primary health care will mean an annual outlay of $50 billion to the year 2000. This is 14 times more than all health spending by international agencies to date. But if we are to ensure that all people enjoy the most basic right of health, it is surely a straightforward challenge that is a measure of our common humanity. After all, $50 billion is no more than cigarette companies in the developed world will spend on advertising during the same period.

Fortunately a few countries are pointing the way. Malawi is one of the poorest countries in Africa, yet thanks to judicious spending of its meagre funds, its citizens enjoy some of the best basic health on that continent. For a heart-bypass operation, apply elsewhere.

Village-level health clinic in Upper Volta (above). Village pharmacist in the Sahel (right).

Education through entertainment

How do you bridge the knowledge gap between health educators and those without basic health information? One answer is to turn health messages into dance, songs, plays, and even comic routines. The influence of the media provides "entertainers with a message" the chance to touch the lives of millions through television, radio, cassettes, books, newspapers, and magazines. Tapes of comedians with a routine on oral rehydration are bestsellers throughout Nepal; in Egypt, dramatized dialogues on the same subject are heard by millions; and a touring Somali play on health care has been seen by more than 70,000 Africans and a video tape of the production by another 2 million. In Malaysia, a counselling organization stages shows in discothèques offering AIDS education.

Child mortality

Each minute of every day more than 25 children die from easily preventable causes, such as diarrhoea, tetanus, and pneumonia – more than a quarter of a million a week. But each week almost 60,000 are saved by immunization programmes and oral re-hydration therapy (ORT) alone. If this rate is increased, then the Health for All aim of saving 100 million children by the year 2000 could be achieved – an unprecedented advance in our capacity to care for each other. Three major measures are in question. First is mass immunization of *all* children against the great killer diseases, such as measles, tetanus, and whooping cough, at a cost of $1.50 per child. Such a five-year programme would cost about the same as a single Trident submarine. According to UNICEF, 50% of all babies in the South already receive multi-immuniz-ation for the six main killer diseases. This now saves 2 million children a year and represents a tenfold in-crease since the mid-1970s. In Africa since 1986 immunization coverage has grown from less than 10% to more than 60% today.

Second is combatting the 10,000 deaths daily from the effects of diarrhoea, using ORT. This therapy, consisting of a sugar-and-salt-water solution, costs 10 cents a child, and saves 1 million children a year.

Third is a mass education campaign to support breast feeding. Bottle-fed infants, being more prone to illness, are 25 times more likely to die prematurely than breast-fed ones. The total cost of a save-the-child effort: $2.5 billion a year – less than a single day's global military expenditure.

The medicine man and modern medicine

Ironically the "total health" insights have often been more relevant in developing-world societies than in the North. Medicine men and other traditional healers, even witch doctors and shamans, have long recognized that sickness can be a psychic as well a physical affair. It can even have social overtones re-quiring the involvement of the community in support of the suf-ferer. Fortunately, these folkloric insights into holistic healing are now being incorporated into modern systems of health care in many developing countries.

Work and leisure

These two very words point up a revolution underway as concerns our attitude to work and nonwork. If people have no work can they then have no leisure either? The two categories are becoming increasingly blurred, after two centuries of increasing differentiation. People have always had to work to gain their livelihood, but the Industrial Revolution established the notion that work for most people would be work for other people, on their terms too. Thus work has tended to be equated with paid employment, and at the end of the working day one becomes free to resume one's own life. Working to live is a world away from living to work.

How different today when there is scope as well as desire for an increasing number of people to undertake work that is fulfilling in much the way that leisure meets needs beyond material wants. As the futurist James Robertson has put it, we can now look forward to something better than "to work 40 hours a week for 48 weeks a year for 40 years in a lifetime". Instead of other people's work, Robertson asks, how about "own-work", or activity that matters to us, not necessarily remunerated?

In the US managers 50 years ago changed companies once in their careers. Today managers on average make seven job changes in their career. The future will see more workers engaging in "portfolio lives" – carrying out a range of activities and con-tracted jobs of which paid work is only one aspect. Fortunately the means are now at hand to enable much professional work to be done from home. The computer linked to the telephone network becomes an electro-nic mailbox for the world; the fax machine can digitize our notes and diagrams and transmit them anywhere on the planet. With such a fast-expanding array of devices, it is now possible to engage in "teleworking" – a breakthrough for much of the services sector. In Britain an estimated 4 million people are likely to be performing home-based telework by 1998, accounting for about one job in five.

Work in the South

Debates about work and leisure will remain academic in much of the South for decades to come. During the 1990s developing economies will need to generate an additional 400 million jobs simply to accommodate new arrivals into the workforce, and during the follow-ing three decades, another 800 million jobs – by comparison with 400 million jobs in the developed world today. Even this effort, if achievable, will do nothing to counter existing unemployment and under-employment in the South, both of which often run at 20 to 30%.

As the traditional workforce of the North ages, employers will focus their attention on other sources of labour. These will include the mobile workforces of countries at its fringes – a process that will increase the brain and skill drain of the educated élites from regions such as Africa, Latin America, and Asia.

The demographic timebomb

In the year 2000 the balance of power will have shifted from employer to employee. The declining birth rate in the North will mean that fewer young people will be available to take up jobs and thus will find themselves in a seller's market. These demographic changes in the workforce may assist women in achieving equality in the workplace. Increasingly, employers are offering job sharing, child-care facilities, and extended career breaks. Governments are also co-operating, either by providing direct funding or by abolishing tax disincentives. Hence, true equality may come about not through simple business necessities as much as through a sense of fairness.

A new work ethos

Those fortunate enough to have professional skills in the North will enjoy "portfolio lives" – mixing paid work with free work. As well as earning a "salary" (for time given) there will be "fees" (for freelance work). In addition, "gift work" will be done for free (perhaps for charities or for the community) and "home" work (housework or child care in the home) will be another component, as will "study" work (learning a new skill or language). Money will come in bits and pieces from various sources, and such people will pursue "cash-flow" lives as opposed to "salary-led" lives. These will be individuals with saleable skills running their lives as mini-businesses.

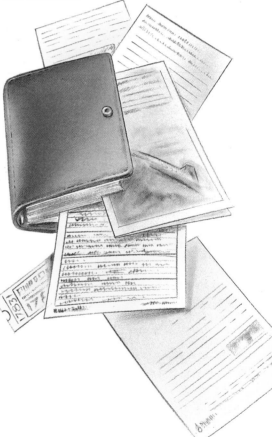

The underground economy

In Italy it is estimated that one job in four is outside the official economy – one reason why Italy can be characterized as a poor country populated by rich people. This underground employment is even more important in many developing countries, and will become more significant as people turn their hands and their wits to "street" work – low-tech, nil-capital industry such as bicycle repair work or bottle/scrap metal collections for recycling (see left). This work is not to be deplored, however unorthodox it might seem to economic planners. Rather it is to be promoted in that it gives outlet to entrepreneurial talents of millions satisfied with other than formal employment.

A day in the life

How shall we envisage a day in the life of year-2000 people? How far will it be enriched or otherwise expanded, or possibly depleted and impoverished, by the changes we are witnessing today?

A businessperson of the North, whether in Manchester, Sydney, Chicago, Frankfurt, or Osaka, may awaken to an automated household of instant convenience. The family may check its electronic mail and overnight faxes, plus the few oddments that still fall through the letterbox. After dropping the children off at their learning-to-learn centre and his/her spouse at an iterative career facility, the businessperson may return home to activate a domestic office for a morning of teleconferencing with colleagues on networks around the world. If face-to-face meetings are necessary in a central office, then fast freeway buses may be the best way to travel, private cars having become punitively expensive.

How different the day of a poorer citizen of the South, illustrated by typical experiences in a shanty town in Nairobi, Bombay, or Rio de Janeiro. Not much will have changed from today, except that conditions will be far more crowded and hopeless. The husband will rise from a sack-covered straw bed before light and stumble along a garbage-strewn track to use the ablutions-and-sanitation block that he and his family share with scores of other families. His wife will be cooking a thin stew over an open fire or, if they are lucky, a paraffin stove, the smoke drifting upward to add to the pall that pollutes as much as the traffic smog overhanging the city. He will then leave on a several-kilometres walk to his work in a backstreet clothing sweatshop producing denims for export. After ten hours of labour for a wage that equals what the Northern businessperson earns in five minutes, he returns home to greet his younger children. He will not have seen his older children for a few days, since they will be scavenging and begging down-town, returning to base only to make contributions to the family kitty. The family will count for all, and hospitality will flow freely – in spirit at least.

The work ethic

To many Northerners work will still supply not only income but also identity. There will never be enough of it, despite the protestations of being overloaded. If the day were suddenly extended by ten hours, the time would be instantly filled with more work. But to most Southerners work will still often be a means to an end, a better life – and that life will tend to revolve more around relationships, not only with an extended family but also friends, for whom there will always be time. This is in contrast with the Northerner's day, which will be dominated by the ticking tyrant on the wrist. Revealingly, an English-Swahili dictionary translates "work" as "kazi", but a Swahili-English dictionary defines "kazi" as "work, activity, occupation, whatever one does".

Contrasting attitudes

Although enjoying a standard of material comfort worlds apart from the Indian flower seller (above), the nightmare levels of stress experienced by these Japanese brokers (left) during the 1987 stock market crash must form part of the equation when calculating the *quality* of life.

Cultural attitudes

Just as our days are dominated by our work, so our Northerners' norms, indeed our essential sense of self, are centred on money-making activities. Although work no longer determines if we live, it is the key factor to where we live and how we live, even if it has less and less to do with how well we live. Income, and hence consumerism, remain the critical factors in our place in the local pecking order. Fortunately there is an emergent shift to other goals and values, as more people recognize the emptiness of wishing they had made more money on their death beds.

The promise of education

Education has hitherto been a childhood/ adolescent affair. From now on it will be a lifelong affair, a case of perpetual retraining to keep pace with an ever-changing world. In the US, an engineer's knowledge is already becoming seriously flawed after a period of only five years, a time-scale that will become more and more telescoped. So learning anew must become an accepted part of daily life.

In turn this means that initial education should not teach children to know specific somethings. Instead it must equip them with the ability to acquire knowledge – to teach themselves. How else will they cope with a world where the body of knowledge will double twice by the year 2000? So knowledge in itself will become less important than an awareness that knowledge exists, where to find it, how to exploit it, and how to relate one field of knowledge to another – in short, to *understand*.

Another revolutionary departure will lie in the fact that by the year 2000 a full 70 per cent of all jobs in developed countries will require mental skills not manual ones, a complete reversal of the situation 50 years ago. At least half of these jobs will demand higher education or a professional qualification; already 50 per cent of Japanese students are taking that track. There will be a premium on computer-related training, and well within 20 years virtually all jobs will need some degree of skill with information-processing technology.

Alongside this specialist-skills training there will fortunately be benefits from learning-by-discovery. If self-education is to be lifelong, it will also be life-empowering, concerned with personal growth, participatory community, leisure, and creativity. Those who are fully aware of the world will realize that there are no categorical divisions in society, the global economy, the environment. Future education must teach all to critique the old assumptions and to create new worldviews, ones without social (let alone environmental) exploitation – and hence to establish a new social ethos.

Education for whom?
Education has the potential to empower. It frees people from dependency and allows them to participate in decisions that affect their lives. In 1990, UN International Literacy Year, more than 960 million people remained illiterate. One-third of all adults in the developing world, most of them women, lack the knowledge or skills to cope with change and help them improve their lives. In real terms, expenditure per primary-school pupil is falling in more than 50% of developing nations, even though economic returns on education are higher than for most other forms of investment; four years of primary education is associated with at least a 10% increase in farm productivity, perhaps even as high as 25%. Some 100 million children currently lack primary schooling and are destined to be the adult illiterates of the 21st century if the UN's goal of eradicating illiteracy by 2000 is not met.

The never-closing school

To cater for new demand, schools may start to stay open 24 hours a day every day of the year. After the children go home, their places will be taken by workers being retrained until late evening, whereupon a night shift will arrive to take advantage of the expensive computer and communications systems that will underpin virtually all fields of learning. We shall witness schools for all seasons, and schools for all reasons.

Multiple careers

The need for incessant retraining will open the way for the adventurous to pursue several different careers. Their awareness of the "systems nature" of the world – induced by, for example, the growing interdependencies of economies, communities, environments, and communications – will allow them to step sideways and explore other areas of endeavour.

Percentages of children enrolled in primary, secondary, tertiary education (1986)

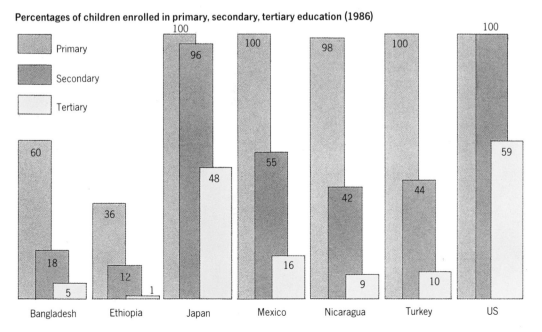

Personal experience

What will life in the future be like at the individual level? What will be some prime features, what new patterns will emerge, how will it feel to be living in a world replete with potential and problems?

In the wake of carbon taxes on fossil fuels, there will be fewer cars and commercial vehicles, many more bicycles, much more mass transport. "Renewables" will be the watchword, recycling will be the norm. We shall not only purchase more green products, we shall simply purchase less. Secondhand retailing will boom, conspicuous consumption will be conspicuously absent. The three-child family will carry special stigma. We shall learn to live with a host of new constraints, which will open up new fields of opportunity, such as sports, arts, and recreation in the sense of "re-creation" through, for example, yoga-style and stress-proofing pursuits.

Equally significant, there will be much more scope for involvement in local initiatives, such as are likely to proliferate when the spreading practice of "governance" spawns self-help communities (see pp. 84-5). This will foster a growing sense of control over one's personal world – a marked advance over the "quack-with-the-flock" spirit of standardized society.

All of this applies only to personal experience of a Northerner. For a Southerner, some things will be similar, many things will be different. There will be the same emphasis on energy efficiency, though more for economic than environmental or climate reasons; plus extensive recycling – though Southerners already practise this out of necessity. In the main, however, and especially in the struggling nations of the Indian subcontinent, sub-Saharan Africa, and the Andean region, life will still be a daily drudge of trying to make ends meet.

What will it be like?
The world is too much with us, especially in the form of our clock-driven schedules. But we may start to heed the idea that the busy person is not necessarily able, the able person not necessarily busy. If we learn to give more attention to the needs of the inner world – and there are many signs already that people wish to nourish this aspect of their lives – we shall place priority value on time that belongs to us, time that is not stolen by the demands of the outer world. At last we shall see cracks appearing in the edifice of the ticking tyrant.

A healthy home
In a world suffering shortages of many natural resources, the home environment is often a prime waster of these precious commodities. In the modern house, basic resources – air, water, energy, and the materials used to construct the shell and furnish the interior – have all become part of a throughput system (see p. 65) that takes and takes but gives little in return. Future homes will need to reflect the new situation, using resources with care and economy. Thus the home will once more become what it was – an acceptable part of the ecosystem, and supportive of environmental sustainability and personal health alike.

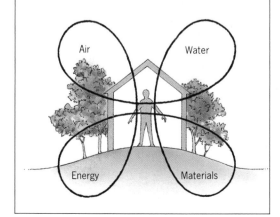

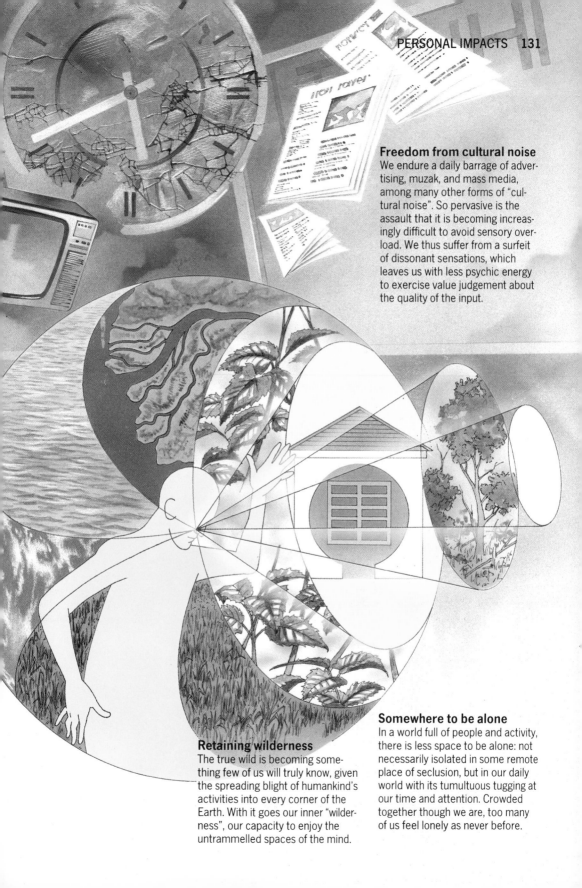

Freedom from cultural noise
We endure a daily barrage of advertising, muzak, and mass media, among many other forms of "cultural noise". So pervasive is the assault that it is becoming increasingly difficult to avoid sensory overload. We thus suffer from a surfeit of dissonant sensations, which leaves us with less psychic energy to exercise value judgement about the quality of the input.

Retaining wilderness
The true wild is becoming something few of us will truly know, given the spreading blight of humankind's activities into every corner of the Earth. With it goes our inner "wilderness", our capacity to enjoy the untrammelled spaces of the mind.

Somewhere to be alone
In a world full of people and activity, there is less space to be alone: not necessarily isolated in some remote place of seclusion, but in our daily world with its tumultuous tugging at our time and attention. Crowded together though we are, too many of us feel lonely as never before.

Surprise – AIDS

Ten years ago AIDS had hardly been heard of. Today it threatens to be one of the greatest disasters ever to overtake humanity, a type of latter-day Black Death. How could a phenomenon of this scale take us by surprise? And what other AIDS-type phenomena might be waiting to catch us out?

According to the World Health Organization there are at least 5 million people infected with the AIDS virus. The total could soar to 20 million by the year 2000 (and conceivably to 50 million or even more), with more than 5 million dying or dead from the disease while the bulk of sufferers will be in developing countries. But there will be sizeable numbers in advanced nations: in Britain, for example, 17,000 dead projected as early as 1992, while in the US the total dead from just the present infections will rise during the early 1990s to over 1 million, or more Americans than have died in all US wars. In New York, AIDS is already the leading cause of death among people under the age of 40; worse, it is thought to have lodged in 1 in 15 of all New Yorkers. By the late 1990s the US death rate could soar to 500,000 a year, and by the year 2000, if not before, the disease could cause the US population growth rate to level off or even decline. Still worse, the concentration of AIDS deaths among young adults, plus the knock-on effects of a devitalized economy, could in the near future prove highly destabilizing for American society.

Yet AIDS need never have been a surprise at all. We know that we cannot beat all diseases; as soon as one is eliminated, another takes its place after merely waiting its turn. More importantly, AIDS would have been a preventable epidemic if we had struck back with full vigour at the first sign of its threat. But we allowed ourselves to be caught with our guard relaxed, and refused to admit that we could in fact be surprised. And thus we set ourselves up for further surprises in the future – a host of them, some perhaps even more apocalyptic than AIDS.

The spread of AIDS
AIDS has now reached 152 countries, the great majority of all countries on Earth. Present preventative measures are not likely to have much impact on slowing the epidemic's spread until the mid-1990s. Nor is there a prospect of a cure or a vaccine within the next ten years.

Another Black Death?
During the years 1348–52 the Black Death swept through Europe killing some three-quarters of the entire population of 75 million. AIDS is like the Black Death in slow motion. After emerging in the mid-1970s, it will entrain a projected 100 million infections by the early 1990s, leading to total deaths in the late 1990s of as many as 50 million. If the number infected eventually climbs to 20% of world population – a far from impossible prospect – the overall mortality could eventually cancel out rapid population growth worldwide.

"We all say it can't happen to us. The more we keep saying it, the more likely we are to be proved fatally wrong."

Dr Jonathon Mann, former Director of WHO's Global Programme on AIDS

- Not affected/not tested
- Less than 10,000 HIV carriers
- 10,000–100,000 HIV carriers
- 100,000–2 million HIV carriers

A 100-year epidemic?

The AIDS virus is a lethal "sleeper" that incubates for up to ten years before starting to wreak havoc on the body's immune system. In sub-Saharan Africa at least 250,000 babies have been born infected, and there is virtually no ultimate hope for them. Because of the virus's lengthy incubation period and its capacity for built-in momentum of growth among its prey communities, we could be facing a 100-year epidemic: as is already the case, the disease will be passed on from generation to generation, its survival guaranteed by our own procreation.

The scourge of Africa

In some urban communities of Central Africa, one person in five is now thought to carry the AIDS virus. Most of these Africans are in their 20s and 30s and include as many men as women. They are their nations' breadwinners, many of them educated professionals – precisely the people in whom their countries have invested so many resources and so much hope, a youthful élite that represents Africa's first post-independence generation to come to power. The impact of their deaths could cause the collapse of some countries within another 20 years; at the very least, their deaths will scar Africa for generations. Whereas direct health-related costs in the US will be over $8 billion in 1991, the cost of testing one African for the virus is more than the annual per-capita health budget in many African countries.

What new AIDS in the works?

AIDS has sprung on us without warning. Worse, it continues to spring on us ever-more heavily because we refuse to heed its multidecibel warnings. If we had moved resolutely in the early days, it need never have become an epidemic. What new catastrophe may be lurking in the wings, waiting to catch us unawares and then to traumatize an all-too-aware society? Not only some new disease, but an economic cataclysm, a climate dislocation, or an international upheaval? We shall be surprised because of our refusal to believe we can be surprised.

Part Three

Creating the future

The future can still be *our* future. We can possess the future, provided we do not let it possess us. All we have to do is to choose. Or rather, to choose to choose.

To do that we shall need to keep an eye better fixed on the long-term future. This is hard, since we have grown adapted to thinking about the short-term future. When the marketplace decrees an interest rate of 10 per cent, investors must recoup their investment within seven years, which is akin to saying there is no future to bother about thereafter. Our political systems proclaim the future extends only till the next election. To enable us to cater for the future beyond this foreshortened perspective, we shall have to engage in much restructuring of society. Otherwise we run the risk of an unguided future descending on us, a future with upheaval abounding. Make no mistake: for the first time in human history, the next generation could find itself worse off than the previous one to an extent without parallel. A worst-case outcome – a prospect far from impossible – would entail the end of civilization as we know it. The only way to avoid that is to reconstruct our civilization from top to bottom.

Many of our options are already foreclosed through our penchant for muddling through. As a result, we face an immediate bottleneck of restricted choices. Much of Part Three presents ways for us to squeeze through this bottleneck. We look at measures to contain the greenhouse effect, to move to new energy paths, to reverse biomass shifts, to halt deforestation, to defuse the population bomb, to refashion our economies, to promote "soft" technologies, to build an organic agriculture, to establish green governance, to devise planetary medicine, to foster dynamic peace, and to undertake the many other prerequisites of a sustainable world.

Most of all, these changes in our outer world depend on still more revolutionary changes in our inner world. So the concluding pages look at the greatest transitions of all: from knowledge to wisdom, and from constant chatter to a readiness to listen – to listen to each other, to ourselves, and to Gaia.

We shall gain the future we deserve. Part Three points the way, a way with portents, pitfalls, and hopes. Whatever tough times lie immediately ahead, this book, like the expansive promise of the longer-term future, is for optimists.

Two moods of optimism
A rushing stream in Utah, USA (main picture). A CND balloon (inset) flies over Catherine the Great's summer palace in Leningrad at the first international hot air balloon rally to be held in the Soviet Union.

Toward 2000

As we head toward the new millennium, a number of organizations have been making ambitious plans. Well might they be ambitious: only by thinking a great deal bigger than we have in the past will we be ready to tackle the challenges ahead.

Health for All
This World Health Organization plan aims to: counter the malnutrition suffered by at least 1 billion people; supply primary health care to everyone; ensure life expectancy reaches 60 years; cut infant mortality to 50 per 1000 live births; ensure all infants and children enjoy proper weight (half of developing-world children are poorly nourished); and supply safe water within 15 minutes' walk. All this is to be accomplished by the year 2000. Just to provide primary health care for all would cost $50 billion a year, and safe water plus sanitation would cost $30 billion a year. The plan also proposes much greater attention to the greying communities in the developed world.

Education for All
This UNESCO plan aims to supply basic education for every person on Earth by the year 2000. Today, 105 million developing-world children enjoy no schooling at all, and more than 900 million adults, or one out of every four, are illiterate. Cost: around $5 billion a year.

Population 2000
According to the International Forum on Population in the 21st Century, convened in late 1989 by the UN Fund for Population Activities, the aim is to "hold the line" on the medium population projection of 6.25 billion people by the year 2000. To achieve this, we need to: reduce developing-world fertility to 3.2 children per family; increase developing-world use of contraceptives to 56%; upgrade the status of women, especially their literacy; and achieve universal enrolment of girls in primary schools. In order to accomplish just the first two items, we shall need to increase the budget for family-planning services in developing countries to $9 billion annually, or twice as much as today.

Anti-Desertification Action Plan
The United Nations' plan seeks to halt the spread of human-made deserts, now threatening one-third of the Earth's land surface. There has been next to no progress on this issue since it was first formulated in 1978, due to government indifference. Yet it would be an unusually sound investment at $6 billion a year for 20 years, against the continuing costs of inaction worth $32 billion a year in agricultural losses alone. In 1986 the world spent more than $100 billion in drought-relief operations that saved lives but did nothing to halt further desertification.

Tropical Forestry Action Plan

The plan, already in action, seeks to slow deforestation by supplying: tree farms for commercial timber; village woodlots and agroforestry plots for fuelwood; more protected areas for threatened species; more research and training, plus public education; and better management all round. Cost: $1.6 billion per year. But the plan does next to nothing to address the main source of deforestation, the slash-and-burn cultivator, who reflects an array of nonforestry problems such as population growth, pervasive poverty, maldistribution of existing farmlands, lack of agrarian reform, and hopelessly inadequate development for rural communities generally.

Climate Change Programme

Focused on global warming, and undertaken by the Intergovernmental Panel on Climate Change leading up to a proposed global-warming treaty, the Programme proposes to stabilize the concentration of greenhouse gases in the atmosphere by cutting emissions of carbon dioxide by 80%, of methane by 15-20%, of nitrous oxide by 70-80%, and of CFCs and related HCFCs by 70-85%. In the case of carbon dioxide, which accounts for roughly half the greenhouse effect, developed nations would have to reduce their fossil-fuel burning by 20% by 2005, by 50% by 2015, and by 75% by 2030. Developing nations would have to stabilize their emissions by 2010, allowing them to rise to no more than double today's levels as they continue to industrialize (developing nations would also have to halt deforestation by 2010 and engage in grand-scale tree planting). All this would mean that global emissions of greenhouse gases would fall to one-quarter of their present levels by 2050, limiting the rate of warming to 0.1° C per decade, and eventually holding it at 2° C above today's average temperatures – still a highly disruptive outcome.

Global Change Programme

Formerly known as the International Geosphere-Biosphere Programme, this research effort aims to provide the information we need to assess the future of the planet for the next 100 years, with emphasis on such areas as biogeochemical cycles, the upper layer of the oceans, Earth's soil stocks, and the sun's radiation. With an operational phase beginning in the early 1990s, the plan will last for ten years.

Beyond 2000?

As worthy as all these organizations' plans are, they all suffer from a serious shortcoming. They are targetted at the year 2000: what about longer-term goals, which must be established *now* if we are to avoid much costlier efforts later on, with much less prospect of success? Regrettably the plans reflect the timid and short-term attitudes of the governments that approve the strategies. It is not in the nature of governments to see beyond the end of their noses, let alone beyond the end of the decade.

Greenhouse tactics: options for response

The greatest environmental upheaval of all, the greenhouse effect, offers much scope for positive response. While it is not possible to tame the problem entirely – there is already too much change in the pipeline – there is still time to slow it, perhaps even to stabilize it, and buy ourselves precious decades in which to devise longer-term answers. But this will require immediate and vigorous action on a broad front, plus international collaboration and individual initiatives on an unprecedented scale.

First and foremost we need to consume less energy, through energy conservation and more efficient use of energy. In fact these two strategies represent our best energy source: from 1973 to 1978 some 95 per cent of all new energy supplies in Europe came from more efficient use of

available supplies – an amount 20 times more than from all other new sources of energy combined.

Since the oil crises of 1973 and 1979, most of the fuel-guzzling industrialized countries have expanded their economies by a full 30 per cent while actually cutting back on total energy consumption. In 1985 came a third oil shock, this one of plunging oil prices, whereupon we quickly reverted to our energy-wasting ways.

But the energy-saving technologies are still there, waiting to be mobilized (see below). And at the same time as we cut back on fossil-fuel burning, so we reduce acid rain, among many other forms of environmental pollution.

Burning fossil fuel for energy, however, is only about one-third of the greenhouse

A climate convention
A worldwide convention (see p.140) will need to decide how much greenhouse effect we are prepared to live with and the degree of remedial action to be taken, and by whom, in order to reduce the problem. This will mean a cap on greenhouse-gas emissions by all nations. But how hefty a cap for such disparate cases as Britain and Bangladesh, the US and Brazil,

Changing energy policies
To mitigate the effects of the greenhouse we must reduce fossil-fuel burning. In the short term the greatest savings will come from buildings and products that use energy more efficiently. Many US electricity utilities offer their customers energy surveys, rebates on energy-efficient appliances, and loans to finance energy-saving improvements. In the long term we need to replace fossil fuels with environmentally benign renewables, such as wind, wave, and solar. As for nuclear power, and leaving aside the unacceptable risks in its use, plus its uncompetitive price in the marketplace, to replace the world's coal-burning stations would entail building one nuclear plant every three days for the next 36 years at a cost of $150 billion annually.

problem. Another source is agriculture:
nitrous oxide from nitrogen-based fertilizers; methane from rice paddies and rumi-
nant livestock. With more mouths to feed
around the world, we cannot allow food
production to plateau – though we could do it
differently and more productively with
genetically engineered breeds. A halt to
tropical deforestation would prevent at least
2.4 billion tonnes of carbon from entering
the atmosphere each year, while reforestation would soak up carbon as well as
restore vital watershed functions among
many other purposes.

Through multiple linkages, then, the
greenhouse problem reflects the myriad
ways we all live. It will only be through
myriad shifts in economic sectors and lifestyles alike that we shall get on top of the

Public perception
Look out of a window and you view
a world in the thrall of climatic
upheaval. Although nothing can be
seen, the world is undergoing an
environmental shift of a type and
scale to rival a geological cataclysm
– and one of the most rapid ever to
overtake the Earth. To confront it
we need a parallel change in our
inner world, our world of perception
and understanding.

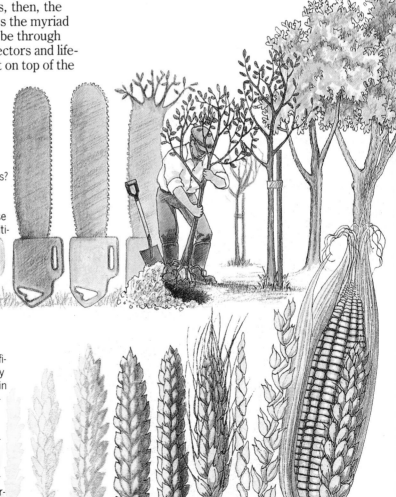

Germany and China, the Soviet
Union, and India? Should the industrialized nations indemnify the
industrializing nations in order to
safeguard the climate of all nations?
Should there be special dispen-
sations on the part of the entire
community of nations to help those
worst affected? The questions multiply and ramify, and we have no
precedents to guide us.

Rethinking agricultural practices
Population growth and the intensifi-
cation of food production are likely
to set limits to reductions in certain
greenhouse gases. Actively reducing the extent of intensive cattle-
rearing operations would curtail
some methane production; reducing fertilizer use, or implementing
more efficient means of fertilizer
application would do the same for
nitrous oxide. An even more important answer lies with new varieties
of crops that require less fertilizer.

Greenhouse tactics: options for response

problem and start to minimize its unavoidable impacts on the environment. It will demand an extraordinary effort from each and every one of us.

There are, however, plausible scenarios to the effect that over the next 30 years the North's economies could continue to grow, while per-capita energy consumption falls to half 1980 levels; and the South's economies could grow to match the living levels of some more advanced countries with only marginally increased energy consumption.

True, a counter-greenhouse strategy depends on us doing most things right, despite our penchant for doing most things wrong. So to prevent a catastrophic decline in climatic conditions, we must engage in a crucial advance in human ingenuity, commitment, and collective endeavour.

A climate convention will shortly be achieved, grounded in a common concern for humanity's common climate. But its detailed workings will be more than difficult to implement over the decades ahead. The greenhouse problem has been primarily brought about by the industrialized nations so far, yet many developing countries will suffer grievously through droughts, sea-level rise, and other forms of gross dislocation. Moreover certain developing nations, such as India and China, plan to burn huge amounts of coal to fuel their development plans. Should not the developed nations accept some special degree of responsibility for global climate – on the grounds of their past energy record, their stake in future climate, and their growing expertise in nonpolluting sources of energy?

Deforestation to reforestation
The destruction of tropical forests contributes 30% of the build-up of carbon dioxide in the atmosphere. Reversing the policies that encourage deforestation and implementing land reforms will require the commitment not only of tropical nations but also of international agencies involved and the global community at large. Tropical nations should be helped to shift to sustainable harvests of timber and beef from formerly forested zones; and they should be offered more equitable terms of trade, plus an easing of the debt burden. One of the best ways to counter the build-up of carbon dioxide is through reforestation. About 1 million sq km (approximately the area of Egypt) of fast-growing trees absorb 1 billion tonnes of carbon annually during their major growth period of up to several decades. Reforestation on this scale would absorb one-quarter of the net annual build-up of carbon dioxide in the atmosphere.

There will be many such acute complications arising, demanding large-scale adaptations, not only technological but also political and social adaptations. The worst outcome would be one where certain nations perceive themselves as "winners" and others as "losers": in a greenhouse-affected world, with its extreme economic upheavals and profound political destabilization, there can only be losers.

So there could be positive benefit, in that by tackling the greenhouse effect the world's nations will have to learn many new modes of collaborative endeavour. The lesson will stand us in good stead as we then move to confront other major issues of One-Earth living.

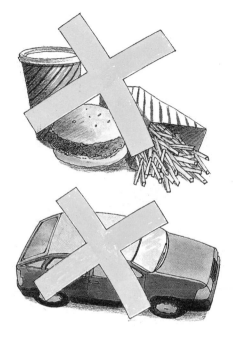

The social backlash

As the greenhouse effect starts to bite, could we witness outbursts of angry citizens against "energy laggards"? For example, attacks on single-occupant cars and grosser gas-guzzlers, on blatantly energy-inefficient buildings, or even fossil-fuel power plants. Will we see "energy wardens" authorized to issue on-the-spot fines to energy abusers? Will there be public pressure for governments to impose punitive carbon taxes on a host of energy-wasteful activities, both commercial and domestic?

Rolling down the highway

Each working day, 126,000 cars roll off the production lines – nearly 33 million annually. Carbon dioxide, nitrous oxide, methane, and ozone are byproducts of burning petrol in the internal combustion engine. Carmakers have been quick to climb aboard the green bandwagon, but even a high-mileage-per-gallon car is an inefficient mode of transport when it carries just the driver.

New transport policies to counter the car culture will play a leading role in tackling the greenhouse problem. A resurgence of flexible public-transport systems and the development of nonpolluting vehicles is just one side of the equation. Integrated urban design in future transport policies will be needed to make private cars far less necessary.

Return of the wild

We urgently need to reverse the devegetation of the Earth. Could the planet in the 21st century start to feature its proper spread of forests, grasslands, and the rest, together with their assemblages of animal life? Are we in fact ready to restore the panoply of the wild to its rightful place in a human-dominated scheme of things?

This challenge is among the most searching of all, linked as it is with soaring human numbers and their food demands, the greenhouse effect, and our out-dated methods of planet management. But it is surely a challenge we cannot any longer defer – even though we have hitherto given all too little attention to its nature, let alone its scale. Without a fresh start on our relations with the wild, we shall end up with a planet on which we shall look out and see nothing but our own activities reflected back on every side. Is this what we truly want? Key questions: and anyone is as well equipped as the next to supply answers that address some of the most valuable of our values.

By the middle of the next century we shall probably have no parks and reserves. Either they will have been finally overrun by throngs of land-hungry people – not only the poor but also the rich, who, by their consumerist demands, are effectively as land hungry as the impoverished. Alternatively there will be no more protected areas because we have finally learned to manage our total landscapes in a manner that, as a spin-off benefit, accords space to wildlife communities in full measure. For this latter option, we must find ways to engage in rational and Gaia-esque planning for all

The wild's view of the wild

From a nonhuman perspective, there are no weeds, pests, or vermin. All life forms play their part, all have their place. True, this is a human-centric world, that is our myopic view of things. We wear our prejudices on our sleeves, right from swaddling clothes to shroud.

But to reiterate the central thesis, we shall serve our own welfare better by adopting a more harmonious relationship with other creatures. To achieve this new perspective, we might try to see the world as wild creatures do: how would our insights and perceptions alter if we could see humankind as does a rabbit, bird, insect, or fish?

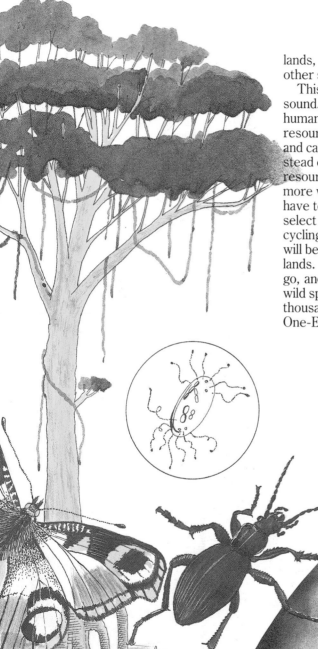

lands, thus making adequate provision for all other species.

This prospect is not as unlikely as it may sound. If we are to devise strategies for humankind to sustain itself from the land-resource base, this will entail a more careful and caring use of Earth's ecosystems. Instead of extensive, wasteful exploitation of resources, with a spirit of "there's always more where that came from", there will have to be intensive, self-sustaining use of select resources, with emphasis on re-cycling and renewables. As a result, there will be less rather than more use of wild-lands. There is no other long-term way to go, and we would need to follow it even if wild species had been reduced to a final few thousands. In terms of our overall use of the One-Earth habitat, we have no option.

Getting from here to there

First, there must be an end to the idea of living with nature as if it were an appurtenance that adds a pleasant diversion along our road. Second, and in related manner, we must move beyond the concept of protected areas, an approach that has served us well so far, but one that reinforces an "us-versus-them" attitude: it ill becomes the status of co-traveller we must attain if we are to appreciate nature's true value. Third, we need to learn more of the elements of nature's functioning, where humans are just a part of the whole. As daunting as this is, the world has become such that the idealistic is necessarily converging with the realistic.

Human aesthetics

Our conventional value system postulates there is no aesthetics without human perception. But that notion betrays the lack of system in the "system". Is a swallowtail butterfly any less beautiful when there is no human to behold it? And is there no beauty in the whole of creation, in its intrinsic complete-ness, in its limitless creativity? If it is difficult even to apprehend the sheer scope of creation, how much more challenging is it to compre-hend its detailed make-up?

Natural justice

"I speak for the microbes and the less attractive forms of life, because they have none to speak for them." Professor James Lovelock

The time could be arriving when we accord some form of rights to the 30 million species that share the planet with us, and perhaps even to the rest of nature. After all, without the unwitting support of the entire natural world – rocks, landscapes, ecosystems – we would not be able to sustain the human enterprise. We cannot continue to misuse and overuse nature as we have thus far: if only for our own self-interest, let alone the interests of our planetary fellow travellers, we need to develop a more purposeful relationship with nature. And to make it secure and productive, there is a case for the relationship to be formalized through some measure of legal guarantee.

As revolutionary as this may sound, it is no more mould breaking than certain other shifts in human perception that have occurred in the past. We have, for example, moved from a position of regarding some people as being mere objects and possessions, to be disposed of as their owner wished; over a period of centuries we have extended basic rights to all humans.

As an extension, then, do not animals and plants also have natural rights? Each species is a unique manifestation of creation, and each species is subject to "unnatural" (human-made), ultimate injury via extinction. For a start, then, should we not assure them future survival on the planet for the term of their natural existence? Even the

Animal cultures

Recent research suggests that whales, through their songs and other complex communications, express a form of community far more advanced and refined than we had earlier supposed. They even show signs of a collective memory and other attributes of a whale culture. Similarly baboons reveal behaviour patterns that imply they are on the verge of a degree of consciousness and planning capacity that extend way beyond what we have conventionally credited them with; their social systems likewise argue an incipient culture. Elephants, too, are now suspected of having the ability to conceptualize and analyse. Individual elephants have been radio-tracked as they go on lengthy walk-abouts during the wet season, when there is ample food in their immediate environs. Could they be investigating potential food stocks to meet their needs during the subsequent dry season – and if so, does this not postulate a capacity to anticipate and plan ahead? By extension, and given the complex nature of their herd interactions, could elephants be displaying their own form of society?

lowliest microbe, with its distinctive attributes, and being the product of the formative pressures of evolution, surely deserves to go its own way without terminal opposition from the human species.

These same considerations apply to forests, grasslands, and coral reefs – hence to their inanimate constituents, such as soil, water, and rocks, as to the entire ecosystems of which they are a part and in which they have their being. Eventually, we should extend the same formal recognition to the rights of Gaia itself, as the ultimate organism and the organizing principle for all life on Earth.

Legal status for Gaia?

On a practical level there should be little problem in recognizing the legal rights of the planetary ecosystem as an independent entity, insofar as there are already inanimate rights-holders accepted by the world of law: corporations, trusts, and nation-states. Should we not accord similar status to Gaia? Thereafter its rights could be articulated through representatives with voting power in the councils of government and international agencies, on boards of corporations and banks, and in the regulatory forums of whatever body exercises significant impact on the workings of Gaia.

Three grey whales

When three grey whales became trapped in the Alaskan ice in 1988, the outpouring of public concern indicated a bond between human cultures as diverse as Inuit, American, and Russian. Did the sentiments of millions of people indicate a conscience over what humanity has done to the whales? Yet in the same year as humans managed to free two of them, hundreds of others fell prey to the harpoons.

From management to medicine

Management postulates that we can adjust, adapt, and otherwise compensate for any deficiencies in a field of organized activity, such as government, business, or the local supermarket. In many circumstances, management structures work wonders, and the field of management is developing into a fully fledged science with all the methodical endeavour that characterizes any science. But management is essentially an attempt to make a given system work better – to organize, to fine tune. It implicitly accepts the system and its workings. It asserts that with sufficient effort we can work better: we shall somehow manage to manage.

Unfortunately the malfunctions of the global system are becoming so pervasive and profound they are now endemic to the system. Management, generally a reduct-

ionist process – reducing an entity to "manageable" parts – does not often address the problems inherent in the system. When we confront the planetary prospect and the myriad maladies that threaten the heart of the system, we find that management tends to tackle the symptoms of problems rather than the sources of problems.

What we must envisage is no less than some form of planetary medicine. There is certainly no shortage of planetary ills, some of which promise to be uniquely debilitating. Or, to put the situation more directly, the planet could well be suffering from a type of deep-seated disorder that embraces the entire biosphere, a meta-disease that penetrates all parts of the system. If this diagnosis is correct, it will not be sufficient to

The "fix-it" mentality
Traditional management is problem-orientated. It is chiefly concerned with making the most of the materials to hand and then directing activity to be more productive. Yet all too often this is a process of crisis management, which forever seeks to rectify the symptoms without addressing the root causes of the problems. In terms of effectiveness on a planetary scale, this can be likened to stuffing sandbags into a breach in the sea wall, and hoping (but not really believing) that the next surge tide does not simply brush them aside.

turn to climatologists or biogeochemists or any other category of single-discipline expert: instead the need will be for a full-blown planetary doctor – and there are not many of them around.

Professor James Lovelock, the originator of the Gaia hypothesis, proposes that a systems approach to Earth science should serve as an essential basis (in theory at least) for the profession of planetary medicine. It should be grounded in the field of "geophysiology": physiology is the systems science of people and animals, and has played a central role in the evolution of medicine; the "geo" aspect adds a vital Earth dimension. This holistic science could supply the practical means to design procedures for the analysis and hence the treatment of planetary maladies.

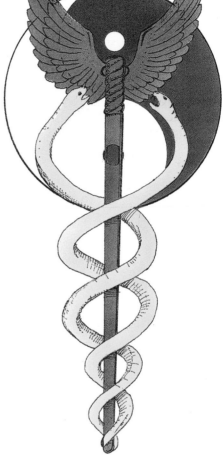

Physiology of a planet

It was the Scottish geologist James Hutton (1726-97), regarded as the founder of modern geology, who first expressed the notion that the Earth was a superorganism, and that its proper study would be physiology. Gaia has many features in common with the physiology of warm-blooded animals. Rivers and oceans act like the blood in an animal's circulatory system. The atmosphere acts like the lungs. All the components of Gaia can be likened to the cells and tissues that aggregate to make up a complete organism, and each component has its unique part to play in the functioning of the whole.

Gaian medicine in practice

As Lovelock points out, Gaia's disability does not stem from the patient itself but comes from the presence of the intelligent fleas that infest the organism. "There is nothing to stop us, however, from going through the temperature charts and the biochemical analyses of the body fluids" – and then assessing the acid indigestion, the overdose of nuclear radiation, the global-warming fever, the skin disease of ozonemia, and whatever other sicknesses threaten the life-support system itself.

Enough is enough

According to the United Nations' medium population projection, there will be 10.6 billion people on the planet by the time population growth finally levels out in about a hundred years' time.

The worst news is that if more countries follow the population path of the Philippines, most countries of sub-Saharan Africa, and a few Muslim countries, where fertility rates are still rising, there will ultimately be more than 14 billion people. The better news is that if more countries follow the example of Thailand, China, South Korea, Taiwan, Java, Kerala state in India, Tunisia, Cuba, and urban communities of Mexico and Colombia, all of which have brought their family sizes plunging in record time, we shall end up with only a little more than 8 billion people. The difference between the projections is a measure of the manoeuvring room still available to us if we move fast enough and vigorously enough to provide basic livelihoods and family-planning facilities for all. The success stories represent a remarkable range of cultures, political systems, and economic advancement. If they can do it, surely all the rest can too.

Fortunately the great majority of countries of the developing world now seem ready to come to grips with the population problem. How much easier would the present task have been if we had moved to get to firm grips with the problem 20 years ago. All except a dozen governments now agree they need to tackle the population issue with specific family-planning targets and carefully planned activities to achieve their goals.

2020 8.9 bn

8.25 bn

7.4 bn

1990 5.3 bn

Family planning in the North
Should not wealthy countries decide how many people they want in the long run? One of the most radical changes ahead for the North is that population planning will become as essential as it already is in the South. What total could be deemed enough for, say, Britain, and for Britain's place in the world? Who would bet that in 25 years Britons might not be deciding that 30 million is about "right" – little more than half today's total? In that case, how many Americans or Russians can the world afford?

Green stamps for babies
Government population-control policies using strong economic and social incentives have been effective in China and Singapore. Extensive government resources have been devoted to expanding services and providing contraception. Additionally, in China strong social pressure has been brought to bear to practise vigorous birth control. Is it too far-fetched to imagine that one day people might be issued with a warrant entitling them to have a single child – a type of green stamp? This warrant might even carry commercial value, allowing individuals to decide not to have children at all and to sell their entitlements to others wanting larger families.

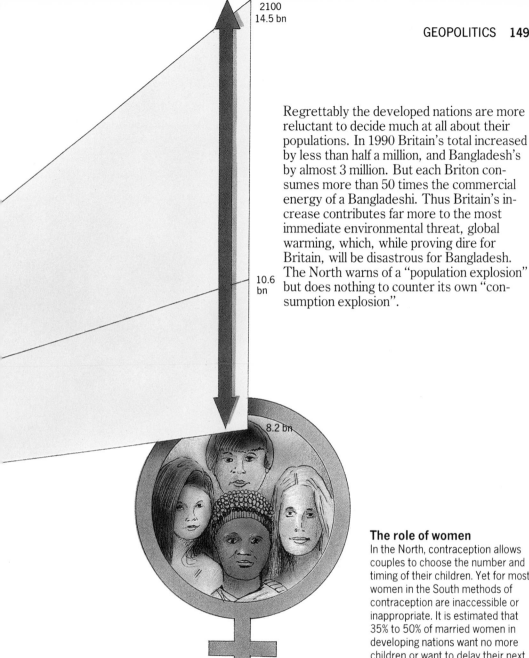

2100
14.5 bn

10.6
bn

8.2 bn

Regrettably the developed nations are more reluctant to decide much at all about their populations. In 1990 Britain's total increased by less than half a million, and Bangladesh's by almost 3 million. But each Briton consumes more than 50 times the commercial energy of a Bangladeshi. Thus Britain's increase contributes far more to the most immediate environmental threat, global warming, which, while proving dire for Britain, will be disastrous for Bangladesh. The North warns of a "population explosion" but does nothing to counter its own "consumption explosion".

The role of women
In the North, contraception allows couples to choose the number and timing of their children. Yet for most women in the South methods of contraception are inaccessible or inappropriate. It is estimated that 35% to 50% of married women in developing nations want no more children or want to delay their next pregnancy. Yet their low status, literacy, and income, as well as ill health, are factors accompanying high fertility. Unless society's attitudes change, fertility levels are unlikely to fall. At present Zimbabwe leads sub-Saharan Africa in its use of contraception methods. Its family-planning efforts have been successfully integrated into programmes to improve women's abilities for self-organization and income earning.

Population planning worldwide
What would it cost to engage in a beefed-up family-planning campaign for the global community? In terms of birth-control facilities alone, we currently spend about $3 billion a year, of which more than $1 billion on the part of China, $550 million on the part of India, and $500 million on the part of international donors (regrettably the US contribution has actually declined since the mid-1980s). To achieve an increase in the number of contraceptive-using couples from 663 million in 1987 to 1 billion in the year 2000, we shall have to triple the annual family-planning budget. But even $9 billion is a trifling amount, being equivalent to only three days of military spending worldwide.

Sharing power and freedom

Of the world's 150-plus nations, only 20 or so enjoy a fully democratic form of government, and at least 50 live under military rule of one sort or another. But only one South American country still labours under dictatorship, while in Eastern Europe and South Africa there have been sudden breakthroughs that have long been thought impossible by the rest of the world – though in China a fledgling popular movement in support of more accountable government was suddenly and brutally crushed in 1989.

What prospect for the "unthinkable", not only in China but also the Middle East, Northern Ireland, Kampuchea, and the other numerous flashpoints around the world – and not forgetting such new "Middle Easts" as may erupt in the decades ahead? The recent outburst of political freedom in

Eastern Europe has already triggered stirrings in certain Arab countries of the Middle East as well as brought the Baltic states to near crisis point. These same processes apply as well to such little-regarded communities as the Basques, Tamils, Karens, and Inuits. How long before the clamour for social justice, in the shape of equitably shared power, self-determination, and political freedom, becomes a crescendo that can no longer be resisted.

But when more of the world's population becomes free from nondemocratic systems of government, will they then become free to practise democracy in its full sense? Having fought and gained "freedom from", will they know how to enjoy "freedom for"? Democracy implies not only more personal rights but also more personal responsibili-

The rulers and the ruled
As increasing numbers of citizens question the nature of the laws that control their lives, the positions of those that hold power become less secure. To what extent do we individually identify with "the state"? Do our senses of value, justice, and democracy coincide? How does authority cope with workers who strike for their rights, "dissidents", and "refuseniks"? There are limits to the tactics governments can employ to maintain the status quo in the face of moral legitimacy.

Direct/indirect democracy

In a democracy, power may be exercised directly through active participation, as it was in ancient Athens, or indirectly through elected representatives, as in modern democracies. In the current system, political apathy is understandable. For example, Ronald Reagan was elected US president by less than 25% of all eligible voters; and out of a total of 3.5 million US government employees, only 537 are publicly elected. All too often, those holding power in a free-market democracy are outside public control. Only if people are more willing and enabled to participate actively in government can a more consensual democracy come into being.

ties, and certainly more involvement than simply casting an occasional vote in favour of representatives. It means exploiting the panoply of opportunities provided through the organs of government, the press and other media, the legal system, and so on, available to all. The more these responsibilities are utilized, the more they will flourish, diversify, and proliferate until eventually they constitute a true democratic system, fashioned by democrats for democrats. Or, more succinctly, we need responsive systems for responsible participants. To this extent, few countries or communities are truly democratic, or indeed free, in the proper sense of the term. Most are limited by the limited perceptions of individuals.

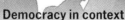

Democracy in context

Given the environmental crises of our future, we shall have to accept a number of constraints on our erstwhile freedom in the wake of new environmental realities. These may well include a greater readiness to comply with recommendations of scientists and other experts: increasingly we shall have to defer to the wisdom of the "wise". As well, the growing urgency of environmental challenges will sometimes leave even less scope for democratic debate. Will this mean a reduction of certain democratic procedures? Not necessarily. Indeed there will be all the greater need for government participation by informed citizenry. But equally it will mean more acceptance of active government with the consent of the governed.

Active democrat

Passive democrat

Clamour for justice

Worldwide there is a rising clamour for justice on all levels – political, social, and economic. The desire for participatory democracy may be spreading farther and faster than was dreamed possible just a few years ago (see pp. 150-1), and by the turn of the millennium it may be possible to look out on a world where more than half the nations of the planet enjoy at least a parliamentary form of democracy.

But when we turn our attention to economic justice, what do we find? We cannot persist with a world where 20 per cent of the global population consumes a full 80 per cent of its resources. Yet economic injustice exists not only between countries: in the North and South alike there are countries where the top 15 per cent of the population enjoy income and wealth equal to all the bottom 85 per cent. The strains this inequality places on the community will simply become too great: a resource in ever-shorter supply is the patience of the poor and disadvantaged. Nor shall we enjoy economic justice until we are all free from the blight of unemployment, inflation, and a host of other economic ills that diminish our personal liberties just as much as do political restrictions.

Similarly, social justice demands a system that assures health, education, security in old age, indeed comprehensive social safeguards for all in whatever country. The time is long past when most developed nations took it for granted that it was a community responsibility to care for all members, whatever their plight and however it came about. The time is surely ripening when we shall

Resource distribution

Resource distribution is a key to social justice worldwide. Large reductions in per-capita resource- and energy-use rates in the rich nations can be achieved through efficient and renewable-energy technologies. Yet this would be only the first step toward a "conserver" society. Maximum recycling of resources, eliminating unnecessary production, and decentralizing to more self-sufficient, small-scale regional economies will form the basis for such a society. If the developed countries would reduce their resource consumption by just one-third, it could mean a ninefold increase in the quantities available for the developing world.

"The rich must live more simply so that the poor may simply live."
Mahatma Ghandi

Developed world
20% population
80% resources

Developing world
80% population
20% resources

look on a broadly similar status as an unquestionable right for all members of the global community. How can, for example, Europeans enjoy full "health", including spiritual health, when millions of Africans and Asians face a bleak future of basic needs and human dignity denied? Will this not eventually engender an infection of the soul?

After enjoying centuries of material growth, society has suddenly been confronted by a new *Zeitgeist* of problems and uncertainty. This presents an unprecedented opportunity to move on to a more just and sustainable world.

Media power

We can thank the media for blowing the whistle on many instances of social and economic injustice. In India, for example, the unfettered functioning of the press hounds officials into action for reform. In China, by contrast, the persistent bungling by officials and ensuing famines have been allowed to continue with little in the way of free reporting by the media. Fortunately the media has the power to interpret news as well as to report it.

Health

* Education
* Security in old age
* Social safeguards

Global inequities

US citizens spend $5 billion a year on slimming aids, a sum that would help reduce much of the malnutrition in developing countries. American and European farmers receive $60 billion in government subsidies each year to persuade them to produce still bigger beef mountains and milk lakes, while developing-world farming languishes for a similar sum that would go far to upgrading peasant agriculture.

Green governance

Environmentalism is now appearing on political agendas around the world, as witness the rise of the Greens in Europe, North America, India, Kenya, Brazil, and many other places. But it has yet to be incorporated as an integral part of governance. How will future management systems look when the environmental cause becomes entrenched in governments, businesses, banking, academia, and other major forums of public affairs? What is the best way to foster genuine green awareness in institutions right across the board?

Certainly politicians and business leaders are vying with each other to demonstrate their "greenness". But the cosmetic approach is epitomized by the airline that, wanting to prove its commitment, plans to recycle passengers' debris, without doing a thing about the carbon dioxide and other pollutants its aircrafts spew out. If airlines were to internalize the spillover costs of their operations, the price of a ticket would almost double and so put an end to the semifree ride we have been enjoying. No airline has yet announced plans to anticipate the soon-to-come carbon tax and adapt its planning strategies accordingly. Just how thin is the green veneer?

Our environmental efforts represent no more than a solid start. There is a danger that environmentalism will continue to be an appurtenance of workaday-world activities, to be viewed as just another important concern that is being dealt with along with trade, interest rates, and the like. But the environmental imperative will increasingly strike at the heart of all our activities – powerfully if unperceived for the most part. Indeed, until Gaian-scope environmentalism

Great transitions

As Gus Speth, President of the World Resources Institute, states, the arrival of the green millennium requires a series of transitions: a demographic transition toward zero-growth populations; a technological transition from resource-intensive and pollution-prone technologies, to environmentally benign ones; an economic transition based on reliance on nature's income rather than depletion of its capital; a social transition to more equitable sharing of the Earth's resources; and an institutional transition, both national and international, to promote global stability.

A week in October

The British Prime Minister, Mrs Thatcher, instructed her Cabinet on an October Monday in 1989 that the greenhouse effect was to be tackled forthwith. Yet the next day her Chancellor expanded a business perk giving greater tax exemptions for executive cars. On Wednesday her Transport Minister announced a plan to expand the roads network, further subsidizing petrol consumption. On Friday her government slashed the budget of the Energy Efficiency Research Office. Of course other governments share this problem: government departments are typically "territorial" and like to go their own unheeding way.

ranks on a par with human-centred ideologies, we shall fail to recognize it for what it ultimately is, a necessity in the functioning of the Earth and our world. Herein lies the essence of environmentalism: Gaia will remain green in its own way regardless of what we do, and thus our sole course will be to govern greenly on Gaia's terms. Gaia is a democratic entity, all species and their ecosystems making up the true electorate.

Greenery in full flower

As Professor David Pearce has documented in his book *Blueprint for a Green Economy*, environmental governance will require an array of incentives, laws, and other institutional initiatives in order to enshrine the dictates of new environmental realities into our daily lives. They will range from taxes on carbon to fiscal incentives for CFC substitutes and subsidies for efficient energy systems. There will be an end to depletion allowances for oil and coal exploitation, along with other environmentally perverse policies. Car owners, for example, will have to pay the true costs of motoring, while cyclists could be rewarded. Supermarket items will be required to reflect the real costs of manufacturing, transportation, etc, which thus far have been subsidized by, for example, government support for artificially cheap energy. This is all light years ahead of "green consumerism", useful as that has been in enabling the public to take a first tentative step toward the environmental cause. The impact too will be light years ahead of what the public may be expecting in the way of paying its environmental bills. There will be profound repercussions for the economy overall. Much of it will be inflationary, since we shall be paying more for goods and services with the benefit often deferred far into the future. But that will no more than compensate for the free lunches we have been enjoying for decades. Above all, let us bear in mind that the key question is not "Can we afford to do it eventually?" but "How can we not afford to do it immediately?".

Nobody in charge?

Governance – being the aggregate of processes, systems, relationships, and arrangements, both governmental and nongovernmental, by which human communities interact – tends to be a confused, sometimes "messy" affair. It works largely through countless channels of activity and obscure linkages that lie beyond government authority. But while it is often supposed to be a "nobody-in-charge" process, it is rather an "everybody-involved" affair. Because the web of interconnections stretches out in many diverse directions, all manner of people are in a position to contribute. In fact, all in the global village can have a voice in the village square.

So while uncontrolled in any formal fashion and seemingly random, the process is far from unregulated. It is from this very aspect that it draws its strength, since it is free to operate in whatever new manner meets new needs. Far from postulating a leaderless world, it supplies an arena for leaders of multiple types, operating at multiple levels. And instead of being overcentralized, it is polycentric. Such a network of sectoral and functional organizations, with appropriate linkages and "switchboard" mechanisms, is capable of providing a higher degree of self-regulating stability than a galaxy of governments – and even more than could ever be provided by some form of global super-agency.

Note especially the factor of multiple levels. Internationally there is need for supranational organizations that can handle questions of regional or global scope. Governments with their outmoded views of

The grassrooter at work
As more people become engaged in governance through locally based networks that reach around the world, there will be an accretion of "people power" to these grass-rooters. They will best understand local-level problems, both through their own experience and through sharing views with similarly situated people in other lands. By the same token, they will be best placed to devise locally attuned solutions. This will be a welcome departure from remote government with its inflexible and insensitive responses (if responses at all).

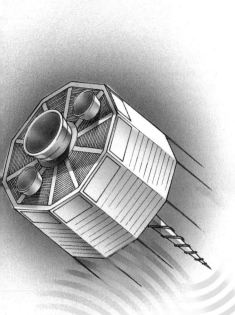

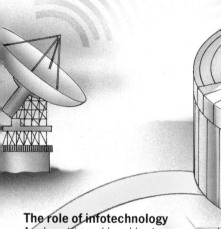

sovereignty will steadily rule themselves out of the game unless they can demonstrate far greater co-operation than hitherto. Fortunately certain of the collaborative functions have already been taken over by international financiers; for example, while several European governments insist the time is not yet ripe for a European Central Bank, the bankers through their co-ordinated exchange rates have already gone far to establishing it in fact if not in name. Equally there will be expanded scope for governance at local level, particularly on the part of citizenry organizations, community councils, and self-help bodies. There should emerge a system where participants interact both horizontally *and* vertically.

The role of infotechnology

A polycentric world could not emerge without the support of infotechnology. Thanks to ultra-rapid computers and communications satellites, there has been an outburst of decentralized networks of common-interest citizens. These "new networkers" know how to make best use of cheap teleconferencing, data-transmission techniques, on-line roundtables, resource-sharing collectives, volunteer-talent pools, and a dozen other innovative forms of intellectual outreach. The upshot should be a light-year's advance in participatory organization – and thus the revolution in information technology is spawning another revolution, the emergent politics of super-participation. It serves to create societies with multitudes of informed people, leading to a diffusion of power. The twin processes serve to promote egalitarian decision-making bolstered by exceptional feedback capacities. In short, computer networks are becoming an increasingly important force for social and political change.

New eco-nomics

Our established approach to assessing our economies is based on gross national product (GNP), the sum total of goods and services produced in the economy. This indicator is, however, increasingly off target, since it takes no account of the natural-resource underpinnings of our economies. It ignores the use, or rather misuse, of capital stocks such as soils, vegetation, water, and climate. So while there is much talk about rates of economic growth, we hear much less, in equally systematized form at least, about rates of environmental decline and the economic consequences. Result: GNP accounting presents a distorted picture of our economic health.

When we make use of resources and assets, such as buildings and equipment that derive from human activity, we write off our use as depreciation. Unfortunately we do not view the environment as productive capital, even though it is used as such. When forests are overharvested, farmlands overworked until the topsoil is spent, and rivers and oceans treated as free garbage sites, GNP actually records an increase in our national fortune. Even more ironically, our efforts to put right the damaged environment are likewise reckoned as economic activities, and thus take GNP up yet another notch. Plainly we need to adapt our conventional accounting procedures to reflect the environmental dimension of our economies.

In short, we require an accounting system that reflects the workings of both our economic activities and their sustaining resource base. Within the near future we shall surely hope to see a government spokes-

Soil erosion

Reforestation

Deforestation

Natural-resource accounting
Developing-nation economies depend heavily on their natural resources. At the same time, these resources are often unduly vulnerable to severe depletion due to the ecological sensitivity of many tropical environments. Ethiopia's forests have been reduced from 25% to 3% of the country, leading to massive soil erosion and a decrease in food production of 1 million tonnes plus per year (equivalent to two-thirds of relief food shipped to that country during the 1985 famine). To have reforested when the problem was readily controllable would have cost $50 million a year – by contrast with the $500 million assigned by the outside world to relief food alone in 1985.

Acid rain
An area of forests in Europe equivalent in size to Britain is injured or dying. Throughout the EC, acid rain damages crops worth about $1 billion annually. Yet its sources, largely power stations and motor vehicles, are reflected as only generating net additions to GNP. With acid rain now affecting large sectors of Eastern Europe, the Soviet Union, Japan, China, and Brazil, the pollution problem is graphic evidence of the need to integrate the environment into economics.

person presenting an overall picture of the national economy in conjunction with its environmental underpinnings.

To illustrate the way we are consuming our environmental capital, consider the case of West Germany in the mid-1980s. Total pollution was running up costs for the economy of at least $51 billion per annum, equivalent at that time to about 5 per cent of GNP. Similarly developing nations have been experiencing desertification resulting in agricultural losses totalling at least $32 billion a year – reflecting the concealed costs of inaction on the UN Anti-Desertification Campaign with its budget of less than $6 billion a year.

GNP   NNP

Environmental cost

Adjusted national product

A new approach proposes that accounting of both "economic flows" and "environmental flows" be integrated into a single system. In France and Norway, depletion of natural resources is now reflected in national economic analyses. In the US and Japan a modified technique focuses on economic quantification of environmental quality as a key component of national welfare. The aim is to produce a *net national product (NNP)*.

Gaian values

Economics has more to say about the environment than its critics sometimes are aware of. But environmental economics are ultimately limited in a way that many economists are reluctant to recognize. Like all economics, it is inherently centred on a single criterion, human welfare: that is the way the world works, and we are primarily motivated by concern for our own wellbeing. Don't worry too much about future generations, since we shall leave them a better world than we came into. But that is not the way the real world works, and never has done. This applies all the more today when we are modifying the world in ways that entrain uniquely profound impacts. Aren't there larger-scope issues at stake than human-centred values? To grapple with these suprahuman issues will require superhuman effort. Again, the future demands of us a visionary leap to match the scale of our impacts on the Gaian world.

Diversity

We are homogenizing both nature and the way we live. Petro-agriculture employs chemicals to create the monoculture ideal for crop growing but highly harmful for most else in the field. The widespread destruction of wildlife habitats grossly reduces genetic diversity, and these trends are mirrored by the pervasive consumer culture.

Our world is becoming one for the masses, with its mass tastes, mass products, mass trends, and mass cultures for mass minds. Hamburgers and cola are standard fare in all major cities. Jeans are a universal uniform, and millions know the words of the latest hit record within days of its release, even though many would not know the words of their national anthems.

Conformism has been a perpetual theme of human societies, not only in oppressive states but in "liberal" countries, by virtue of unvaried materialism, advertising, and the "mechanistic" world view (see pp. 50-1). In salient senses the conformist urge is becoming an unwitting form of cultural repression. Airports, hotels, shopping precincts, housing developments, and even parks are growing increasingly alike. Nor can we look with confidence to education for possible salvation, since many schools simply purvey the dominant culture.

Our future world must emphasize diversity – both cultural as well as genetic. Fortunately there is already a discernible trend in this direction. The more homogenized our lifestyles become, the more we seem inclined to cling to the deeper values, those of language, literature, art, and religion. To quote the well-known American futurists

The fast-food culture
In almost as many countries as not, you can enjoy (or not) one of the proliferating examples of fast-food meals – hamburgers, pizzas, fries, and so on. The aim of these outlets is to produce a standard product of acceptable quality that appeals to the broadest spectrum of population, and do so in the shortest possible time. But is the competition from the fast-food culture in effect curtailing the distinctive regional services that enrich life with variety and choice?

Fostering diversity
Will diversity come to be appreciated as the future currency? Today we witness token diversity in the form of multicultural education, a few networks of wilderness parks, and wild flowers in the corners of fields or at the bottom of gardens. Tomorrow we shall find it to our enduring advantage to live in societies as diverse and polycultural as possible, ones that foster rather than repress the differences enhancing our quality of life. We need to develop a range of options for living, tailored to the local environment to provide models for appropriate education, conservation, work, and leisure.

John Naisbitt and Patricia Aburdene: "As our outer worlds grow more similar, we will increasingly treasure the traditions that spring from within."

Examples abound, even though often in small pockets. In northeastern Spain, for instance, the Catalan language has been reinstated as the official language; in French-speaking Quebec, there are no English-language street signs. Welsh, Basque, Maori, and native American cultures are not making a comeback, they have always been there but largely ignored. Now they are simply reasserting themselves.

The modern *mauvaise foi*
The belief in the "One True Way", with its missionaries for the Dream World or religious fundamentalism, is the *mauvaise foi* of the modern world, giving rise to a basic conflict in the modern mind: packaged predictability versus people doing things in their own way. Likewise, single-mindedness versus diversity of cultures or species.

Dynamic peace

Just as health is more than the absence of disease, so peace is much more than the absence of war. It is a state of dynamic stability that has to be actively maintained. It is an end to violence among human beings and, by extension, to the planet. When this relationship is understood and accepted and when basic needs are met, there exists the opportunity for positive peace. While many people talk about peace building, they rarely specify what it means. Not that they have had much chance to practise it, since peace-building activities have not received even 1 per cent of 1 per cent of what has been spent on war activities.

First and foremost, peace on Earth means peace with the Earth. As this book has repeatedly made plain, we are engaged in World War III, a war against the planet, a war that is no contest. We must negotiate terms of surrender to the new environmental dictates, recognizing that victory over the Earth would be a no-win outcome. In turn, this postulates a new form of security, environmental security. As President Gorbachev was one of the first to point out, the threat from the sky is no longer missiles but climate change. Stealth bombers cannot be launched against this uniquely threatening adversary – just as tanks cannot be mobilized to counter rising sea levels, nor troops despatched to block the advance of the encroaching desert.

So peace with the Earth implies peace with each other, a peace comprising three essential components: relations of harmony among people in society; co-operation for the common good; and justice based on the

Green security
With the thawing of the Cold War, some of the erstwhile military outlays could be directed toward building a more secure world. According to Robert McNamara and other experts, NATO countries could soon release $175 billion a year from military budgets. Soviet leaders indicate they could release perhaps $100 billion a year, funds needed to rebuild the Soviet economy. According to Lester Brown, President of the Worldwatch Institute, to restore environmental security would cost: protecting topsoil around $9 billion in 1991; restoring forests $3 billion; halting the spread of deserts $4 billion; supplying clean water $30 billion; raising energy efficiency $10 billion; developing renewable energy $5 billion; slowing population growth $18 billion; and retiring developing world debt $30 billion. This total of $109 billion would need to rise to $170 billion a year by 2000 – still no more than eight weeks' military spending at late 1980s levels.

The role of nonviolence
Nuclear power has forced us to contemplate both extinction and new forms of conflict resolution. The latter could soon become much more common. Nonviolence however goes far beyond ensuring peace by reducing military budgets or halting environmental destruction. As well as the weapons, we must also eliminate the "mind" that brought them into being and contemplated their use.

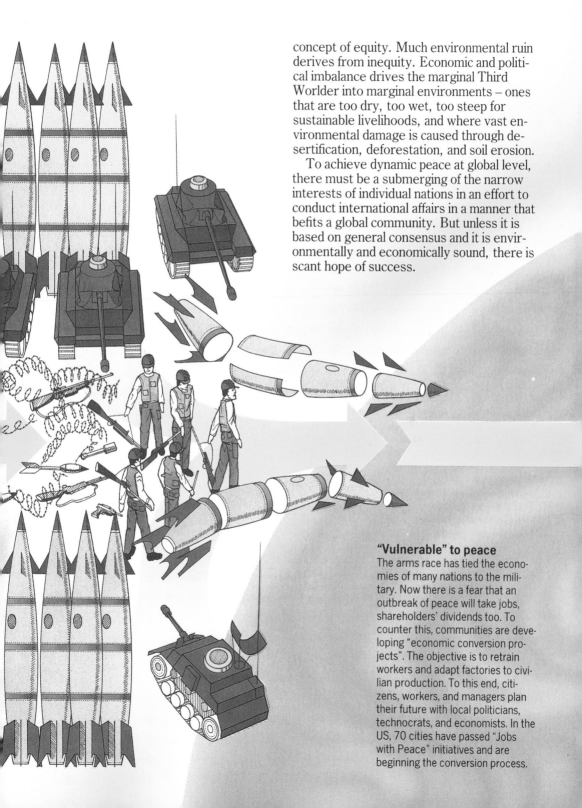

concept of equity. Much environmental ruin
derives from inequity. Economic and political imbalance drives the marginal Third
Worlder into marginal environments – ones
that are too dry, too wet, too steep for
sustainable livelihoods, and where vast environmental damage is caused through desertification, deforestation, and soil erosion.

To achieve dynamic peace at global level,
there must be a submerging of the narrow
interests of individual nations in an effort to
conduct international affairs in a manner that
befits a global community. But unless it is
based on general consensus and it is environmentally and economically sound, there is
scant hope of success.

"Vulnerable" to peace

The arms race has tied the economies of many nations to the military. Now there is a fear that an
outbreak of peace will take jobs,
shareholders' dividends too. To
counter this, communities are developing "economic conversion projects". The objective is to retrain
workers and adapt factories to civilian production. To this end, citizens, workers, and managers plan
their future with local politicians,
technocrats, and economists. In the
US, 70 cities have passed "Jobs
with Peace" initiatives and are
beginning the conversion process.

Planetary citizenship

We started out on our human enterprise with loyalty to a hunting band of a few dozen people. From there we successively expanded our allegiance to the village, town, city, region, and eventually the nation. At each stage our sense of community grew, until today we feel a part of societies of millions. Yet the greatest loyalty leap awaits us. Can we now raise our vision to embrace the whole of humanity, Gaia too? So great is this challenge that it will rank as the second true step away from the cave's threshold.

First, we need to identify with a global community of individuals whose names we do not know, whose faces we shall never see, whose traditions we may not share, and whose hopes we shall not know, but who are all, whether they are aware of it or not, *de facto* members of a single society. Second, we must foster a super-allegiance to Gaia, and frame our actions accordingly. Can we learn in time to identify with these two ultimate communities?

This need not present any conflict of interest. When we salute our countries' flags, we are not thereby denying bonds with families or neighbourhoods. We are simply acknowledging a greater context of kindred spirits, a loftier level of allegiance. So our new planetary loyalty will not diminish established links; rather it will enhance them by adding perspective to local attachments.

There could, however, be some exceptions. What when a country asks us to do something against the global good? To hold back for the sake of the national economy on

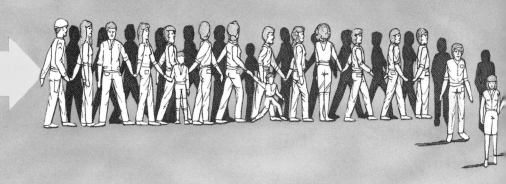

Transcending politics

Traditional politics concerns itself with the managing of social systems. This view will need to be considerably broadened to take into account the concept of planetary citizenship. The best politics will enable people and communities to create their own solutions to their own problems within a larger context. But a prerequisite will be the moulding of a new environmental/political consensus from the pre-sent anti-environmental world. Among initiatives that could soon become commonplace is an Earth Corps, an organization providing a framework for people, young and old, to make a personal contribution to the planet. The potential is vast, not only in terms of work to be done but the reservoir of people and energy waiting to be mobilized on behalf of the Earth.

Rising above the nation-state

We are suspended at a hinge of history, between two ages – that of competitive nationalism and that of co-operative internationalism. Nationhood is becoming a pernicious anachronism, a primitive phenomenon like feudalism or slavery. Future generations will surely consider that nationhood was a transient phase in society's development, a holding measure until the emergence of planetary citizenship.

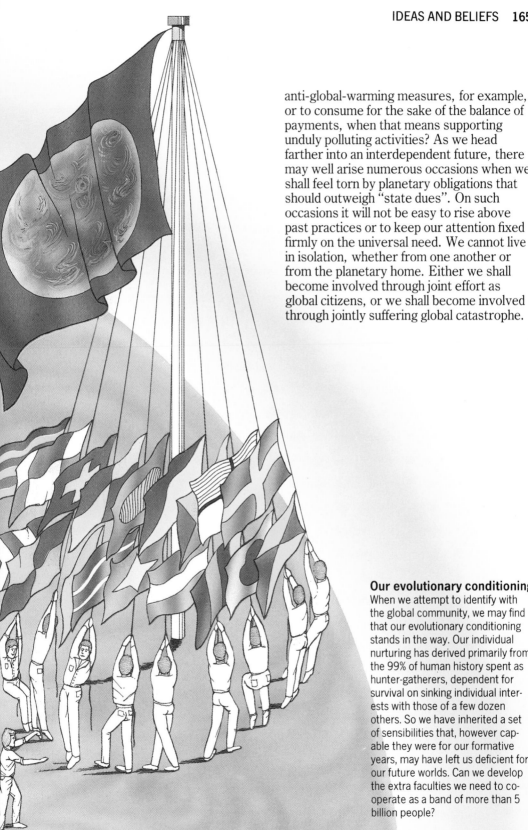

anti-global-warming measures, for example, or to consume for the sake of the balance of payments, when that means supporting unduly polluting activities? As we head farther into an interdependent future, there may well arise numerous occasions when we shall feel torn by planetary obligations that should outweigh "state dues". On such occasions it will not be easy to rise above past practices or to keep our attention fixed firmly on the universal need. We cannot live in isolation, whether from one another or from the planetary home. Either we shall become involved through joint effort as global citizens, or we shall become involved through jointly suffering global catastrophe.

Our evolutionary conditioning

When we attempt to identify with the global community, we may find that our evolutionary conditioning stands in the way. Our individual nurturing has derived primarily from the 99% of human history spent as hunter-gatherers, dependent for survival on sinking individual interests with those of a few dozen others. So we have inherited a set of sensibilities that, however capable they were for our formative years, may have left us deficient for our future worlds. Can we develop the extra faculties we need to cooperate as a band of more than 5 billion people?

A law unto ourselves

In a new-age world we shall learn to be our own legal experts, in that we shall have to devise rules for living in a crowded global community without treading on anybody else's prerogatives. We shall need to recognize that planetary citizenship entails responsibilities as well as rights; and we shall have to learn that it is in our own best interests to be our own private law enforcer. Not that this concept is anything new in itself. The rule of law has always depended on a strong supporting consensus of the citizenry, without which the best-intentioned laws fail. Consider, for example, the debacle of the Prohibition years in America. But this time around there will be such an abundance and complexity of laws, regulations, and rules, whether formal or unwritten, that there cannot be enough

police to keep everyone on the straight and narrow. We must devise our own path ahead, and follow it because it is in our own best interests.

This mode of behaviour will be in stark contrast to the free-wheeling years of a simpler and less vulnerable world, one where there was no threat of terminal breakdown in society through outright environmental collapse. With multiplying numbers of people, multiplying demands, and multiplying linkages through our increasing interdependency, both environmental and economic, there will be multiplying scope for disruption and dislocation. The answer will lie with the dictum of "Mutual coercion, mutually agreed upon". But this need not be a fraction as "Big Brotherish" as it may sound. It will replace the unlicensed

Roundabouts or traffic lights?
Law-abiding societies of the future must operate by consensus, rather than by the threat of punishment. Communally agreed codes will be the order of the day, not dictates passed down from some distant national assembly. When we all agree to drive on the same side of the road we make no sacrifice of personal freedom – rather our freedom is enhanced by communal consensus. As we progress into the future we shall find that we will be driving ever-more sophisticated models (of the figurative type) at higher speeds, and sharing the road with ever-more drivers. This will necessitate more "traffic control" to facilitate everybody's journey. These controls can take the form of roundabouts (communal codes with which people have licence to assess, evaluate, and make decisions) or traffic lights (specific laws that require simple acquiescence).

liberty of yesterday with new forms of freedom for tomorrow – an expansive and a disciplined freedom.

Above all, the new "world of laws" will be all the more acceptable in that it will not be a top-down affair, by contrast with the situation in the past. It will be a grass-roots process, a home-grown homage to largely local imperatives. Communal laws will be more like social codes, finely tuned to local needs – a world away from the rigidity of conventional laws.

Local control in Sweden
Flexible, local systems of sharing and control are becoming a feature of codes of conduct of certain smaller nations. In Sweden, for example, most of the unionized workforce is solidly behind its government's new programme of economic decentralization. In each one of Sweden's two dozen counties, a proportion of the workforce's earnings is automatically paid into a public fund administered by an elected board. The accumulated funds are used to purchase shares in local industries, which are then publicly controlled. Local economic control is thus back in the hands of the community, where decisions can be made in light of local needs.

"Law and order exist for the purpose of establishing justice. . . . When they fail to do this they become the dangerously structured dams that block the flow of social justice . . ."
Martin Luther King

The genie out of the bottle

Our technological capacities are such that it is now possible to reshape our world from top to bottom – not only our planetary living space and the Gaian system itself, but our social relations, our individual inner worlds, all that we are and do. The record to date does not presage a future as constructive and bountiful as we might wish. Unbridled technology already threatens our very life-support systems. Yet technology could be one of the greatest boons for the human condition, for Gaia too, provided we ensure that it serves our overall interests. We need to take a long look at the role of technology in our future world and to ask how we can take systematic control of its multifarious impacts. We have released the genie from its bottle, and even if we perversely wished, we cannot return it. The present challenge

is to control the genie before it controls us in unwitting ways that we cannot remotely discern.

What then is to be the future role of technology, as of its scientific underpinnings? The new physics (see pp. 50-1) shows us that what scientists observe in nature is intimately conditioned by their minds. Hence scientific and technological applications are also conditioned by the mind and thus by human values. Scientists are not only intellectually responsible for their research, they are also morally responsible. In turn, should not scientists and technologists now be required to take methodical cognizance of the impacts of their endeavours, whether environmental, social, or even political?

True, this would mark a profound change

Human hubris

Our overweening attitude toward the natural world is a recurring theme in cultures right from the Ancient World. For stealing fire from the gods, Prometheus was chained and tortured. It seems always to have been accepted that there are some areas of enquiry that are simply off limits in view of the potential costs they entrain. The question now is to determine which precisely these areas are. While we understand so little of the world about us, especially the expanding world of the future, we must move from hubris to humility and practise a cautious rather than a Promethean approach.

Self-imposed audits

Already some ecology professors are proposing that students' dissertations should include a chapter on the social implications of their findings. In some cases, these implications will be virtually nil, in many others they will be of marginal consequence, in certain others they will be significant. Whatever the outcome, the exercise will induce an explicit awareness that science and technology can no longer be practised in a vacuum.

in our attitudes to science, as to its role in society. Many scientists would be aghast at the notion that their research should somehow be trammelled. But this is not to assert that all science should be subject to detailed constraints. There must always be abundant place for the pursuit of knowledge and understanding, whatever it reveals. Yet the overall context of science should surely be examined to see whether we can determine some limits to its unfortunate technological by-products. It is this new dimension, placing a check on undesirable fall-out, that is the key to controlling the genie.

Genetic engineering

To date, genetic engineering has caused no regrettable spillovers on to the environment. The potential, however, is certainly there as new organisms are introduced into natural communities at an increasing rate. After all, an earlier effort at improved breeding of livestock in the form of a goat variety adapted to harsh environments – hailed as an undoubted success at the time – led to semi-arid lands becoming arid lands. The new breeders, for example, gene splicers using recombinant DNA technology, need to exercise far more scrupulous care as they release multitudes of entirely new organisms. While it is unlikely that the newcomers could ever become dominant on a broad scale, they could well cause local ecological disasters that could not readily be controlled. Unfortunately there is a tendency for expectations and benefits to be overestimated, while costs and problems receive short shrift – as is often the case during the early stages of the development of any new technology. The prospect of hosts of newly minted organisms warrants exceptional caution rather than a "rush-in" approach. Yet we have scarcely started to assess the legal, let alone ethical, issues at stake.

Responsible technology

Modern society is hooked on technology, one that gives us life-saving hospital units and liberating communications, also nuclear weapons and soulless production lines. We are led to believe that there is a technofix for every social ill and global problem – and if technology goes wrong, then technology will put it right again. Yet we continue to feed off ecodestructive agriculture, to use products from energy-wasteful industries, and to live lives in technology-ravaged environments.

Our notions of wealth and welfare, competition and efficiency, are grounded in technology. The progress of technology is supposed to be unstoppable: it represents the crowning achievement of human enterprise, and other notions of progress come second. But our resource-intensive, overcentralized technology is making itself obsolete. Petro-

chemical agribusiness, nuclear power, fuel-guzzling cars are environmental disasters. Yet we still have to devise guidelines for our present technology, let alone the fast-expanding technology of the future. What technology is "right"?

The answer lies with technology that supports humankind in our need to live in accord *with* the planet rather than in dominion *over* it: technology with a planetary face. Many technologies for sustainability already exist in the form of so-called "soft technologies", for instance those that utilize renewable resources and recycled materials. A good number of these technologies are already familiar to us: energy-saving devices; ultra-efficient motors; solar energy conversion; wind, wave, and tidal power utilization; organic farming; semiconductors; and super-

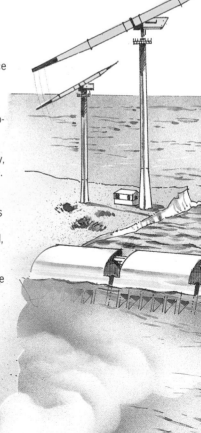

A new orientation
To solve the multiple crises we face, we don't need more energy-intensive technologies. We need to shift our emphasis from nonrenewable to renewable resources, from hard to soft technologies. But this alone will not be sufficient without a thorough-going cultural change – a move away from the mechanistic "we can fix it" mentality to a more careful and caring approach. This in turn will require the most basic retooling of all: wholescale shifts in our attitudes, lifestyles, and values.

The solar future
The planet's principal energy source is the sun, with its potential for limitless, nonpolluting energy. Life has evolved to make optimum use of this form of energy. Plants photosynthesize food with the aid of the sun's radiation, and in turn provide the conditions, directly or indirectly, for practically all other forms of life. Solar energy can either be "passive", as when the fabric of a building heats up and then releases its energy, or "active", as in the example of solar collectors. As well, the sun's energy raises air masses that drive wind turbines, and it also energizes the water cycle, which we harness as hydropower. Bear in mind that solar energy is not only available everywhere, it is a source of diverse energy types, hence adapted to decentralized technologies in local communities.

chips. The challenge is to create a flexible, benign, and humane technology – a process that will also allow us to exercise our full creativity. Indeed a crucial factor in this new technology will be its readiness to draw much more on a resource we already possess in abundance – human ingenuity.

In this regard, the soft technologies are often ideal, since they tend to be small scale and decentralized. And, being generally labour intensive, they help to establish a local economy, one that is flexible and sensitive to local conditions.

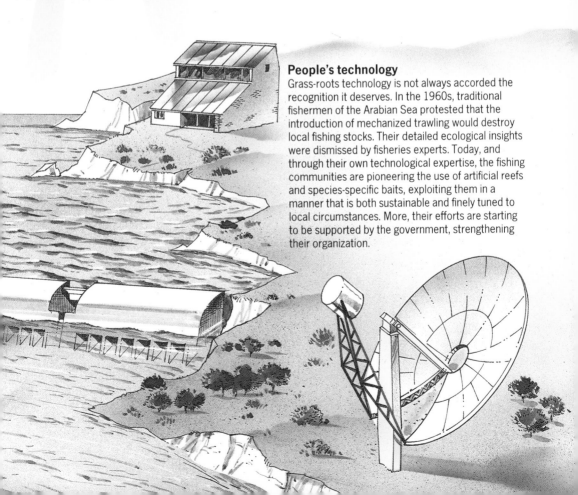

People's technology

Grass-roots technology is not always accorded the recognition it deserves. In the 1960s, traditional fishermen of the Arabian Sea protested that the introduction of mechanized trawling would destroy local fishing stocks. Their detailed ecological insights were dismissed by fisheries experts. Today, and through their own technological expertise, the fishing communities are pioneering the use of artificial reefs and species-specific baits, exploiting them in a manner that is both sustainable and finely tuned to local circumstances. More, their efforts are starting to be supported by the government, strengthening their organization.

From agriculture to Gaiaculture

For millennia human agriculture has been based on the idea that we only need to simplify ecosystems in order to make them more productive for food growing. Unfortunately agro-ecosystems then become vulnerable to diseases and pests: the miracle grains of the Green Revolution have spawned miracle blights and rats. When we try to subdue nature instead of working with it, nature eventually has its emphatic way.

Thus our agriculture has attempted to override the critical and inexorable laws of ecosystems. We have even supposed we could engage in industrial agriculture based on fossil-fuel energy – a mode of eating oil. Now we need to shift to an approach that deploys scientific skills to enhance "natural" agriculture, with emphasis on lower inputs and reduced energy. In turn this new-age

agriculture will expand to embrace even more radical strategies, such as greater dependence on perennial crops, which require less intervention in nature's systems through, for example, annual ploughing and sowing for single-season harvests. Of course we shall still need grain crops to supply most of our food, and being grass-type plants they will require major manipulation of ecosystems. But grain crops can be grown through polyculture rather than monoculture. This will be all the more essential as we try to grow more food on croplands that are likely to have declined to one-third less per person than in today's inadequately fed world.

Thus the new agriculture will be a case of working with nature rather than against it. Instead of bending the environment to suit

An ecological agriculture

As an American agricultural expert, Edward Kormondy, points out: "We have proposed, but nature has disposed, often in unexpected ways counter to our intent. Simple ecosystems such as a cornfield are youthful ones, and like our own youth, are volatile, unpredictable, and unstable. Young ecosystems do not conserve nutrients, and lack resistance to pests and disease, so they have to be protected artificially and expensively by fertilizers and pesticides. Must not our proposals for managing agricultural systems be mindful of nature's managerial strategy of providing biological diversity to help sustain most complex ecosystems? What of our own manicured lawns?"

the plant through cultivation, irrigation, fertilizers, and the rest of the massive inputs of modern agriculture, the aim should be to bend the plant to suit the environment. Thanks to the breakthroughs of genetic engineering (see pp. 60-1), there is now prospect of a Gene-Revolution agriculture where we tailor crop species to fit in with ecosystems. The peat soils of the Great Lakes area in North America, for example, hitherto offering little agricultural potential, now feature soil-adapted strains of blueberries that support a multimillion-dollar agro-industry. While this radical approach is still in its infancy, it offers eventual hope for us to reap the benefits of nature's bounty in more productive manner than our heavy-handed techniques to date – and in far more sustainable fashion.

A lesson from the East

China, Japan, and Taiwan practise a more biological than industrial agriculture. While not so productive per worker as the European and North American model, it gives higher yields per hectare and requires fewer additives. This approach could form part of a shift from a demand-driven to a resource-limited agriculture.

Less meat

If we were to stop feeding one-third of the global grain harvest to livestock and poultry, we would find that we could afford less meat. This would mean that the affluent minority would have to shift down the food chain and adopt a diet with a higher proportion of grains and vegetables – which will also be better for their health.

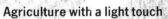

Agriculture with a light touch

Rather than ploughing deep furrows, the low-till farmer scrapes the soil's surface before planting seeds. To counteract weeds, more mulches and herbicides may be used. But "light touch" agriculture maximizes crop-residue cover on the land, and conserves soil, organic matter, water, fertilizer, and energy. Steep lands can also be utilized without fear of erosion. In the US as much as one-third of croplands feature the low-till approach, a figure expected to exceed half within ten years. Other innovations entail the application of traditional principles: crop rotation, multiple cropping, and agroforestry.

Science for people and planet

Beyond "responsible technology" the need is to establish a science that is intrinsically holistic (see pp. 56-7), a science that addresses the needs of both people and planet. Incorporating the findings of the new physics and new maths (see pp. 50-1 and 54-5), it should adopt a systems approach to knowledge, hence embracing psychology, sociology, ethics, whatever is germane to the superscience that is required to meet the expansive needs of our future worlds.

This new science will inevitably be interdisciplinary, with emphasis on the so-called grey areas between established disciplines: after all, the world does not run in discrete compartments, nor should our efforts to understand it. It is precisely because we have disregarded these grey areas, with their dynamic interactions, that many of our environmental problems have arisen (solve a problem in one area, and create a problem in another). Yet interdisciplinary subjects are still viewed by traditionalists as less than true science. As a result, the comparative amount of funding to, for example, ecology, an intrinsically interdisciplinary endeavour, is trifling: in the US, it is not 1 per cent of what is assigned to molecular biology. And we are a long way from seeing the awarding of a Nobel Prize for ecology.

Fortunately there are signs that established science can still pause and check its foundations. Holistic medicine proclaims there is more to a sick person than a body; there is a person whose nonphysical makeup may be contributing to the sickness. Chaos

Science for whom?

Science seeks to mobilize the resources of the planet to serve humankind. The time has come when we should mobilize human resources to serve the planet (if only for our own sake). This will require a profound reorientation in those aspects of science that are inherently human-centred, a feature common to science from the Ancient Greeks, through the Renaissance, and right up to modern times. By contrast, aspects of Oriental science focus first on the planet, then on humanity's place in it.

Science and society

Because of its preoccupation with serving the human cause first and last, Western science has never been as "value free" as is traditionally supposed. At the same time, it is often reluctant to acknowledge the built-in factor of social responsibility. It asserts that it does not want to be trammelled by considerations of its impacts on society, even though it is deeply involved with social issues. While science should not be unreasonably limited in its endeavours – pure science has produced many spinoff benefits – we need a newly expansive framework within which science can pursue its new mission, to safeguard the planet, and society within it, at a time of wholly new threat.

theory is calling into question certain of the central tenets of physics and maths. Biology and agriculture are finding they could well join hands with anthropology: much is to be learned from "primitive" peoples with their folkloric insights from centuries of experiments with their environments. A few pioneering economists, brave souls that they are, are recognizing that there are critical environmental constraints to conventional analyses, and that "standard economic growth forever" cannot have that much longer to run.

Indeed the time is long past when it was urgent for the new superscience to get to grips with the demands of a world facing super-threats.

Demography in a vacuum

As an example of single-disciplinary science, hence restrictive science, consider demography. Many demographers continue with their projections of population growth, ostensibly indifferent to such factors as the need for present communities to find the wherewithal to support themselves throughout a normal lifespan: it is demography in an "environmental vacuum". Who can realistically suppose that sub-Saharan Africa's population will expand five times over, as is projected? The continued publication of this projection lends credence to the idea that it could somehow be possible, and damps down the urgent need for African leaders to move more vigorously with family-planning efforts. True, demographers object that they are coming up with projections of past trends, not predictions of future outcomes. But they should indicate as well that cogent environmental factors also pertain to their findings – to which demographers are inclined to respond that they are not environmentalists.

From knowledge to wisdom

As T S Eliot once asked: "Where is the knowledge we have lost in information? Where is the wisdom we have lost in knowledge?" Obviously knowledge is an essential component of wisdom, but there is more to it than that. While we possess knowledge in abundance, the world about us proclaims that we are falling woefully short of the step from knowledge to wisdom.

Our long tradition of reductionist analysis has brought us to a state where we often find that we are learning more and more about less and less. Result: our attention is diverted from the whole that is more than the sum of its parts. Confronted with the disjunct pieces of a watch, would we guess that when reassembled they would make up a mechanism for telling the time? Yet we meddle with the intricate components of our planetary ecosystem, no less, and suppose we can do so with impunity, even concluding that certain pieces are forever dispensable. We are unwittingly engaged in global-scale experiments, not only environmental but technological and social experiments, without a thought for their global consequences. Yet these grandiose experiments demand the most scrupulous care, and would tax the faculties of the wisest.

Moreover there is much that we, whether scientist or not, can discern in terms of values without understanding the details. We do not need to understand the physical or chemical make-up of a weapon to realize it is designed to destroy. We do not need endless reports on the influence of the media to see their power to misinform.

Thus far we have tended to head blithely

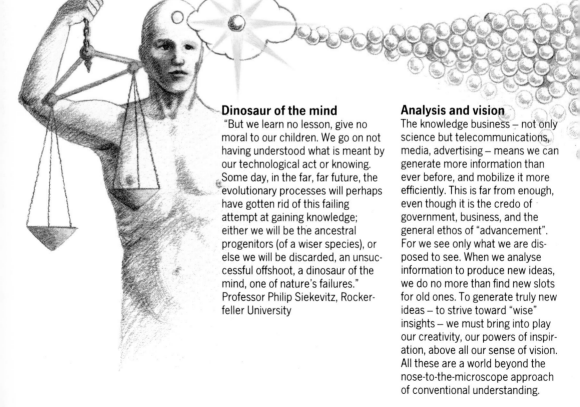

Dinosaur of the mind

"But we learn no lesson, give no moral to our children. We go on not having understood what is meant by our technological act or knowing. Some day, in the far, far future, the evolutionary processes will perhaps have gotten rid of this failing attempt at gaining knowledge; either we will be the ancestral progenitors (of a wiser species), or else we will be discarded, an unsuccessful offshoot, a dinosaur of the mind, one of nature's failures."
Professor Philip Siekevitz, Rockerfeller University

Analysis and vision

The knowledge business – not only science but telecommunications, media, advertising – means we can generate more information than ever before, and mobilize it more efficiently. This is far from enough, even though it is the credo of government, business, and the general ethos of "advancement". For we see only what we are disposed to see. When we analyse information to produce new ideas, we do no more than find new slots for old ones. To generate truly new ideas – to strive toward "wise" insights – we must bring into play our creativity, our powers of inspiration, above all our sense of vision. All these are a world beyond the nose-to-the-microscope approach of conventional understanding.

toward a "universal horizon" and have
limited ourselves to doing a better job in
getting from here to there – "there" being
something that reflects the common understanding of most people. We make sure that
we travel along smoothly in a car that is in
good order and with enough fuel. Beyond
our present crossroads, however, that will
not suffice. Often enough we shall need to
consider the proper road to follow. The
landscape ahead is no longer preordained by
"where we have always been going before".
Increasingly we shall find that we need to
choose a different route, change the car,
even ask whether we want to travel at all.
All the fast-growing knowledge in the world
will not help us if we do not have the wisdom
to look out all over the world, and to decide
where we feel most at home.

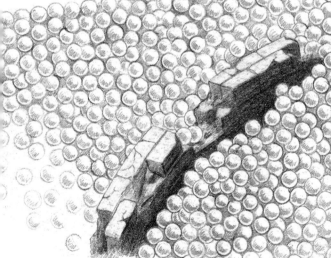

Knowledge as private property

The trend toward privatized knowledge is regrettable. While the
patenting of ideas is a valid safeguard, the wholesale locking away
of knowledge as private property,
walled by legal defences, can only
redound to our collective detriment.
Instance the North-South gap:
whether wittingly or not, the technological underpinnings of the
knowledge explosion in the developed nations are acting to exclude
developing nations from one of the
most productive phenomena of our
age. How ironic if the knowledge
resources in the North serve to
impoverish further the South. Surely
we will recognize that knowledge
should be generally available in the
public domain, serving the needs of
everyone. Only as the walls around
knowledge crumble away will the
shared experience of all contribute
to dawnings of wisdom.

From talking to listening

We talk interminably. We tell each other that the quality of life depends on the quantity of livelihood; that more possessions confer fulfilment; that the problems of technology can be solved by still more technology; that weaponry is the path to peace; and that the Earth is made for humans above all other life. Amid this babble, we need to pause and try what we do all too little – to listen.

Listening is not a passive affair. Rather, there can be active, involved listening, listening with all our senses. Then we may hear new messages, not only from each other (from within ourselves too) but also from the natural world around us. We have been inclined to view the natural world with utilitarian spirit, bent on exploiting it for all it is worth. Instead of "shouting at the planet", what if we were to "listen to ecosystems"

and hear whatever they have to say? This is not as fanciful as it sounds. Our approach has been too targeted, predetermined by what we want to hear, what they should be telling us. What about more simple observation after the style of the early naturalists with their open-ended approach, preconceptions left at home? Then we might hear all manner of answers to questions we have not even thought to ask.

We could also do a better job of listening to each other. Politics, law, the marketplace, and the nation-state all place a premium on confrontation and arguing down the "other side". This may have suited bygone times, but today's world places a special premium on joint effort to tackle joint problems – which in turn places an extra-special premium on listening to diverse

From embattled culture to enabling culture

By being at loggerheads with each other and the world, we have permitted our culture to become embattled. It is at odds with itself in the face of conflicting demands, as crass consumerism struggles with the urge for something more. If we could relieve the tensions, we could cultivate a sense of harmony restored – harmony with our separate selves, then with each other and with the world. The result would be an enabling culture that releases our collective capacity, indeed our creativity, to strive toward a society that befits our innate sense of what accords.

views, trying to understand them (even if not agreeing with them), and seeking for common ground.

Above all, we should listen to ourselves. If we can regain contact with our spiritual selves – with what touches our own beings – then we could pick up intuitive insights that are too often lost amid the din within ourselves. Let us not play down, in deference to over-intellectualized analysis, the value of our "instinctive sense" of what fits, what is enduringly right.

In short, we should seek for an enhanced awareness, attained through higher levels of sensitivity – to ourselves, to each other, and to the world around us. We need to develop finer hearing and sharper eyesight among our other senses, leading ultimately to sensation-al understanding.

Treading a new path

"In time of war and misfortune people often turn again to poetry and to wondering how they have gone astray and lost the true path of the Self. In times of prosperity they are often distracted from such philosophical reflection. . . . I predict that as industry and the rational way of life cease to deliver the real goods, we shall turn inward and outward in new ways . . . the local community will once again become important as the best environment for personal life and craftmanship."
Robert Waller, *Be Human or Die*

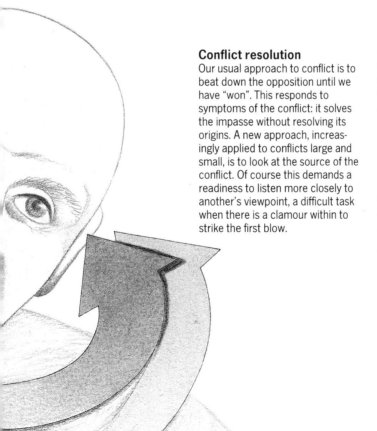

Conflict resolution

Our usual approach to conflict is to beat down the opposition until we have "won". This responds to symptoms of the conflict: it solves the impasse without resolving its origins. A new approach, increasingly applied to conflicts large and small, is to look at the source of the conflict. Of course this demands a readiness to listen more closely to another's viewpoint, a difficult task when there is a clamour within to strike the first blow.

Listening to the birds

We have recently learned that whales and elephants communicate with each other (see pp. 144-5) in all manner of sophisticated ways. But that message for us has long remained beyond our hearing because we have supposed that they have nothing to say. We have also learned that wild creatures are far more attuned to their environment than we have given them credit for – again because we have not "listened" to them or their environment. If we stop telling ourselves that we have a sufficient idea already of what they can and cannot do, we shall find that we can tune in to their networks and pick up unsuspected messages. The more we keep quiet, the more we shall receive them loud and clear.

Conclusion

The future of the future

This book has revealed our future worlds – or rather, some of them. There are many others discernible already, and many more will become apparent as we head into the future. For however much is uncertain about the future, one thing is definite: new worlds will constantly unfold, with their new problems *and* their new possibilities. In some senses, in fact, there will be as many possible futures as there are people. We are all deeply involved, whether we appreciate it or not; we shall all play our individual parts. Indeed there has never been a time like the present when the individual can *count*. So a prime aim of this book has been to show the reader how to envision the future, and to decide how to contribute – if only at the local level, which will often be the best level.

The shadows over our future remind us that the optimist proclaims this is the best of all possible worlds, while the pessimist responds that is regrettably true. We must stay hopeful, otherwise we might as well go to the beach until the sky falls in. But let us not be seduced by an airy hope that somehow all will work out in the wash: the laundry water likely contains too many pollutants. There are prophets who assert we should not worry about the prospect of feeding 10 billion people when it is theoretically possible to feed four times as many. As Paul and Anne Ehrlich point out, it is theoretically possible too for your favourite football team to win every game for the next ten years. In any case, the Ehrlichs continue, what is the sense in converting the Earth into a gigantic human feedlot? How about more quality of life for fewer people? Moreover a future of "the same as usual, only more so" would be a future that for many people would simply not arrive.

If further persuasion is necessary, recall that of the 31 major civilizations in history, only one remains a dominant force, so-called Western civilization. As the historian Arnold Toynbee demonstrates, the rest disappeared because they tried to become dominant on every side – over their neighbours, their environments, whatever else they cast their eyes on. Western civilization, materialist to beat any other, shows plenty of signs of dominating the entire world into an ultimate crunch.

No doubt about it, we stand at a hiatus in the human enterprise. The present is so different from the past, and the present so different from the future, that it is as if we are at a hiatus in the course of human affairs. It is a unique time: a time of breakdown or breakthrough.

To break through into a future of undreamed potential, we must enable a new sort of society to be born. Indeed the stresses of the present are like the stresses of being born, a time of utmost threat yet with new life ahead. Or, to shift the analogy, our society is like a human being growing up. From the start it shows boundless appetite for resources of every type. This appetite continues throughout the first two decades of physical growth, expanding all the while. Then it suddenly levels off. This does not mean the person's growth is at an end. On the contrary, the richest stage of growth begins – mental, intellectual, emotional, and spiritual growth, growth that extends many times longer than the early phase.

Our global society is still adolescent – lusty, vigorous, and assertive. Can we move on to maturity – assured, stable, and sensitive, displaying all the attributes of adulthood? Are we ready to grow up? To shift from egosystem to eco-system, to social compact and whatever else is needed for us to become citizens of the globe and of Gaia?

Are we ready, in fact, to engage in the most salient experience of adulthood, the mutuality of love? Nothing less will do. Finally we can recognize that there is no longer any "we" and "they". For the first time, and for all time, there is only "us" – all of us humans, together with all our fellow species and other members of the Gaian community.

This will be the greatest of our global experiments. As we measure up to the challenge, we shall need to become giants of the human condition. As we approach our climacteric – never attempted before, surely never to be repeated with such instantaneous speed – let us count ourselves fortunate to be living at this hour. No generation of the past has been presented with such a chance to rise above the tide of human history. No generation of the future will have our chance, because if we do not do the job they will have little left but to pick up the pieces. What a privileged generation we are.

What's possible; what's probable

What lies ahead? This section looks at an array of possibilities that may prompt us to speculate on what else is in store. The following list is highly selective and no more than illustrative. The items derive from analyses of experts who use techniques such as scenario planning to think methodically about the future. Futurists based at universities have set up entire departments for futures studies. There are commissions on the future, established by individual governments, United Nations agencies, the City of Tokyo, and the like. The World Future Society, based in Washington DC, organizes regular conferences on all aspects of the future. But the most remarkable feature of this futurist community is not that there are so many people thinking about what the future holds, but that there are so few.

Among some prospective developments are the following:

Global environment

During the 1990s and as the greenhouse effect takes hold, we could witness persistent droughts over much of North America, sub-Saharan Africa, and China. Together with repeated failures of the Indian monsoon and other climatic quirks, plus the most expansive phase of the population explosion, there could ensue a greater outbreak of starvation in a single year early next century than throughout the 1980s, even culminating in the deaths of one billion people in just one decade. This worst-case scenario, by no means implausible, would amount to a human catastrophe of unique proportions.

In the longer-term future, a one-metre rise in sea level by the middle of next century could, when combined with storm surges reaching far inland, plus saltwater intrusions up rivers, threaten a total area of 5 million sq km – or one-third of today's croplands and home to one billion people already. Also on the cards is the prospect of mass migrations in the wake of the greenhouse effect. On the Chinese side of the Sino-Soviet border there are already acute pressures from 1300 persons per square kilometre, by contrast with only one person to every 2.5 square kilometres on the Siberian side. What when China starts to suffer the full rigours of global warming?

Geopolitics

Consider the following scenario. In the year 2000 the world has 350 billionaires, at least 4 million millionaires, and 250 million homeless. The average income of the top 1 billion people has reached 50 times more than that of the bottom 1 billion. More than 50 nations no longer qualify as developing nations; they are disintegrating nations. Americans spend $10 billion per year on slimming diets, while 1 billion people are so undernourished that they are semi-starving. Water from a single spring in France is still shipped to the affluent around the world, while a full 2.5 billion people lack access to clean water for basic needs. It has become plain that poverty is a luxury we can no longer afford.

Furthermore, in the year 1999 there has been a series of crises on top of widespread starvation. Chernobyl-type accidents have occurred in four nations. The North Sea has been declared beyond foreseeable recovery. The most bountiful marine ecosystem on Earth, the Southern Ocean, has collapsed after UV-B radiation knocks out the phytoplankton. A nuclear terrorist has destroyed Cairo. Drug barons have declared jurisdiction over much of South America. The Pope has been added to Willy Brandt, Stevie Wonder, and Steffi Graf as hostages held by extremists. The latest Live World concert has been watched by two and a half billion people, and has led to mass protests throughout the world.

This all pushes governments into finally acknowledging that there is only one track ahead: global collaboration with a vengeance, and for the first time ever. As European President Joan Ruddock puts it at the World Conference for the World: "The biggest problem is no longer others, it is ourselves. We are suspended at a hinge of history, between two ages – that of competitive nationalism and that of cooperative internationalism. At long glorious last, we recognize that traditional nationhood is an anachronism, a pernicious phenomenon like feudalism or slavery."

What emerges is a system of government based on concentric circles: local councils, regional assemblies, national governments, groupings such as the European Community, and global bodies such as the United Nations (supplied with teeth). This vertical structure is paralleled by a horizontal structure of NGOs with real power, made up of professions, trade unions, Friends of the Earth, major charities, academics, service clubs, Oxfam, and the like. These NGOs receive collective representation through the long-proposed Second Assembly of the United Nations. Under these twin structures of government, citizens can cheer equally for Edinburgh, Scotland, Britain, Europe, the Commonwealth, the world, tropical forests, Antarctica, and Action Aid.

Science and technology

As a result of scientific advances, techno-jumps as early as the year 2000 could include: a breakthrough with photovoltaics that transforms the energy prospect from top to bottom, especially for tropical countries; backpack nuclear weapons, with all that means for terrorism; sex selection on the cheap, leading to a massive majority of male babies; and genetically engineered trees that sprout like mushrooms ("plant the seedling and jump aside"), allowing reforestation to do a better job of soaking up excess carbon dioxide from the atmosphere. But note that genetic engineering could lead to some unfortunate consequences of economic and social sort. It will soon be possible to "grow" cocoa in the laboratory, which could devastate those developing-world countries that now earn $2.6 billion a year from the field-grown crop.

A related technology is nanotechnology, enabling us to redesign cellular structures. This will lead to, for example, exceptionally strong and lightweight alloys, leading in turn to organically manufactured aircraft that fly much more speedily and cheaply than today's dinosaur-style devices. Among more "way out" applications of nanotechnology could be steaks from hay, without the help of cows. These, like many other techno-jumps, will derive in part from the fast-growing capacity of supercomputers. Already the latest Cray model, standing no taller than its human operator, can solve

problems at a sustained rate better than one "gigaflop", or one billion calculations every second (the term gigaflop comes from "giga" meaning one billion, and FLOP for "floating point operation", a common form of computerized arithmetic). Soon to become available is a computer capable of 22 gigaflops per second, while by the mid-1990s we should see a machine speeding along at 128 gigaflops per second.

As for the car of the future, that is already with us. A Volvo prototype, with lightweight synthetic materials, weighs only half as much as a conventional model. Its lean-and-clean engine, backed up by a continuously variable transmission and a flywheel energy-storage unit, achieves almost 150 km per gallon in average traffic conditions. A further prospect for the petrol-driven car is that there will simply be far fewer of them in urban areas, their place having been taken by vehicles powered by electricity or hydrogen fuel. In any case, there will be far less need for them in the face of competition from efficient and cheap mass-transit systems (in Tokyo today, only 15% of commuters drive cars to the office). Moreover there will be an increasing trend for offices to be connected by electronic lines rather than crowded highways. Note too that if China were to devote as much land to asphalt as the United States does per head, it would lose over 40% of its croplands.

Health

What price an end to drug addiction by the year 2000? There is prospect of a final solution in the form of "opiate antagonists" that block the effects of, for example, cocaine for a month or so, whereafter the euphoric impact dissipates and the addict loses interest.

More broadly, we can anticipate a growing disaffection with established ideas about health. As more people recognize that health is in-

trinsically a holistic affair, so they will be inclined to accept personal responsibility for cures of "disease". There will thus be an increase in wholesome diets, exercise, and sports, stress-reducing activities, self-rehabilitation, and recreation in the sense of re-creation. Sooner than we might suppose, self-help health will become mainstream.

In developing countries the technique of oral rehydration therapy (ORT) could soon become as familiar as cola – otherwise we shall witness 25 million children die of dehydration during the 1990s. Ironically, as we bring about an end to the human haemorrhage represented by child mortality in developing countries – one of the great success stories in human history – we may well witness another scourge overtaking hundreds of millions, the ravages of tobacco, as cigarette corporations of the developed world, losing their clientele at home, peddle their wares to the last corners of the developing world.

Lifestyles

Already many households feature a personal computer. A child has hardly learned to read and write before he or she starts to work with a device that, a couple of decades earlier, would have had to be as big as a house to contain the computing power of the tabletop model. It is this new skill, backed by global-scope telecommunications networks, that is opening up worlds for youngsters way beyond the dreams of their parents.

Within just a few years a majority of women will be engaged in paid work, whether in a formal workplace or in homes linked to offices by computer networks. At the same time, many men will accept a greater role in the family and home. In response to the cocktail party question, "What do you do?" the answer will increasingly be, "I'm a househusband".

Personal experience

Shall we soon see a time when consumerism is not only recognized as bad for the planet, but eventually fades from fashion as many people come to sense that the good life does not lie in endless goodies? According to Louis Harris polls, a majority of American adults already rank family life, friends, and the environment as their main priorities, ahead of career, income, and other materialist factors. So it is entirely possible that for the first time in human history there will soon be a widespread retreat from material-ism, with people content with the "sufficient affluence" of the 1950s.

Moreover, as we steadily achieve greater control over our outward worlds, many people will become aware of a disarray within – an uneasy sense that external afflu-ence is not matched by internal richness. This will spark a multitude of gropings toward semi-spiritual enlightenment: a quasi-religious movement to accept responsibility for our ravaged planet, a yearning for the "certainty" offered by vari-ous faiths, even a mystical orien-tation toward the "something more" that becomes an imperative in daily living. Eventually people will come to realize the paramount need for a personal sorting out of priorities. To the extent there is a religious revival, there will be as many religions as there are sensi-tized individuals.

"If you are thinking a year ahead, sow seed. If you are thinking ten years ahead, plant a tree. If you are thinking 100 years ahead, make people aware. By sowing seed once, you will harvest once. By planting a tree, you will harvest ten-fold. By opening the minds of people, you will harvest 100-fold."
                                    (of Chinese origin)

The Center for Futures Research at the University of Southern California has come up with a lengthy list of possibilities, all qualified with a probability factor ranging from 0 (impossible) to 1 (certain).

"Intelligent" home terminals are developed at low cost, with print-and-display capability that can connect to TV, telephone, and microprocessor software for such functions as remote data-based in-quiries and payment of bills. **0.99**

Major mineral deposits are dis-covered on the ocean floor (i.e. under the surface, not as nodules), including bauxite, chromite, and nickel, by the mid-1990s. **0.8**

Pocket-sized computers come into widespread use with the capability of current IBM PCs. **0.8**

A satellite-based, pocket-sized "pager" system is widely used, able to pick up signals from thousands of miles away. **0.8**

A drug becomes available, in the form of an "eat but don't gain weight" pill, that temporarily pre-vents food from being absorbed by the body. **0.75**

A combination of improved food-storage and processing techniques (such as irradiation and drying) leads to a reduction in food spoil-age in developing countries, worth at least 20% of their crops. **0.75**

Terrorists use a sophisticated ground-to-air missile to shoot down a commercial jet in a leading indus-trialized nation. **0.75**

Personal identification systems are developed, via foolproof computer-ized technology, depending on characteristics such as finger- or voice-prints. **0.75**

A short war erupts between Israel and one or more Arab nations, causing numerous casualties all round and reinforcing a stale-mate. **0.75**

Automated health examinations for self-administered routine checkups, employing only noninvasive tech-niques, enable people to watch out for abnormalities. **0.75**

Ultra-effective drugs become avail-able to clear blocked arteries, thus eliminating most bypass surgery. **0.7**

So much for some front-runner pre-dictions. Slightly less probable are the following:

A super-battery is devised, with 10 times the energy-density ratio of present lead/acid batteries. **0.6**

Scientists learn to convert solar energy into cells, producing about 3% of developed-world energy con-sumption. **0.6**

Scientists devise a way to dispose of nuclear waste. **0.6**

As monocultural, chemical-intensive farming becomes increasingly un-profitable in North America and Western Europe, many farmers shift to diversified and "natural" farming systems ("ecological agriculture") until such farms produce at least one-tenth of our food. **0.6**

Single-cell protein for animal feed is produced on a scale that allows it to account for at least 10% of the feed-grain trade.   **0.6**

Scientists understand the chemical basis of mood and behaviour, a research breakthrough that leads to highly potent drugs.   **0.6**

Electromechanical "nannies" make their appearance in many homes, able to handle kitchen functions, such as preparing meals and cleaning up afterward, and communication functions, such as tele-shopping.   **0.6**

A further breakthrough arrives in selective control of the immune response, which facilitates transplant of foreign objects and improves chemical therapy for a wide range of diseases.   **0.6**

Genetic modifications lead to super-fish, for example a 40-kg trout that matures in one-fifth of the normal time.   **0.6**

A cure for most forms of cancer, provided detection is early enough.   **0.5**

Grain-crop types are developed that grow in sandy soils and can be irrigated with seawater, opening up many areas, especially along coasts (Israel, Saudi Arabia, Chile, Namibia, Mauritania) that are now considered off limits to agriculture.   **0.5**

A hybrid car goes into mass production, driven by batteries with only a boost from an auxiliary petrol engine.   **0.5**

A low-energy and cost-effective process is developed to desalinize large quantities of seawater.   **0.5**

An artificial womb is foreseen, capable of carrying an animal, such as a calf or a lamb, from conception to full-term fetus.   **0.45**

Consumer lobbyists establish a communications network that can conduct a "national referendum" within a day, the system being designed to influence government regulations.   **0.45**

A four-day working week becomes standard, with 7-10 hour working days.   **0.4**

A North American Common Market is established, encompassing Canada, the United States and Mexico.   **0.4**

Several Western governments adopt constitutional amendments or similar mechanisms to limit government expenditures to no more than a specified percentage of GNP, for example 35%.   **0.3**

Industrialized nations try to stem pervasive types of pollution by severely taxing imports from polluting nations.   **0.3**

Corporation directors become personally liable for the safety of their products, as for the polluting impacts of their enterprises.   **0.3**

A medical cure for alcoholism is developed, permanently eliminating addiction.   **0.3**

A populist revolution overtakes Saudi Arabia, bringing in a socialist government.   **0.3**

Inflation of at least 20% returns to afflict a number of developed-world economies for several years.   **0.3**

The Catholic Church accepts birth control in whatever form.   **0.3**

A woman is elected president of the USA.   **0.25**

Mexico is shaken by revolution.   **0.2**

A scientific breakthrough enables large-scale production of hydrogen and oxygen from water, at a more cost-effective rate (in terms of dollars per British Thermal Unit) than any other form of energy.   **0.2**

The USA launches a satellite that returns about five megawatts of electricity to the Earth's surface.   **0.2**

Japan revises its constitution and re-arms.   **0.2**

The 100-year lifespan becomes not uncommon.   **0.2**

Average unemployment rates in North America, Western Europe, and Japan exceed 20% for at least two years, bringing on worldwide depression.   **0.2**

After a blackmail attempt fails, a nuclear bomb is detonated in a major Western-world city.   **0.2**

Quebec secedes politically from Canada.   **0.2**

British Columbia becomes a US state.   **0.1**

The Catholic Church allows women to be ordained as priests.   **0.1**

At least one large American city, probably New York, makes public transportation free.   **0.1**

Further reading

Asimov, I (ed), *Living in the Future*, New English Library, Sevenoaks, Kent, UK, 1985

Barnaby, F (gen ed), *The Gaia Peace Atlas: Survival into the Third Millennium*, Pan Books, London, and Doubleday, New York, 1988

Beckwith, B P, *Beyond Tomorrow: A Rational Utopia*, B P Beckwith, Palo Alto, California, 1986

Benjamin, M and Freedman, A, *Bridging the Global Gap: A Handbook to Linking Citizens of the First and Third Worlds*, Seven Locks Press, Maryland, 1989

Bhaskara, H et al., *Against All Odds: Breaking the Poverty Trap*, Panos Publications Ltd, London, 1989

Boulding, K E, *Three Faces of Power*, Sage Publications, San Francisco, 1989

Boyle, S and Ardill J, *The Greenhouse Effect: A Practical Guide to Our Changing Climate*, Hodder and Stoughton, Sevenoaks, Kent, UK, 1989

Brown, L R et al., *State of the World 1990*, W W Norton, New York, 1990

Burger, J, *The Gaia Atlas of First Peoples: A Future for the Indigenous World*, Robertson McCarta, London, and Doubleday, New York, 1990

Cadman, D and Payne, G (eds), *The Living City: Towards a Sustainable Future*, Routledge, London, 1990

Calder, C and Newell, J (eds), *On the Frontiers of Science: How Scientists See Our Future*, Facts on File, New York, 1989

Cappo, J, *FutureScope: Success Stories for the 1990s and Beyond*, Longman Publishing, New York, 1989

Capra, F, *Uncommon Wisdom*, Century Hutchinson, London, 1988

Cetron, M J and Davies, O, *American Renaissance: Our Life at the Turn of the Twenty-first Century*, St. Martin's Press, New York, 1989

Cetron, M J, *America at the Turn of the Century*, St. Martin's Press, New York, 1989

Christensen, K E (ed), *The New Era of Home-Based Work; Directions and Policies*, Westview Press, Boulder, Colorado, 1988

Clark, M E, *Ariadne's Thread: The Search for New Modes of Thinking*, St. Martin's Press, New York, 1989

Coates, J F and Jarratt, J, *What Futurists Believe*, World Future Society and Lomond Publications, Maryland, 1989

Cornish, E (ed), *The 1990s and Beyond*, World Future Society, Maryland, 1990

Didsbury, H F (ed), *The Future: Opportunity Not Destiny*, World Future Society, Maryland, 1989

Diebold, J, *The Innovators: the Discoveries, Inventions, and Breakthroughs of Our Time*, E P Dutton, New York, 1990

Drexler, K E, *Engines of Creation: The Coming Era of Nanotechnology*, Anchor Press, New York, 1986

Dychtwald, K and Flower, J, *Age Wave: The Challenges and Opportunities of an Ageing America*, Tarcher Publications, Los Angeles, 1989

Ehrlich, P R and A H, *The Population Explosion*, Simon and Schuster, New York, 1990

Engelberger, J F, *Robotics in Service*, MIT Press, Cambridge, Massachusetts, 1989

Etzioni, A, *The Moral Dimension: Toward a New Economics*, The Free Press, New York, 1988

Finkelstein, J (ed), *Windows on a New World: The Third Industrial Revolution*, Greenwood Press, New York, 1989

Forester, T (ed), *The Materials Revolution*, Basil Blackwell, Oxford, 1988

Gleick, J, *Chaos: Making a New Science*, Cardinal, London, 1988

Glenn, J C, *Future Mind: Artificial Intelligence*, Acropolis Books, New York, 1989

Goldemberg, J, Johansson, T B, Reddy A K N, and Williams R. H., *Energy for a Sustainable World*, World Resources Institute, Washington DC, 1987

Gorman, R F (ed), *Private Voluntary Organizations as Agents for Development*, Westview Press, Boulder, Colorado, 1984

Gribben, J, *The Hole in the Sky: Man's Threat to the Ozone Layer*, Corgi Books, London, 1988

Grobstein, C, *Science and the Unborn: Choosing Human Futures*, Basic Books, New York, 1988

Heaword, R and Larke, C, *The Directory of Appropriate Technology*, Routledge, London, 1989

Hohmeyer, O, *Social Costs of Energy Consumption*, Springer-Verlag, Berlin, 1988

Hubbard, B M, *The Hunger of Eve: One Woman's Odyssey Toward the Future*, Island Press, Washington DC, 1989

Hubbard, H M, "Photovoltaics Today and Tomorrow", *Science* 244: 297-304, 1989

Jastrow, R, *Journey to the Stars: Space Exploration – Tomorrow and Beyond*, Bantam Books, New York, 1989

Kidder, R, *Reinventing the Future: Global Goals for the Twenty-first Century*, MIT Press, Cambridge, Massachusetts, 1989

Kinsman, F, *Millennium 2000: Toward Tomorrow's Society*, W H Allen, London, 1990

Krannich, R L, *Careering and Re-Careering for the 1990s: The Complete Guide to Planning Your Future*, Impact Publications, Manassas, Virginia, 1989

Kurtz, P (ed), *Building a World Community: Humanism in the Twenty-first Century*, Prometheus Books, New York, 1989

Laszlo, E, *The Inner Limits of Mankind*, Oneworld Publications, London, 1989

Lorie, P and Murray-Clark, S, *History of the Future: A Chronology*, Doubleday, New York, 1989

Lovelock, J, *The Ages of Gaia*, Oxford University Press, Oxford, 1988

Manzini, E, *The Material of Invention: Materials and Design*, MIT Press, Cambridge, Massachusetts, 1989

Marien, M and Jennings, L (eds), *What I Have Learned: Thinking About the Future Then and Now*, Greenwood Press, New York, 1987

Marx, J L (ed), *A Revolution in Biotechnology*, Cambridge University Press, Cambridge and New York, 1989

McLuhan, M and Powers, B RT, *The Global Village: Transformations in World Life and Media in the Twenty-first Century*, Oxford University Press, London and New York, 1989

Milbrath, L W, *Envisioning a Sustainable Society: Learning Our Way Out*, State University of New York Press, New York, 1989

Moravec, H, *Mind Children: The Future of Robot and Human Intelligence*, Harvard University Press, Cambridge, Massachusetts, 1988

Myers, N (gen ed), *The Gaia Atlas of Planet Management*, Pan Books, London, and Doubleday, New York, 1985

Myers, N, "The United States and global environment: policy linkages", *Foreign Policy* 74:23-41, 1989

Myers, N, *Deforestation Rates in Tropical Forests and Their Climatic Implications*, Friends of the Earth, London, 1989

Nadler, G and Hibino, S, *Breakthrough Thinking*, Prima Publishing and Communications, New York, 1990

Nanus, B, *The Leader's Edge: The Seven Keys to Leadership in a Turbulent World*, Contemporary Books, Los Angeles, 1989

Nash, R F, *The Rights of Nature: The History of Environmental Ethics*, University of Wisconsin Press, Madison, Wisconsin, 1989

Naisbitt, J and Aburdene, P, *Megatrends 2000: Ten New Directions for the 1990s*, William Morrow and Co., New York

Odum, E P, *Ecology and Our Endangered Life-Support Systems*, Sinauer Associates, Sunderland, Massachusetts, 1989

Olson, S, *Shaping the Future: Biology and Human Values*, National Academy Press, Washington DC, 1989

Ornstein, R and Ehrlich P, *New World, New Mind: Moving Toward Conscious Evolution*, Doubleday, New York, 1989

Paehlke, *Environmentalism and the Future of Progressive Politics*, Yale University Press, Connecticut, 1989

Parkin, S, *Green Parties*, Heretic Books/GMP Publications, London, 1989

Pearce, D, Markandya A and Barbier E B, *Blueprint for a Green Economy*, Earthscan Publications, London, 1989

Pearson, D, *The Natural House Book: Creating a Healthy, Harmonious, and Ecologically Sound Home*, Conran Octopus, London, and Simon and Schuster, New York, 1990

Platt, C, *When You Can Live Twice as Long, What Will You Do: and 99 Other Questions You May Have to Answer ... Sooner Than You Think*, Morrow, New York, 1989

Platt, J, "The acceleration of evolution", *The Futurist* (Feb):14-23, 1981

Postle, D *The Mind Gymnasium*, Macdonald, London and McGraw Hill, New York, 1989

Ravetz, J R, *The Merger of Knowledge with Power: Essays in Critical Science*, Cassell, London, 1990

Robertson, J, *Future Wealth: New Economics for the Twenty-first Century,*, Cassell, London, 1990

Schneider, S H, *Global Warming: Are We Entering the Greenhouse Century?*, Sierra Club Books, San Francisco, 1989

Shipman, H L, *Humans in Space, Twenty-first Century Frontiers*, Plenum Press, New York, 1989

Silverstein, M, *The Environmental Factor: Its Impact on the Future of the World Economy and Your Investments*, Longman Financial Services Publishing, Chicago, 1990

Simon, R and Smith, A, *Superconductors: Conquering Technology's New Frontier*, Plenum Press, New York, 1988

Stallibrass, A, *Being Me and Also Us*, Scottish Academic Press, Edinburgh, 1989

Soroos, M S, *Beyond Sovereignty: The Challenge of Global Policy*, University of South Carolina Press, Columbia, 1986

Stewart, H B, *Recollecting the Future: A View of Business, Technology and Innovation in the Next Thirty Years*, Dow Jones-Irwin, Homewood, Illinois, 1989

Stewart, I, *Does God Play Dice?*, Basil Blackwell, Oxford, 1989

Suzuki, D and Knudtson, P, *Genethics: The Clash Between the New Genetics and Human Values*, Harvard University Press, Cambridge, Massachusetts, 1989

Theobold, R, *The Rapids of Change: Entrepreneurship in Turbulent Times*, Knowledge Systems Inc., Chicago, 1987

Toffler, A, *Previews and Premises*, South End Press, Boston, 1983

Toulmin, S, *Cosmopolis: The Hidden Agenda of Modernity*, Free Press, New York, 1990

Tudge, C, *Food Crops for the Future*, Basil Blackwell, Oxford, 1988

Van de Veer, D and Pierce, C, *People, Penguins and Plastic Trees: Basic Issues in Environmental Ethics*, Wadsworth Publishing Company, Belmont, California, 1986

Veatch, R M, *Death, Dying, and the Biological Revolution: Our Last Quest for Responsibility*, Yale University Press, New Haven, Connecticut, 1989

Wagar, W W, *A Short History of the Future*, University of Chicago Press, Chicago, 1989

Weiss, J, *The Asian Century: The Economic Ascent of the Pacific Rim – and What it Means for the West*, Facts on File, New York, 1989

Western, D, and Pearl, M (eds), *Conservation for the Twenty-first Century*, Oxford University Press, New York, 1989

Wilkinson, G, *What Lies Ahead: Countdown to the Twenty-first Century*, United Way Strategic Institute, Alexandria, Virginia, 1989

Willoughby, K W, *Technology Choice: A Critique of the Appropriate Technology Movement*, Westview Press, Boulder, Colorado, 1990

World Commission on Environment and Development, *Our Common Future*, Oxford University Press, Oxford, 1987

Wygant, A C, and Markley, O W, *Information and the Future: A Handbook of Sources and Strategies*, Greenwood Press, New York, 1988

Journals

Futures: The Journal of Planning and Forecasting, Butterworths, London

Futures Survey, World Future Society, Bethesda, Maryland

The Futurist, World Future Society, Bethesda, Maryland

Technological Forecasting and Social Change Elsevier, New York

Turning Point 2000, The Old Bakehouse, Cholsey, Nr Wallingford, Oxon, OX10 9NU, UK

Index

Acknowledgements

Publisher's acknowledgements

The production of this book has been a co-operative affair involving many individuals and organizations around the world. Gaia Books would like to extend warm thanks to all those who contributed so unstintingly of their time and knowledge. In particular, our thanks go to those organizations that provided invaluable sources and references including: the Campaign for Nuclear Disarmament, UK Commonwealth Secretariat Expert Group on Climatic Change and Sea-Level Rise, *The Ecologist* magazine, *The Economist* magazine, Friends of the Earth (UK), *Geographical* magazine, *New Internationalist* magazine, *New Scientist* magazine, Novosti Press Agency, Oxfam (UK), Juliet Heller at The Panos Institute (UK), Population Reference Bureau (USA), UN Information Office, UNESCO Centre (UK), War on Want (UK), World Wide Fund for Nature (UK), Worldwatch Institute (USA), and the organizers and members of the World Future Society. We would also particularly like to thank Susan Walby and Alison Jones for their production expertise; Susan Mennell assisted by Samantha Nunn for picture research; Lesley Gilbert for text preparation; James Lovelock for his inspiration; Jonathon Porritt; Jennie Kent for unfailing assistance; Rosanne Hooper for initial research and development; Erik Ness for research assistance; Alison Gadsby and Philip Gamble for design assistance; and Lynette Beckford, Libby Hoseason, Fiona Trent, Denis Dawson, On Yer Bike, Cambridge Photosetting Services, and Technographic Design and Print Ltd. Our thanks also go to Friends of the Earth, Rotary International, and Oxfam for allowing us to reproduce their logos.

Author's acknowledgements

In early 1989 I went to Gaia Books with an idea I had been brooding over for a year. The two Gaia leaders, Joss Pearson and Patrick Nugent, gave my idea a thorough going-over, and out of our discussions emerged a much expanded concept for *The Gaia Atlas of Future Worlds.*

Joss Pearson is one of the most creative people I have come across in the publishing field. She took the *Future Worlds* idea and started to shape it into a synoptic outline. I compared her efforts with what I had already drafted by way of structure, and found a fine degree of agreement. At the same time Patrick Nugent, as Artistic Director, started to apply his design talents to fleshing out the spread-by-spread topics, bringing vague notions to graphic life.

Along the way my assistant, Jennie Kent, typed wads of notes and drafts and undertook a massive amount of fact chasing. Thank you, Jennie, for contributing much more than you realize.

A book of this one's scope cannot be produced without the support of friends and professional colleagues in many fields. To list them all would take a couple of pages; so I can only record my collective thanks – no less emphatic for that. It would be invidious, however, to omit mention of my exceptional debt to a handful of key contributors: Stewart Boyle of the Association for Conservation of Energy, London; Lester Brown and his associates, Worldwatch Institute, Washington DC; Paul and Anne Ehrlich, Stanford University; David Hall, London University; Jeremy Hamand, International Planned Parenthood Federation, London; John Platt, futurist extraordinary, Cambridge, Massachusetts; Peter Raven, Missouri Botanical Garden; and M. S. Swaminathan, Centre for Research on Sustainable Agriculture, Madras. You all have my warm thanks.

Other Gaia books published by Anchor/Doubleday:

Gaia: an Atlas of Planet Management
gen ed: Dr Norman Myers
0-385-19072-7

Gaia State of the Ark Atlas
by Lee Durrell
0-385-23668-9

The Gaia Atlas of First Peoples
by Julian Burger
0-385-26652-9 (hardcover)
0-385-26653-7 (paperback)